CITY BELLE

Relax, watch the world go by

Previous page Aerial in 4ply Cotton by Kim Hargreaves, pattern page 114, this page Mia in Cotton Glace by Debbie Bliss, pattern page 94, opposite Charm in 4ply Cotton by Kim Hargreaves, pattern page 100

This page Flourish in Cotton Glace, pattern page 72, opposite Frolic in 4ply Cotton, pattern page 82, both by Kim Hargreaves

This page Wicked in 4ply Cotton, pattern page 76, opposite Tune in 4ply Cotton, pattern page 93, both by Kim Hargreaves

This page Curls in 4ply Cotton, by Susan Duckworth, pattern page 104, opposite Swank in All Seasons Cotton pattern page 111 & Aerial in 4ply Cotton, pattern page 114, both by Kim Hargreaves

10

This page Flourish in Cotton
Glace by Kim Hargreaves,
pattern page 72, opposite
Brocade in Wool Cotton by
Kaffe Fassett, pattern page 84

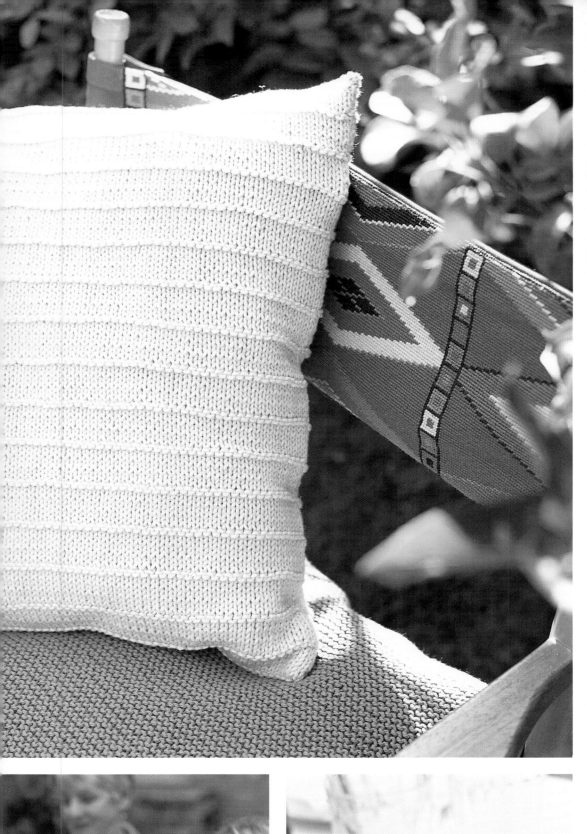

16

Photography by Pia Tryde/Conran Octopus

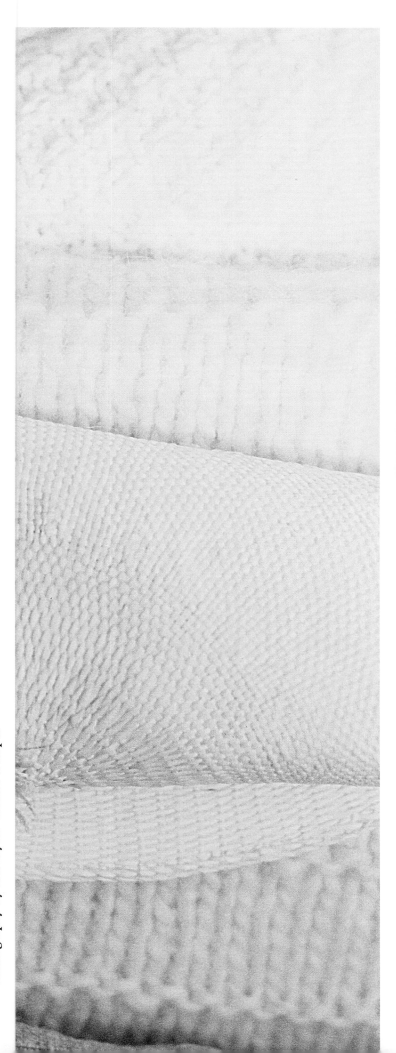

Photograph by Mark Scott

MARY NORDEN

Never one to resist a challenge, Mary Norden

has made a special niche for herself through

her quiet determination and sparkling talent,

Gail Abbott went to meet her at home

*Far left: With it's cool, lofty rooms and tall windows, the house
now has a spare elegance that is thoroughly contemporary
Above: Mary in Hunter by Kim Hargreaves, pattern page 79.
Left: Simple stitches add texture to knitted cushions.
Find instructions on page 116*

Photographer Joey Toller
Stylist Kim Hargreaves
Hair & Make-up
Annabel Hobbs
Model Helena Costa
Thank you to Jorge Sousa
& Hotel Estalagem do Farol,
Cascais for allowing us to
photograph in the hotel,
Tel: 00351 21 483 01 73

This page Marcia in Cotton Glace by Debbie Abrahams, pattern page 88, opposite Nancy in Wool Cotton by Debbie Bliss, pattern page 110

'I spend hours at car boots sales and am always on the lookout for bargains'

The pile of rubble waiting to be carried away from the front of Mary Norden's house is testament to the gentrification that has been taking place up and down this leafy north London street in recent years, as well as being a good indication of it's owners' love of a challenge. 'We bought the house three years ago when it was a total wreck,' says Mary. 'It's taken us ages as we've done it all ourselves.' With its cool, lofty rooms and rows of tall windows, the house now has a spare elegance that is thoroughly contemporary, without losing any of its early-nineteenth century character. It's just about finished. 'Well – all but the kitchen', laughs Mary as we contemplate the empty basement space. 'We make do with the tiny scullery for now, so we tend to eat in the garden whenever it's warm enough.' The large, peaceful garden at the back of the house, hidden away from the city street, is a haven for Mary, her husband Charles and their friends. 'We have so much space, which is lovely when we entertain. Ella and Jamie, the children of my friend Anne, often come round to play.'

Mary's name will be familiar to long-time Rowan knitters as a knitwear designer with a talent for classic stitch patterns. 'I've always been excited by colour and texture,' she says. 'I loved taking a stitch pattern like Fairisle and giving it a whole new look by reworking it in a new colourway, or using traditional Arans with a modern twist.' When Mary's work was spotted by Rowan's Stephen Sheard in the 1980s, he was quick to commision her for the early magazines. 'I was impressed by Mary's use of stitch detail,' says Stephen. 'So I asked her to design two garments for Rowan Knitting Book number two.' More editorial work followed, and soon Mary was designing regularly for magazines like Essentials and Prima, as well as her own ready-to-wear collections. Even as a child living in Somerset, Mary recalls, she was forever making things out of felt and scraps of fabric. 'There were nine of us children, so

there was no way we could all be taken out and entertained, and we had no television. We just had to make our own amusement. I used to disappear into my room and completely lose myself in my own fantasy world.' Her love of materials led Mary to take a printed textiles degree at Farnham art school in Surrey, where her second subject was hand knitting. For three years she was free to experiment and play to her heart's content, and her final degree show proved such a success that the whole lot was bought outright by an agent who took her work out to Japan. 'After college I won a Crafts Council grant for a year, so I set up a studio and concentrated on designing printed textiles for the fashion industry,' she tells me. But after a few years she began to miss seeing her projects through from beginning to end. 'My painted ideas would go off to Japan, New York and Paris, but I would never see the finished result.' So back to knitting, with its hands-on approach and the satisfaction of thinking a garment through from its original conception to the final sewing-up.

Mary's more recent success, as an interior stylist and journalist, grew out of her experience of working on her own design books. 'I started to get interested in needlepoint,' she remembers. 'It's a marvellous medium for concentrating on colour and pattern, so when I was asked to work on my own book I jumped at the chance.'

With no budget for a stylist, Mary found herself searching for props to put in the pictures alongside her cushions and chair seats. 'I'd never styled a photograph before,' she comments. 'But I was so naive I took it on anyway, and with a lot of hard work, just managed to do it.' More books followed, and to date she has written and designed a dozen titles ranging from 'Ethnic needlepoint', inspired by world textiles, 'Embroidery with wool', with its ideas on decorated textiles, to

Far left: from top, clockwise: Mary prepares lunch in the garden wearing Nancy by Debbie Bliss, pattern page 110. Ella wears Tiger Lily by Carol Meldrum, pattern page 90. Jamie tucks in wearing Native by Kim Hargreaves, pattern page 102 Simple cotton cushions, pattern page 116 sit on a director's chair designed by Mary in needlepoint. Below: Gail talks to Mary wearing Charm by Kim Hargreaves, pattern page 100. Mary has always been excited by colour and texture, patterns for knitted cushions page 116

Photographs Mark Scott

Photographs Mark Scott

Above: Jamie plays boules in the garden wearing Raewyn by Debbie Bliss, pattern page 98. Top right: Mary comes into the house wearing Enchant by Kim Hargreaves, pattern page 70, Kate wears Sheriff by Louisa Harding, pattern page 68. Bottom right: Ella takes a quiet moment to sit with Mary in Navigator by Kim Hargreaves, pattern page 113.

'Modern Country', simple natural interiors for the urban home. But where does she find all those battered garden chairs, distressed bedside tables and modern accessories that give her pictures such style? 'I beg and borrow from friends, spend hours at car boot sales and am always on the lookout for bargains,' she confesses. 'Mind you, I often have a stall at a car boot myself, just to get rid of everything before I start again.'

Her latest project involves flying round the world with Ann Grafton, Design Director of Colefax and Fowler, as they work on a new book together. 'We are using the best of the old and the new', explains Mary. 'Mixing textiles like vintage French linen sheets with fabrics from the latest collections. Ann and I discuss the look she wants to achieve, and then I organise the location, props and work with the photographer on

the shoot.' The book has already entailed working all round England and in France, and soon Mary is off to the States, and maybe South Africa before it's finished.

It all sounds like a lot of hard work to me, so does she manage to make any time for herself? 'It's easy to focus on nothing else when I'm in London,' she agrees. 'I often find myself working too hard, and even when we're abroad I don't get time to do much else.' But plans are in the pipeline to take time out later in the year, to do something completely different and revitalise her own inspiration. But, being Mary, it's not likely to be the easy option of a beach holiday. She looks excited at the prospect of another challenge – 'I'm hoping to take two months to ride across Mongolia on horseback, it's something I've always wanted to do, and this feels like the right time.'

modern country mary norden

'MODERN COUNTRY'
BY MARY NORDEN
published by Conran Octopus, £18.99 (UK)
ISBN 1 84091 092 5

Contemporary design looks to the natural
world for inspiration, and Mary Norden's
latest book recaptures the essential values
of nature's shapes, materials and colours.
Practical projects ranging from simple
knitted cushions to easy window dressings
are provided with step-by-step
instructions and photographed in modern
pared-down interiors.

**Photography this page by
Pia Tryde/Conran Octopus**
taken from 'Modern Country'

Opposite Core i
Handknit DK Cotton &
Denim by Kim Hargreave
pattern page 96, this pag
Raewyn by Debbie Blis
pattern page 98 & Sher
by Louisa Harding, patter
page 68, both in Denim

MARINE LIFE

Double impact with a nautical note

This page Frolic in 4ply Cotton, pattern page 82 & Moonbeam in Linen Drape, pattern page 69, opposite Hope in All Seasons Cotton, pattern page 92, all by Kim Hargreaves

This page Spellbound, pattern page 83 & Navigator, pattern page 113, both in All Seasons Cotton, opposite Tune in 4ply cotton, pattern page 93 & Hunter in Linen Drape pattern page 79, all by Kim Hargeaves

This page Spruce, pattern page 115 & Prance, pattern page 107 both in Linen Drape, opposite Core in Handknit Cotton or Denim, pattern page 96, all by Kim Hargreaves

Photograher Joey Toller
Stylist Kim Hargreaves
Hair & Make-up
Annabel Hobbs
Models Helena Costa
& Ines Castel – Branco
Thank you to Marina De
Cascais for allowing us to
photograph at the marina,
Tel: 00351 21 482 48 00

EVERYTHING YOU NEED TO KNOW ABOUT INTARSIA

If you've ever longed to knit a complicated, multi-coloured design but been put off by the

thought of all those ends, take heart, Kate Buller's guide will get you started

Intarsia is the term used for knitting blocks of pattern that require separate balls of yarn for each area of colour to create a single thickness fabric. The secret of intarsia knitting lies in the preparation. It is important to take time to organise yourself before you start knitting, and prepare yarns carefully in order to avoid tangles. The beauty of knitting with intarsia is that absolutely anything is possible. Delicate motifs like hearts and flowers, geometric patterns in rich colours or allover designs using intertwining natural forms; all are possible, in any combination, with this versatile knitting technique. If you have never tried intarsia before, get started with a simple motif, or try out designs on a swatch to perfect the colour changes. Once you have got the hang of it, progress to a simple design like Debbie Bliss's Nancy see opposite page and page 110 for full chart and pattern.

CHART TIPS

- Enlarging a chart on a photocopier will help you follow it more easily
- Always remember to read a chart from right to left on odd numbered rows (knit) and from left to right on even numbered (purl) rows
- Mark off each line of the chart as you work.

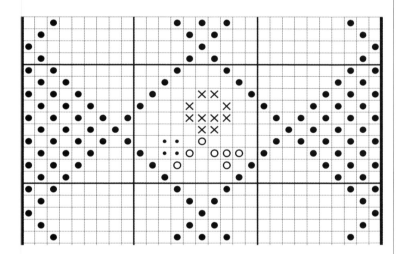

PREPARING THE YARNS

There are lots of different ways to prepare yarn for knitting intarsia, try these different methods for large, medium and small amounts;

1 Prepare balls of yarn for large background areas by placing each ball inside a clear plastic bag. Secure the bags with elastic bands.

2 Wind the yarn for medium-sized areas of colour around bobbins.

3 Cut off short lengths of yarn for small areas of colour as you need them.

MAKING YOUR OWN BOBBINS

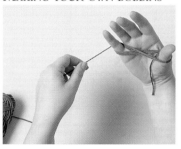

Step 1 Wrap the yarn around your thumb and forefinger in a figure of eight.

Step 2 Cut the yarn and tie a knot around the centre of the figure of eight to secure it.

TIPS

- When using bobbins, only pull out the amount of yarn required, keeping the length as short as possible to stop the yarns from untangling

- To calculate yarn needed for small areas, wind the yarn around the needle the same number of times as the number of stitches, plus a little extra to secure ends

JOINING IN A NEW COLOUR

Don't get a hole in your knitting at the start of a new colour, cross yarns together whenever you join in a new yarn.

Step 1 Insert the right needle into the next stitch. Place the end of the new pink yarn between the tips of the needles and across the blue yarn from left to right.

Step 2 Take the new pink yarn under the blue yarn and knit the next stitch with it. Move the tail of the pink yarn off the right needle as the new stitch is formed.

CHANGING COLOURS

Once you are knitting with different colours, cross yarns together at every colour change

Step 1 On a knit row, insert the right needle into the next stitch. Place the old blue yarn over the new pink yarn. Pull the new pink yarn up and knit the stitch.

Step 2 On a purl row, insert the right needle into the next stitch. Place the old pink yarn over the new blue yarn. Pull the new blue yarn up and purl the next stitch.

CARRYING THE YARN

In order to create different patterns and shapes, you may need to move colours over several stitches across the back of the work

To move a colour to the right
On a knit row, insert the right needle into the next stitch. Take the pink yarn across the back of the work to the right and behind the blue yarn. Knit the stitch.

To move a colour to the left
On a knit row, insert the right needle into the next stitch. Take the pink yarn across the back of the work to the left and across the blue yarn. Knit the stitch.

> **TIP**
> • When carrying yarn to the left, take care not to pull the working yarn too tight, this is because there is no needle in the stitch to anchor it and keep the tension correct

WORKSHOPS
If you have never attended a workshop, give yourself a treat and brush up your skills, learn a new technique, or even get to grips with designing your own sweater. Rowan workshops are run by leading designers like Debbie Bliss, Brandon Mably, Zoe Mellor and Sasha Kagan, as well as the team of Rowan Design Consultants led by Kate Buller. Contact Rowan for details or look on the website www.rowanyarns.co.uk

CARRYING YARN OVER MORE THAN THREE STITCHES

If you carry yarn over more than three stitches you will create a loop, catch this loop in as you go along

ON THE RIGHT SIDE

Step 1 On a knit row, insert the right needle into the next stitch, cross the blue yarn under the pink yarn and knit the next 2 stitches with the blue yarn.

Step 2 To catch in the blue loop that this creates at the back of the work, insert the tip of the right needle into the next stitch and then down to pick up the loop.

Step 3 Knit the stitch, at the same time losing the loop. Do not knit the loop itself.

ON THE WRONG SIDE

Step 1 On a purl row, insert the right needle into the next stitch, cross the blue yarn under the pink yarn and purl the next 2 stitches in the blue yarn.

Step 2 To catch in the blue loop that this creates at the back of the work, insert the tip of the right needle into the next stitch, and then down to pick up the loop.

Step 3 Purl the stitch at the same time losing the loop. Do not purl the loop itself.

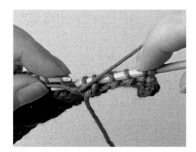

DESIGN WORKSHOP

> **TIP**
> - Always place the right needle into the next stitch before crossing the yarns. This will stop the stitches from becoming distorted. Stop and look at the colour changes at the end of every row. With the tip of a knitting or darning needle even out any distorted stitches

REDUCE THE NUMBER OF ENDS

You will find intarsia knitting more manageable if you keep the number of yarn ends to a minimum. There are several ways to do this.

START A LENGTH OF NEW YARN IN THE CENTRE

 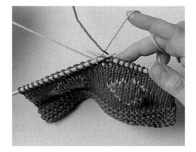

Step 1 Join a new colour by folding it in half and looping it over the needle.

Step 2 On the next row, take one length to the right and one length to the left, twisting it with the main yarn at the edges of the motif so that there are no ends to sew in

USE THE MAIN YARN ACROSS THE BACK OF THE MOTIF

If a yarn is used throughout as a background colour, it may make sense to carry this yarn across the back of the work when not in use

> **TIP**
> - Carrying the background colour across the back of the work is a Fair Isle technique. Remember that it is important not to carry the yarn over too large an area, as this will distort the fabric and create areas of different thickness across the work

TIDYING THE ENDS

Do this job every ten rows rather than leaving it all to the end

Step 1 Darn the ends around shapes of the same colour by darning in one direction first.

Step 2 Then darn the end back on itself, stretching the work before cutting the end

Photograph Hannah Mournemont

Kate Buller is Rowan's Retail Manager and the force behind the team of Design Consultants up and down the UK. She began her career as a freelance knitwear designer and joined Rowan Yarns after travelling in Latin America where she was influenced by the colours and crafts of the country and by the people she met. Kate is passionate about keeping the traditions of hand knitting alive through teaching and writing.

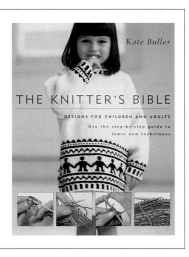

'The Knitter's Bible' is published by Collins & Brown, £16.99 (UK) ISBN 1 85585 8193 and in the US as 'The Ultimate Knitter's Guide' by Martingale, $39.95

Photographs Colin Bowling

*This page Hunter, pattern page 79,
opposite Essence, pattern page 108,
both in Linen Drape, by Kim Hargreaves*

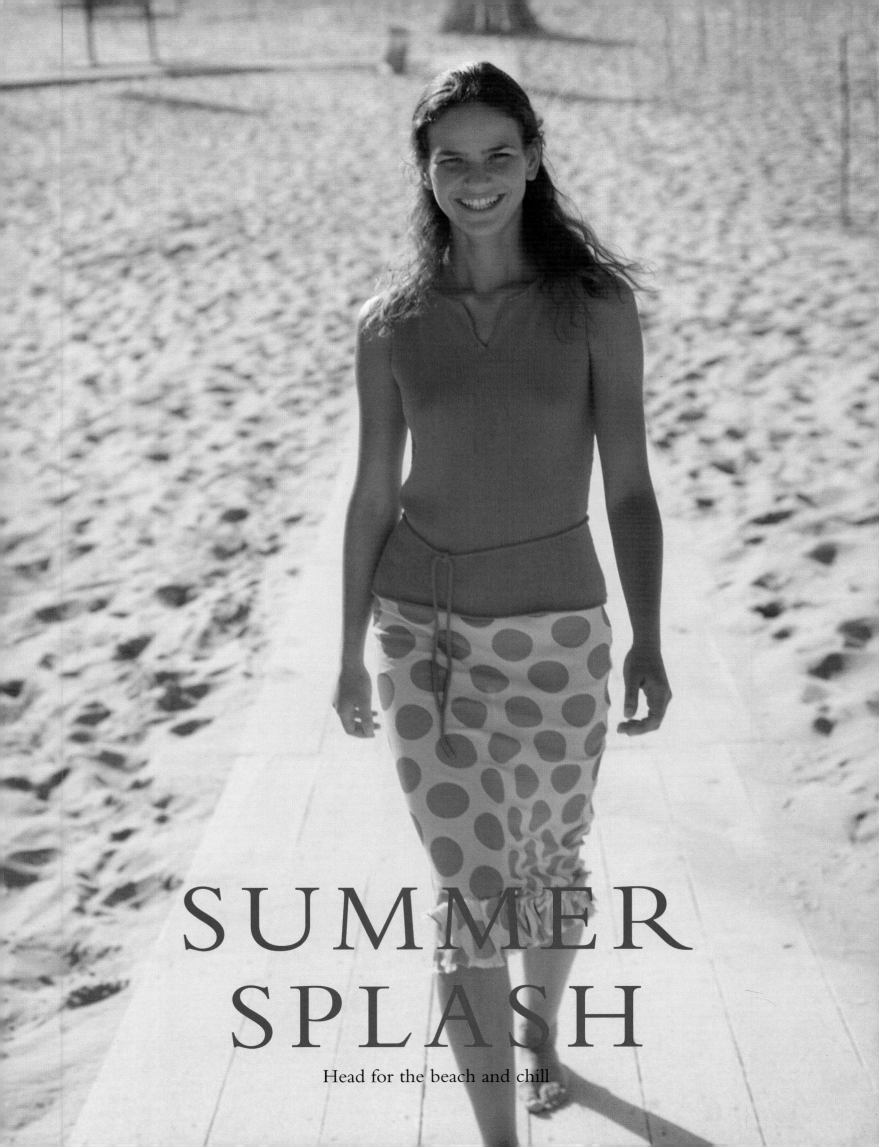

SUMMER
SPLASH

Head for the beach and chill

Courthouse Steps in 4ply Cotton & Cotton Glace by Kaffe Fassett, pattern page 80

Navigator, pattern page 113,
Swank, pattern page 111,
both in All Seasons Cotton
by Kim Hargeaves

This page Native by Kim Hargeaves, pattern page 102, opposite Raewyn by Debbie Bliss, pattern page 98, both in Handknit DK Cotton

This page Puppy Love in All Seasons Cotton, by Julia Ryan Dinner, pattern page 105, opposite Tiger Lily in Cotton Glace by Carol Meldrum, pattern page 90

41

Essence, pattern page 108 & Hunter, pattern page 79, both in Linen Drape by Kim Hargreaves

*Essence, pattern page
108, in Linen Drape
by Kim Hargreaves*

*Native in Handknit DK
Cotton by Kim Hargreaves,
pattern page 102*

Photographer Joey Toller
Stylist Kim Hargreaves
Hair & Make-up
Annabel Hobbs
Models Erika &
Demetrio Ruivo

Feature Gail Abbott photographs Hannah Mourmemont

A New Generation

For the craft of knitting to be kept alive and kicking, it's best to teach children early

Striped rucksack featured in 'Baby Style', by Debbie Bliss, see page 48 for details

Like most things, learning to knit is best attempted when you are young. Not so young that your fingers don't do what you want them to, but young enough for those skills to become second nature. The satisfaction of seeing a ball of yarn slowly and haltingly turn into a wobbly strip of knitting under your still clumsy fingers is not to be underestimated. A pleasure that is doubled when it can be tied around a much-loved teddy bear's neck.

When Nell, Jenie and Sophie, aged 10, and 11 year-old Letoyah came together for a children's knitting workshop they brought with them an assortment of skills. 'I've never knitted at all before today', confessed Sophie, while Letoyah brought with her a piece of brightly striped stocking stitch that she confidently sat down with. 'My mum taught me when I was seven,' she recalled. 'I found it quite hard at first, there were lots of holes and it was all wonky. I make less mistakes now I'm older, but I still sometimes need help.' Nell, too, had a false start at an early age. 'The first thing I knitted was a scarf for Grommit in red, turquoise and blue, that was when I was only seven,' said Nell. 'But the dog ate it and I sort of stopped then.' Jenie found that beginning at ten years old gave her a better start. 'My Nan showed me how to knit about five months ago and I didn't really make many mistakes. '

All the girls agreed that a good way to get started is to make something in wool that is easier to tackle than knitting, like a Friendship Bracelet made with four or five coloured yarns knotted together into a multi-coloured braid. 'We all make them at school,' explained Nell, as she showed ace knitter Kate Buller how to do it. 'We make them for our best friend who has to wear it round her wrist until it falls apart. If she takes it off it means we've broken up.'

When the girls got started on their knitting, they found it took plenty of concentration but was a lot of fun. 'I picked it up really quickly,' said a surprised Sophie at the end of her first strip of knitting. 'I'd like to more now and make things like little rugs for my teddies and stuffed toys. I don't really play with dolls, but I might like to make a bag and maybe a hat for me.' Jenie enjoyed trying out different coloured squares, while Letoyah, with her four years of experience, needed little help to adapt a simple pattern. 'I found a pattern for a pair of Barbie doll trousers in a magazine,' she told Kate. 'I wanted them to be pedal pushers, so I just made them shorter. Now I've started a proper sweater for myself.' Debbie Bliss, hosting the workshop, is keen for young people to learn early. 'There's no time on the National Curriculum for schools to teach knitting these days,' she said. 'So schools rely on voluntary helpers, like mum's with a bit of spare time, to go in and help out.' Debbie runs basic knitting workshops regularly at her shop and is happy for children to come along and join her learn-to-knit classes.

Kate Buller, responsible for the team of Rowan Design Consultants up and down the UK, encouraged the girls to ask for help from people like Jane Bunce, Design Consultant at John Lewis in Oxford Street, London. 'If mum can't knit and gran doesn't live near enough to be able to help, any Design Consultant would be happy to give a young girl one-to-one tuition,' Kate confirmed. 'To get the most out of the time though, they need to be old enough, say ten or eleven.'

With three Friendship Bracelets, one teddy's scarf and two coloured squares completed, Nell, Sophie and Jenie were enthusiastically planning their next projects. A little stripey backpack, a patchwork cot blanket and a padded coat hanger were all desirable items under consideration, while it was hard to get Letoyah to put her work down. 'She started grabbing my knitting when she was tiny,' smiled her mum, Angela. 'I decided the only way to get some peace was to teach her as soon as she was old enough and she's never looked back.'

Left: Kate turns her attention to teaching Nell the basics. Middle: Letoyah is well away with her first sweater, but wanted some help with stranding yarns up the side of the knitting. Right: 'Yes, that's right', Jane Bunce examines Sophie's first attempt

Top left: Jenie takes her time listening and taking it all in. Top middle: A knitted coat hanger cover makes a great present for gran. Find instructions in 'Baby Style, by Debbie Bliss (see page 48 for details). Top right: Debbie Bliss.
Above left: Letoyah wears two colourful friendship bracelets. Find instructions on page 118. Above middle: Sophie is doing well and has never knitted a stitch before. Above right: Nell makes a Friendship bracelet, a simple project to help develop coordination. Right: When you're concentrating, an afternoon passes quickly.

Debbie Bliss runs knitting workshops every alternate Saturday at her shop in London. Workshops run from 10am to 4pm and include all yarn used on the day. Each workshop costs £35.

For details contact Debbie at; Debbie Bliss Shop, 365 St. John's Street, Islington, London EC2. Tel 020 7833 8255, or email her at debbie@debbiebliss.freeserve.co.uk

'Baby Style' is published by Ebury, price £12.99. ISBN 0 09 187082

Find Rowan Design Consultants at John Lewis stores and some independent department stores throughout the UK. For details of your local Design Consultant, call Rowan at 01484 681881

All independent Rowan stockists are happy to help with knitting queries and basic teaching, see the back page for details of your nearest stockist.

Find instructions for Teddy Bear in 'Toy Knits' and 'Teddy Bears' by Debbie Bliss

Feature and styling Gail Abbott Photographs Mark Scott

CLEVER IDEAS

Make the most of the sun with our bright ideas for Rowan cotton fabrics and summer yarns

LEFT: SIMPLE BLIND Fine enough to let in plenty of summer light but not totally sheer, hand woven cotton makes the perfect fabric for a simple Roman blind. For details of how to make curtains and blinds, see The Complete Curtain Book, by Isabella Forbes, published by Conran Octopus, £14.99 (UK). ISBN 1 85029 527 1

RIGHT: SOFTLY CUSHIONED Use a combination of knitted linen and embroidered textures to make a pair of cornflower blue summer cushions for a smart, contemporary armchair. Find the instructions on page 109.

BELOW RIGHT: FRINGED LINEN WRAP Rowan's newest yarn, Linen Drape, is made in a combination of linen and viscose, which knits up into a cool, lightweight fabric perfect for this stylish summer wrap. The simple lines of embroidered cross stitch and tiny glass beads, sewn on just above the moss stitch borders, give the wrap understated texture, defined by the delicate fringing at either end. Find the instructions on page 117.

BELOW: PRANCE CARDIGAN Also knitted in Linen Drape, a moss stitch cardigan with edge-to-edge fronts is fastened with buttonhole loops and tiny mother-of-pearl buttons. Find the instructions on page 107.

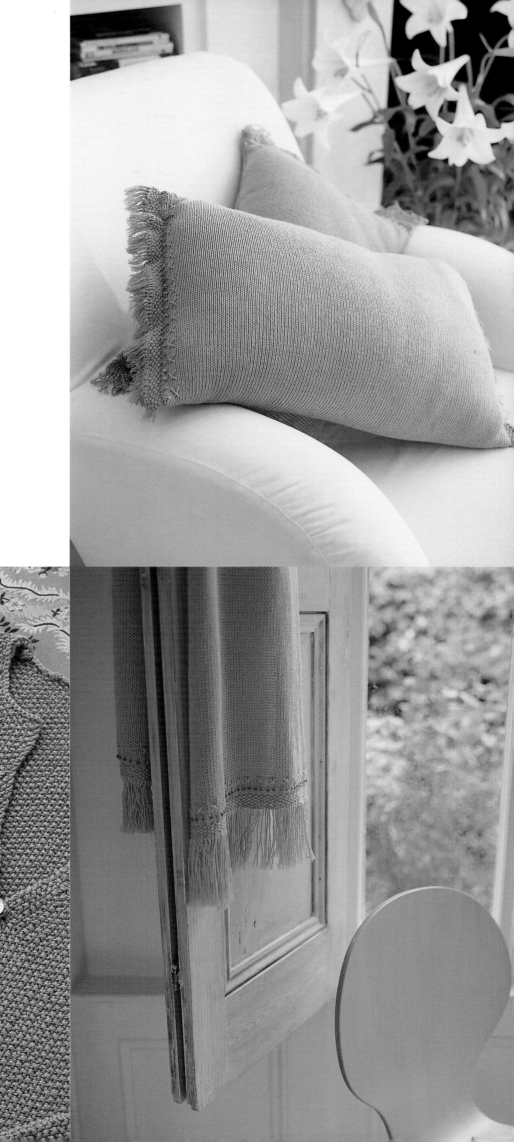

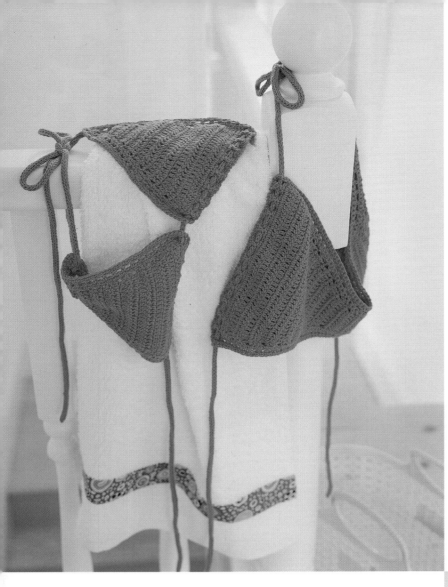

LEFT: NATTY BIKINI AND PERSONALISED TOWEL Show off your tan in this 4ply cotton crochet bikini. Worked only in double and treble crochet, the bikini is made in 3 easy shapes linked together with rouleaux bands. Find the instructions on page 87. Personalise a pure white towel too, with a strip of Roman Glass printed cotton sewn across the ends.

RIGHT: DINING CHAIR COVER Made in Rowan hand woven cotton, a slip cover will smarten up shabby upholstery or pull together an assorted collection of dining chairs into a co-ordinated set to match your interior. Make the whole set in the same colour, or mix and match plains and stripes. Find the instructions on page 118.

BELOW: LOOSELY TIED Make a wide pleat at the back of the chair cover and attach a separate tie to each side, then loop together in a soft bow to keep the cover in place. Find the instructions on page 118.

ABOVE LEFT: BRIGHT COTTON FLOOR CUSHIONS Get the most out of your floor space with these large, squashy floor cushions made in cotton fabrics from the Rowan range designed by Kaffe Fassett . Simple squares of calico are filled with polystyrene beads and a removable cotton cover zipped over the top – just throw them down either indoors or out and get on with some serious relaxing. Find instructions on page 118.

ABOVE: KNITTING BAG Keeping balls of yarn and knitting needles together, as well as essential extras like tape measures and scissors is essential in summer when you are likely to be working in the garden as well as indoors. So why not make your latest project this soft knitting bag made in Handknit DK Cotton. The handles make it easy to hang the bag on a door handle or the back of a chair, and the bag is lined throughout with 'Roman Glass' cotton fabric to stop knitting needles slipping through. Find the instructions on page 117.

LEFT: MOSS STITCH BATHMAT The simplest home furnishings are always the best, and nothing could be simpler than this moss stitch bath mat knitted in cool stripes of Handknit DK cotton. The soft blue of Raindrop contrasts with the lemony green of Zing for an easy project just right for a beginner. Find instructions on page 103.

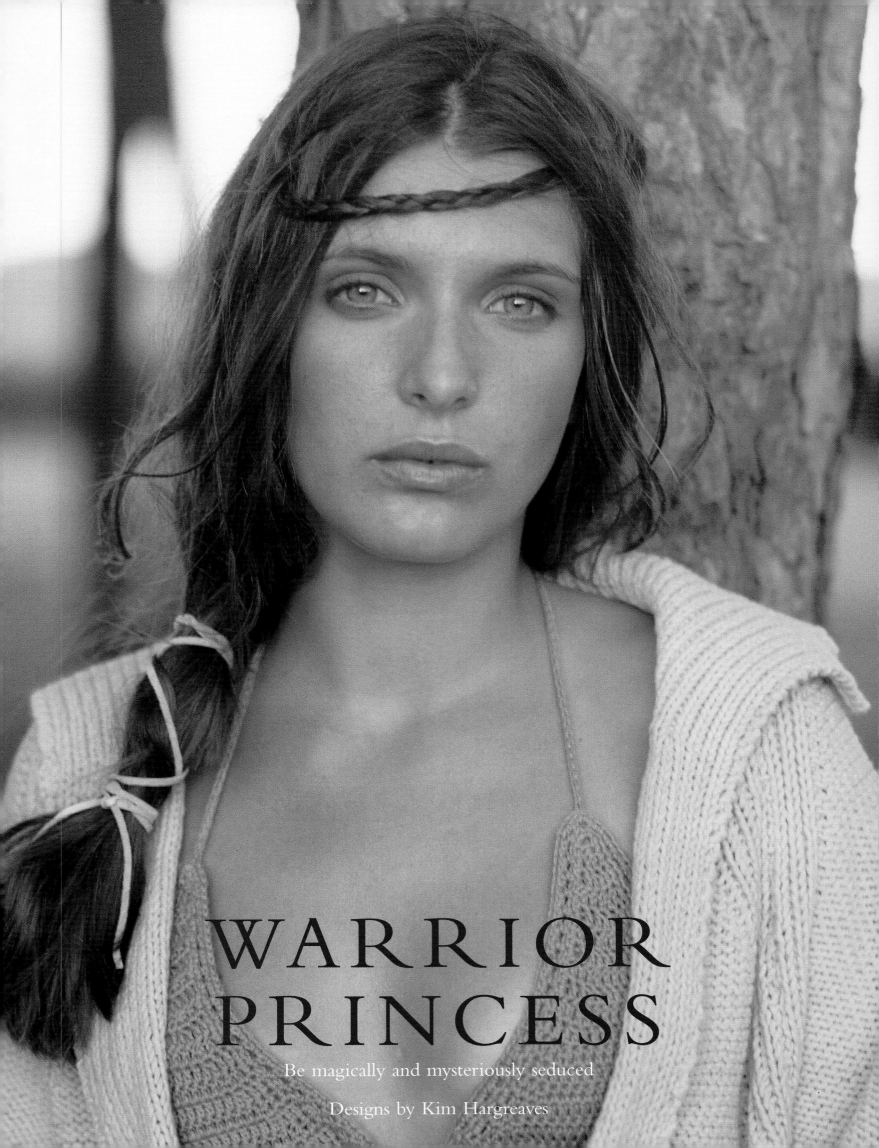

WARRIOR
PRINCESS

Be magically and mysteriously seduced

Designs by Kim Hargreaves

Opposite Earth, pattern page 71, this page Hunter, pattern page 79, both in Linen Drape

Aerial in 4ply Cotton, pattern page 114

Photographer Joey Toller Stylist Kim Hargreaves Hair & Make-up Annabel Hobbs Model Ines Castel - Branco. Thank you to Gerard Sarrouy for all his help

Opposite Moonbeam, pattern page 69, this page Enchant, pattern page 70 both in Line Drape

What's New

We take a look at some of the latest books, knitted blinds and home accessories, as well as focus on three Rowan Design Consultants and hear about an exciting new shop

MINIMAL KNITS

Designer Sarah Dallas is well placed to have her finger on the pulse of modern home textiles. As senior tutor in fashion and textiles at the Royal College of Art in London, Sarah favours a completely understated look, for her own range of felted lambswool home accessories. The designs are based on the simplicity of paintings by artists like Rothko and Sean Scully. The lambswool throws and cushions in Sarah's 2001 collection are knitted in blocks of muted greys, with simple contrasting edgings and just a hint of a tassel. Sarah Dallas's felted cushion costs £45 and the felted throw costs £350.
Contact Sarah on 020 7731 3239 for mail-order details.

SEASIDE SHOPPING

Zoe Mellor's new shop, 'Toby Tiger' has opened in Brighton with a gorgeous selection of Zoe's own designs. Knitted blankets and throws from her books, as well as children's knitwear from newborn to six years old, sit happily alongside Zoe's range of applique fleece wear. 'Bright and groovy', is how Zoe describes the shop, and with embroidered photo albums, gifts and much more, 'Toby Tiger' is well worth a visit. Find her at 15, Montpellier Place, Brighton, or visit Zoe's website, www.tobytiger.com or call Zoe on 01273 731923 for mail-order details.

ROLE PLAY

One of the keenest barometers of social change must surely be the knitting pattern, and Cath Tate has given us even more to chuckle at with her 'Loose knits' greeting cards. Poker-faced models from the 1940s wear their sweaters and balaclavas like a second skin. If you want to poke a little kindly fun at someone who takes himself just a little too seriously, Dickie, (below), is just the man for the job. Find Cath Tate cards at good book sellers and gift shops. Cath Tate, Unit 1, 45 Morrish Road, London SW2 4EE

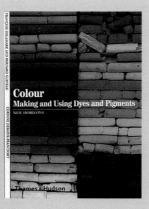

CTFLK02 Loose KNITS CHEST 32" – 44" 6D

"Manhood," thought Dickie "is a very serious business"

COLOUR STORY

If you've ever wondered where indigo and ochre come from, or why purple is the colour of royalty, this new book from Thames & Hudson will answer all your questions. We take colour for granted, but colours are manufactured and the history of pigments, hues and dyes has an ancient and fascinating history. Francois Delamare and Bernard Guineau are both specialists in this field, and this is a book as rich and varied as a painter's palette, tracing the story of how colour has been made, from the 40,000-years-old painted caves at Lascaux to the medieval cloth trade.
'Colour – Making and Using Dyes and Pigments', published by Thames & Hudson, costs £6.95 (UK). ISBN 0 500 301026

ANIMAL MAGIC

If you're a fan of Zoe Mellor's children's designs, with their colourful and wacky motifs, you'll love her latest pattern book. As a young mum herself, Zoe knows what two-year old Toby likes best. 'Toby just loves animals,' she says. 'So I've designed Animal Knits with him in mind.' Borders of bunnies, ladybird blanket and butterfly sweater; these knits will delight any young animal lover, as will the fish hat, tiger print jacket and cowprint scarf. All knitted in Rowan yarns, 'Animal Knits' is published by Collins & Brown, £10.99 (UK), Trafalgar, $19.95 (US) ISBN 1 85585 8703

salt.

SCULPTED BLINDS

Knitting is beginning to encompass every area of interiors and the newest, most innovative ideas around are blinds by textile designers June Swindell and Karina Thomas. Four years ago they set up their own company, *salt*, which designs blinds for clients like architects and interior designers, as well as private clients who want inspirational solutions to light and privacy. Vertical totems, sculptural Roman blinds and woven reflective blinds to be used as room dividers are among the award-winning projects to date, bringing knitting right up to the 21st century. Contact *salt* at: 117 Oxo Tower Wharf, Bargehouse Street, London SE1 9PH, tel 020 7593 0007. www.salt-uk.com

KNITTING WORKBOOK

Following on from her first knitting How-to book, Debbie has been working on another guide to creative knitting. Her 'Knitting Workbook' features over 20 inspiring projects for adults and children, with easy-to-follow step-by-steps to help you get to grips with techniques like Fair Isle, intarsia and shaping. 'Knitting Workshop', by Debbie Bliss, is published by Ebury, £14.99 (UK). ISBN 0 09187 873X

Photograph Sandra Lane

HOME GROWN TALENT

Rowan Design Consultants are a talented bunch. Many of them are designers in their own right, with years of experience behind them, so you know you are getting the best advice when you need help. As well as spending time with knitters in-store, many of the Consultants are forging ahead selling their own designs, either as kits or finished items.

Gaye Hawkins is the Design Consultant in Cambridge's Robert Sayle, and she has brought out a delightful range of knitted gifts and kits inspired by Shaker designs. This padded coat hanger with a heart lavender bag and matching wash bag is knitted in Handknit DK Cotton, and is available as a finished set for £26.50, or £14.00 for the kit, which includes the coat hanger, wadding, sachet of lavender and button, as well as all the yarn needed to knit the items. Both prices are inclusive of post and packing. Call Gaye on 01480 216708 for details and a free leaflet of her other designs

Photograph Mark Scott

Photograph Mark Scott

Since Julie Marchington moved to Edinburgh she has been able to combine her love of hand knitting with her enthusiam for the Scottish landscape. As well as working as Design Consultant in Edinburgh's John Lewis, Julie is running her own business selling knitted garments and kits. 'The Broch' jacket was inspired by the lichen covered walls of Dunn Beag Broch, a ruined fort on the Isle of Skye. Knitted mainly in Magpie Tweed, 'The Broch' is available as a long jacket, price £140, or £65 for the kit, or this smaller, cropped, version, price £110 or £55 for the kit. Please add £3 for post and packing. Call Julie on 0131 447 3627; email, julie.marchington@hot-toast.com or visit her website www.handknit.co.uk.

Debbie Abrahams, from Jessops in Nottingham, is well known for her beaded cushions and bags, but Debbie also makes a stunning collection of hand crafted ceramic buttons. Made from earthenware clay which is then glazed and fired, the buttons come in a wide variety of designs ranging from simple, plain colours, embossed patterns, multi-coloured designs and some charming novelty buttons. Individual buttons start at 80p each. See Debbie's range on her website: www.da-handknits.demon.co.uk or call her on 0115 9161524.

Photograph Mark Scott

A HELPING HAND

Help and advice is always on hand from Debbie, Gaye, Julie and all the team of Rowan Design Consultants up and down the country. For details of your nearest Rowan Design Consultant, to find out when she is in-store and details of their one-day workshops, contact Rowan on 01481 681881, or look on the Rowan website www.rowanyarns.co.uk

ROWAN INTERNATIONAL

If you haven't joined Rowan's unique member's club, you are missing out on a great deal. Rowan International members are spread throughout the world in over forty countries, and every member receives two free newsletters a year which are packed with up-to-date information on knitting events, exhibitions and books, interesting news stories and lots of special offers and discounts. Also included in the Rowan International package is free delivery of two Rowan Knitting Magazines each year and a chance to benefit from the famous Knitting Circle which brings knitters together with like-minded souls in their area. New members get a free gift too, this year's gift is a knitting kit of Kim Hargreaves' embroidered beach bag (see left). Membership for one year costs £14.95 (UK), £19.50 (Europe), $39 (US and Canada) and £24.50 elsewhere. To join, call 01484 681881, or fill in the form on the Rowan website; www.rowanyarns.co.uk

Photograph by Joey Toller

ROWAN ONLINE

If you want all the latest information and products at your fingertips, plus new and exciting developments coming online regularly, don't miss out on the new Rowan website. You can read the story of Rowan and find out how the company started, review all the latest knitting books and order them online, get up to date information on workshops and events and find your nearest stockist at a click of your mouse. But there's more to come. The new website address is about to bring you a complete resource centre, with a pattern library, a chat room in the member's lounge for Rowan International members, bulletin boards for you to paste up your own information and comments, and lots, lots more.

VISIT GREEN LANE MILL

Now's your chance to soak up the unique atmosphere of Rowan's own 19th century Mill, set in the rolling countryside of West Yorkshire. Green Lane Mill has been home to Rowan since the beginning, and now there's a new programme of workshops about to start, held in the spacious showrooms. With displays of all the latest collections to inspire, baskets of colourful yarns to entice, plentiful tea and coffee, plus a delicious lunch to refresh, you will have a lively and special weekend to remember. Stay in Holmfirth, the setting for TV's 'The Last of the Summer Wine', and socialise with other knitters, make new friends and have a great time. Find out more from Rowan.

Photograph Hannah Mournemont

SUMMER LINENS

Just in time for the warmer weather, the newest Rowan yarn is 'Linen Drape', a machine washable combination of 55% linen and 45% viscose. 10 delicious colours include pastels like the pink of 'Petal' and the blue of 'Cornflower' (see the summer wrap and knitted cushions in 'Clever Ideas' on page 49), as well as deeper colours like the rich purple 'Hawaii' and brights like coral red 'Watermelon' and the zingy aqua of 'Splash'. Cool and contemporary, 'Linen Drape' is perfect for knitting into simple home textiles or the latest fitted sweater.

Photograph Mark Scott

ROWAN KNITTING MAGAZINE NUMBER 29

Index

Design number 1

Sheriff

LOUISA HARDING

YARN
Rowan Denim

One size to fit bust | 86–97 | | cm
| | 34–38 | | in

3 colour sweater

A Nashville	225	6	x	50gm
B Memphis	229	11	x	50gm
C Ecru	324	7	x	50gm
One colour sweater		20	x	50gm

(photographed in Ecru 324)

NEEDLES
1 pair 3¼mm (no 10) (US 3) needles
1 pair 4mm (no 8) (US 6) needles

BEADS – Approx 3,250 clear glass beads
(See page 117 for details).

TENSION (before washing)
20 sts and 28 rows to 10 cm measured over stocking stitch using 4mm (US 6) needles.

Tension note: Denim will shrink in length when washed for the first time. Allowances have been made in this pattern for shrinkage (see size diagram for after washing measurements).

Colour note: When 3 colour garment is washed, indigo dye will bleed into ecru blocks, making them appear pale blue (as in photograph.)

Beading note: Thread beads onto yarn before beginning. To make it easier to thread beads onto yarn, try "painting" the first few inches of yarn with nail varnish. Each star motif uses 59 beads – ensure there are sufficient beads threaded onto appropriate yarn before starting the block. Place beads within knitting as folls: bring yarn to front (RS) of work and slip next st purlwise, slide bead along yarn so that it sits in front of st just slipped, then take yarn to back (WS) of work.

3 colour sweater
BACK and FRONT (both alike)
Using 3¼mm (US 3) needles, cast on as folls: (21 sts using yarn A, 21 sts using yarn B) 3 times. 126 sts.
Using colours as set by cast-on, work in garter st for 6 rows.
Using the **intarsia** technique described on the information page and repeating the 42 st patt repeat 3 times, cont in patt from chart as folls:
Work 4 rows.
Change to 4mm (US 6) needles.
Cont as set until chart row 69 has been worked for third time (6th band of blocks nearly completed).
Change to 3¼mm (US 3) needles.
Using colours as set by last row, work in garter st for 8 rows.
Cast off knitwise (on WS).

SLEEVES (both alike)
(**Note**: positioning of blocks on sleeve has been adjusted from that in photograph to give better distribution of colours over entire garment.)
Using 3¼mm (US 3) needles, cast on as folls:
(21 sts using yarn B, 21 sts using yarn C) twice. 84 sts.
Using colours as set by cast-on, work in garter st for 6 rows.
Repeating the 42 st patt repeat twice and **beg with chart row 37**, cont in patt from chart as folls:
Work 4 rows.
Change to 4mm (US 6) needles.
Cont straight until chart row 36 has been worked for second time (4th band of blocks completed).
Cast off knitwise.

UNDERARM GUSSETS (make 2)
Cast on 3 sts using 4mm (US 6) needles and yarn B.
Row 1 (RS): Knit.
Row 2: Purl, inc 1 st at each end of row.
Row 3: Knit, inc 1 st at each end of row.
Row 4: Purl.
Row 5: As row 3.
Row 6: As row 2.
Rep last 6 rows 3 times more. 35 sts.
Row 25 (RS): Knit.
Row 26: P2tog, P to last 2 sts, P2tog.
Row 27: K2tog, K to last 2 sts, K2tog.
Row 28: Purl.
Row 29: As row 27.
Row 30: As row 26.
Rep last 6 rows 3 times more.
Cast off rem 3 sts.

MAKING UP
DO NOT PRESS.
Machine wash all pieces together before sewing together (see ball band for instructions).
Join shoulder seams using back stitch, or mattress stitch if preferred, leaving 30 cm neck opening at centre.

See information page for finishing instructions, setting in sleeves using the straight cast-off method and leaving 10 cm open along underarm/sleeve seam either side of underarm point. Matching cast-on and cast-off ends of gussets to side and sleeve seams and other points to underarm points, sew gussets into seams.

One colour sweater
Work as given for 3 colour sweater, using same colour throughout and replacing "bead 1" with "slip one st purlwise" (so that all stars appear the same).

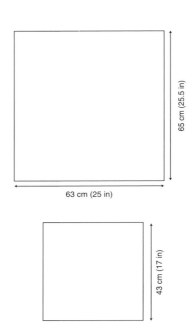

65 cm (25.5 in)
63 cm (25 in)

43 cm (17 in)

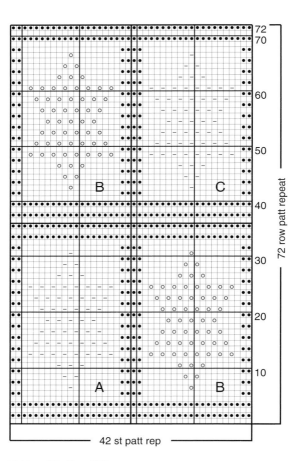

72 row patt repeat
42 st patt rep

□ K on RS, P on WS
● P on RS, K on WS
⊙ Place bead
⊟ Slip st purlwise with yarn at front (RS) of work

Design number 2

Moonbeam

KIM HARGREAVES

YARN
Rowan Linen

	XS	S	M	L	XL	
To fit bust	81	86	91	97	102	cm
	32	34	36	38	40	in
Vest	5	5	6	6	7	x 50gm
Sweater	8	9	9	10	11	x 50gm

(vest photographed in Pewter 841, sweater in Cornflower 846)

NEEDLES
1 pair 3mm (no 11) (US 2/3) needles
1 pair 3¾mm (no 9) (US 5) needles
2 double-pointed 3mm (no 11) (US 2/3) needles

TENSION
23 sts and 30 rows to 10 cm measured over flattened rib pattern using 3¾mm (US 5) needles.

Pattern note: As row end edges around front opening, neck and, for vest, armhole edges form actual finished edges of garment, it is important these edges are kept neat. Therefore all new balls of yarn should be joined in at side seam or, for sweater, armhole edges of rows.

FRONT
Cast on 90 (98: 106: 114: 122) sts using 3mm (US 2/3) needles.
Row 1 (RS): K2, ★P2, K2, rep from ★ to end.
Row 2: P2, ★K2, P2, rep from ★ to end.
These 2 rows form rib.
Work a further 2 (4: 4: 4: 4) rows in rib.
Dec 1 st at each end of next row.
88 (96: 104: 112: 120) sts.
Work 3 (1: 1: 1: 1) rows.
Change to 3¾mm (US 5) needles.
Work 2 (4: 4: 4: 4) rows.
Dec 1 st at each end of next and foll 6th row, then on every foll 4th row until 78 (86: 94: 102: 110) sts rem.
Cont straight until front measures 12 (13: 13: 14: 14) cm, ending with a WS row.
Inc 1 st at each end of next and every foll 10th row to 84 (92: 100: 108: 116) sts, then on every foll 8th row until there are 90 (98: 106: 114: 122) sts, working inc sts in rib.★★
Work 3 rows, ending with a WS row.
Divide for front opening
Next row (RS): Rib 44 (48: 52: 56: 60), K1 and turn, leaving rem sts on a holder.
Work each side of neck separately.
Next row (WS): K1, rib to end.
Last 2 rows set the sts – front opening edge st worked as a K st on every row with all other sts in rib.
Keeping sts correct as set, cont as folls:
Next row (eyelet row) (RS): Rib to last 7 sts, yrn (for eyelet), P2tog, rib 4, K1.
Work 5 rows, ending with a WS row.
Shape armhole
Cast off 5 sts at beg of next row. 40 (44: 48: 52: 56) sts.
Work 1 row.
Next row (RS): K1, P2, K2, P1, P2tog, rib to last 7 sts, yrn (for 2nd eyelet), P2tog, rib 4, K1.
Next row: K1, rib to last 8 sts, K2tog, K1, P2, K3.
Making eyelets in every foll 6th row, working all armhole decreases as set by last 2 rows and working armhole edge st as a K st on every row, cont as folls:
Dec 1 st at armhole edge of next 3 (3: 7: 7: 7) rows, then on foll 3 alt rows. 32 (36: 36: 40: 44) sts.
Work 12 (12: 8: 8: 8) rows, ending 4 rows after 5th eyelet and with a RS row.
Shape neck
Cast off 8 (8: 8: 12: 12) sts at beg of next row.
24 (28: 28: 28: 32) sts.
Next row (RS): Rib to last 8 sts, P2tog, P1, K2, P2, K1.
Next row: K3, P2, K1, K2tog, rib to end.
Working all neck decreases as set by last 2 rows and working first and last st of every row as a K st, cont as folls:
Dec 1 st at neck edge of next 3 rows, then on foll 4 alt rows, then on every foll 4th row until 12 (16: 16: 16: 20) sts rem.
Cont straight until armhole measures 20 (20: 21: 21: 22) cm, ending with a WS row.
Shape shoulder
Cast off 4 (5: 5: 5: 7) sts at beg of next and foll alt row.
Work 1 row.
Cast off rem 4 (6: 6: 6: 6) sts.
With RS facing, rejoin yarn to rem sts and complete to match first side, reversing shaping.

BACK
Work as given for front to ★★.
Cont straight until back matches front to beg of armhole shaping, ending with a WS row.
Shape armholes
Cast off 5 sts at beg of next 2 rows.
80 (88: 96: 104: 112) sts.

Working all armhole decreases 6 sts in from ends of rows as given for front and working first and last st of every row as a K st, cont as folls:
Dec 1 st at armhole edge of next 5 (5: 9: 9: 9) rows, then on foll 3 alt rows. 64 (72: 72: 80: 88) sts.
Cont straight until 2 rows less have been worked than on back to start of shoulder shaping, ending with a WS row.
Shape back neck and shoulders
Next row (RS): Rib 15 (19: 19: 19: 23), K1 and turn, leaving rem sts on a holder.
Work each side of neck separately.
Working all neck decreases in same way as armhole decreases and keeping neck edge st as a K st on every row, cont as folls:
Dec 1 st at neck edge of next row.
Cast off 4 (5: 5: 5: 7) sts at beg and dec 1 st at end of next row.
Rep last 2 rows once more. Work 1 row.
Cast off rem 4 (6: 6: 6: 6) sts.
With RS facing, rejoin yarn to rem sts, cast off centre 32 (32: 32: 40: 40) sts, rib to end.
Work to match first side, reversing shapings.

SWEATER SLEEVES (both alike)
Cast on 58 (58: 58: 62: 62) sts using 3mm (US 2/3) needles.
Work in rib as given for front for 8 rows.
Change to 3¾mm (US 5) needles.
Cont in rib, inc 1 st at each end of next and every foll 8th row to 78 (78: 70: 82: 74) sts, then on every foll 6th (6th: 6th: 10th: 6th) row until there are 80 (80: 84: 84: 88) sts, taking inc sts into rib.
Cont straight until sleeve measures 33 (33: 34: 34: 34) cm, ending with a WS row.
Shape top
Cast off 5 sts at beg of next 2 rows.
70 (70: 74: 74: 78) sts.
Working all decreases in same way as armhole and neck decreases, dec 1 st at each end of next 3 rows, then on foll 3 alt rows, then on every foll 4th row until 46 (46: 52: 52: 58) sts rem.
Work 1 row, ending with a WS row.
Dec 1 st at each end of next and foll 0 (0: 3: 3: 6) alt rows, then on foll 3 rows. 38 sts.
Cast off 5 sts at beg of next 2 rows.
Cast off rem 28 sts.

MAKING UP
PRESS all pieces as described on the info page.
Tie
Using double pointed 3mm (US 2/3) needles, cast on 3 sts.
Next row (RS): K3 – all 3 sts now on right needle, ★slip sts to opposite end of needle and transfer this needle to left hand, without turning work and taking yarn quite tightly across back of work, K same 3 sts again – all 3 sts now on right needle again, rep from ★ until tie is 100 cm long.
Next row: K3tog and fasten off.
Thread tie in and out of front opening eyelet holes.
See information page for finishing instructions, setting in sweater sleeves using the set-in method.

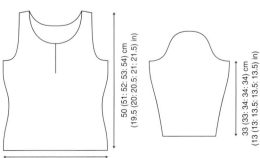

50 (51: 52: 53: 54) cm
(19.5 (20: 20.5: 21: 21.5) in)

39 (42.5: 46: 49.5: 53) cm
(15.5 (16.5: 18: 19.5: 21) in)

33 (33: 34: 34: 34) cm
(13 (13: 13.5: 13.5: 13.5) in)

Design number 3

Enchant

KIM HARGREAVES

YARN

	XS	S	M	L	XL
To fit bust	81	86	91	97	102 cm
	32	34	36	38	40 in

Rowan Linen Drape

| | 11 | 11 | 12 | 13 | 13 x 50gm |

(tie front version photographed in Reed 845, buttoned version in Watery 844)

NEEDLES

1 pair 3mm (no 11) (US 2/3) needles
1 pair 3¾mm (no 9) (US 5) needles

BUTTONS – 5 for buttoned version

BEADS – approx 70 rectangular glass beads for tie front version (See page 117 for details).

TENSION

23 sts and 30 rows to 10 cm measured over stocking stitch using 3¾mm (US 5) needles.

Pattern note: As row end edges of fronts form actual finished edges of garment, it is important these edges are kept neat. Therefore all new balls of yarn should be joined in at side seam or armhole edges of rows.

BACK
Cast on 104 (110: 116: 122: 128) sts using 3mm (US 2/3) needles.
Row 1 (RS): Knit.
Row 2: K2, P to last 2 sts, K2.
Rep rows 1 and 2, 9 times more.
Change to 3¾mm (US 5) needles and work a further 8 rows in patt as set.
Beg with a K row, cont in st st as folls:
Counting from both ends of last row, place markers on 24th (26th: 28th: 30th: 32nd) sts in from ends of row.
Row 29 (RS): K2tog, *K to within 1 st of marker, sl 2 tog as though to K2tog (marked st is 2nd of these sts), K1, p2sso, rep from * once more, K to last 2 sts, K2tog.
Work 15 rows.
Rep last 16 rows once more and then row 29 again. 86 (92: 98: 104: 110) sts.
Work 17 (19: 19: 21: 21) rows.
Next row (RS): Inc in first st, *K to marked st, M1, K marked st, M1, rep from * once more, K to last st, inc in last st.
Work 17 rows.
Rep last 18 rows once more and then first of these rows (the inc row) again. 104 (110: 116: 122: 128) sts.
Cont straight until back measures 42 (43: 43: 44: 44) cm, ending with a WS row.
Shape armholes
Cast off 3 (4: 4: 5: 5) sts at beg of next 2 rows. 98 (102: 108: 112: 118) sts.
Dec 1 st at each end of next 7 (7: 9: 9: 11) rows, then on foll 3 (4: 4: 5: 5) alt rows.
78 (80: 82: 84: 86) sts.
Cont straight until armhole measures 21 (21: 22: 22: 23) cm, ending with a WS row.
Shape shoulders and back neck
Cast off 7 (7: 8: 8: 8) sts at beg of next 3 rows. 57 (59: 58: 60: 62) sts.
Next row (WS): Cast off 7 (7: 8: 8: 8) sts, P until there are 6 (6: 5: 5: 6) sts on right needle, K38 (40: 40: 42: 42), P6 (6: 5: 5: 6).
Next row: Cast off 8 (8: 7: 7: 8) sts, K to end.
Next row: Cast off first 6 (6: 5: 5: 6) sts purlwise, cast off rem sts knitwise.

LEFT FRONT
Cast on 54 (57: 60: 63: 66) sts using 3mm (US 2/3) needles.
Tie front version only
Row 1 (RS): Knit.
Row 2: K2, P to last 2 sts, K2.
These 2 rows set the sts – first and last 2 sts of every row worked in garter st with all other sts in st st.
Buttoned version only
Row 1 (RS): Knit.
Row 2: K4, P to last 2 sts, K2.
These 2 rows set the sts – front opening edge 4 sts and side edge 2 sts of every row worked in garter st with all other sts in st st.
Both versions
Rep rows 1 and 2, 9 times more.
Change to 3¾mm (US 5) needles and work a further 8 rows in patt as set.
Keeping front opening edge sts in garter st as set and now working all other sts in st st, cont as folls:
Counting from side seam, place marker on 24th (26th: 28th: 30th: 32nd) sts in from end of last row.
Row 29 (RS): K2tog, K to within 1 st of marker, sl 2 tog, K1, p2sso, K to end.
Work 15 rows.

Rep last 16 rows once more and then row 29 again.
45 (48: 51: 54: 57) sts.
Work 17 (19: 19: 21: 21) rows.
Next row (RS): Inc in first st, K to marked st, M1, K marked st, M1, K to end.
Work 17 rows.
Rep last 18 rows once more and then first of these rows (the inc row) again. 54 (57: 60: 63: 66) sts.
Cont straight until left front matches back to beg of armhole shaping, ending with a WS row.
Shape armhole
Cast off 3 (4: 4: 5: 5) sts at beg of next row.
51 (53: 56: 58: 61) sts.
Work 1 row.
Dec 1 st at armhole edge of next 4 rows.
47 (49: 52: 54: 57) sts.
Shape neck
Tie front version only
Next row (RS) (dec): K2tog, K to last 5 sts, K2tog, K3.
Next row: K2, P to last 2 sts, P2tog.
Buttoned version only
Next row (RS) (dec): K2tog, K to last 7 sts, K2tog, K5.
Next row: K4, P to last 2 sts, P2tog.
Both versions
Working all neck decreases as set by last 2 rows, dec 1 st at armhole edge of next 1 (1: 3: 3: 5) rows, then on foll 3 (4: 4: 5: 5) alt rows **and at same time** dec 1 st at neck edge of next and every foll alt row. 36 sts.
Work 1 row.
Dec 1 st at neck edge **only** of next and foll 6 (7: 4: 5: 3) alt rows, then on every foll 4th row until 22 (22: 23: 23: 24) sts rem.
Cont straight until left front matches back to start of shoulder shaping, ending with a WS row.
Shape shoulder
Cast off 7 (7: 8: 8: 8) sts at beg of next and foll alt row.
Work 1 row.
Cast off rem 8 (8: 7: 7: 8) sts.
Buttoned version only
Mark positions for 5 buttons along left front opening edge – first to come in 25th row above cast-on edge, last to come just below start of neck shaping and rem 3 buttons evenly spaced between.

RIGHT FRONT
Cast on 54 (57: 60: 63: 66) sts using 3mm (US 2/3) needles.
Tie front version only
Row 1 (RS): Knit.
Row 2: K2, P to last 2 sts, K2.
These 2 rows set the sts – first and last 2 sts of every row worked in garter st with all other sts in st st.
Buttoned version only
Row 1 (RS): Knit.
Row 2: K2, P to last 4 sts, K4.
These 2 rows set the sts – front opening edge 4 sts and side edge 2 sts of every row worked in garter st with all other sts in st st.
Both versions
Rep rows 1 and 2, 9 times more.
Change to 3¾mm (US 5) needles.
Tie front version only
Rep rows 1 and 2, 4 times more.
Buttoned version only
Rep rows 1 and 2 twice more.
Next row (RS) (buttonhole row): K2, yfwd, K2tog, K to end.
Next row: K2, P to last 4 sts, K4.
Working a further 4 buttonholes in this way to correspond with positions marked for buttons on left front, cont as folls:
Rep rows 1 and 2, once more.
Both versions
Keeping front opening edge sts in garter st as set and now working all other sts in st st, complete to match left front, reversing shapings.

SLEEVES (both alike)
Cast on 54 (54: 56: 58: 58) sts using 3mm (US 2/3) needles.
Beg with a K row, work 8 rows in st st.
Row 9 (RS): K3, M1, K to last 3 sts, M1, K3.
Working all increases as set by last row, cont as folls:
Work 1 row.
Change to 3¾mm (US 5) needles.
Cont in st st, inc 1 st at each end of every foll 8th row from previous inc to 74 (80: 82: 84: 82) sts, then on every foll 10th (6th: 10th: 10th: 6th) row until there are 80 (82: 84: 86: 88) sts.
Cont straight until sleeve measures 41 (41: 42: 42: 42) cm, ending with a WS row.

Shape top

Cast off 3 (4: 4: 5: 5) sts at beg of next 2 rows.
74 (74: 76: 76: 78) sts.
Dec 1 st at each end of next 3 rows, then on foll 3 alt rows, then on every foll 4th row until 54 (54: 56: 56: 58) sts rem.
Work 1 row, ending with a WS row.
Dec 1 st at each end of next and foll 2 (2: 3: 3: 4) alt rows, then on foll 5 rows, ending with a WS row.
38 sts.
Cast off 4 sts at beg of next 4 rows.
Cast off rem 22 sts.

MAKING UP
PRESS all pieces as described on the information page.
See information page for finishing instructions, setting in sleeves using the set-in method and leaving side seams open for first 28 rows.

Tie front version only

Using 2 strands of yarn, make 2 twisted cords approx 22 cm long and knot ends, leaving a tassel of approx 6 cm. Thread a bead onto each yarn end of tassel and tie a knot to secure bead. Attach other ends of ties to inside of fronts just below start of front neck shaping. Sew a row of beads around each cuff edge, positioning beads on every other st of 6th row up from cast-on edge.

Buttoned version only

Sew on buttons.

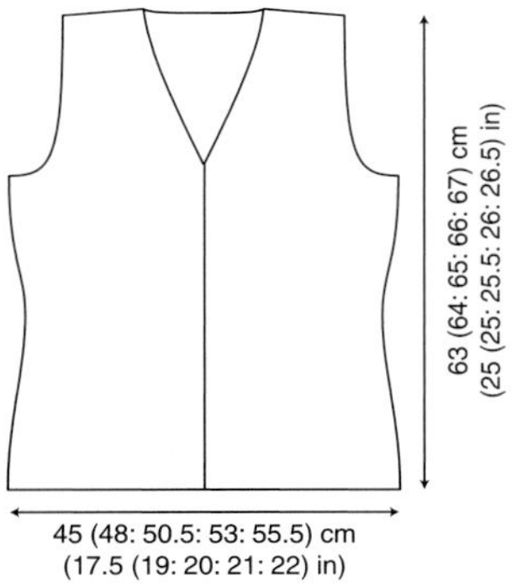
63 (64: 65: 66: 67) cm
(25 (25: 25.5: 26: 26.5) in)
45 (48: 50.5: 53: 55.5) cm
(17.5 (19: 20: 21: 22) in)

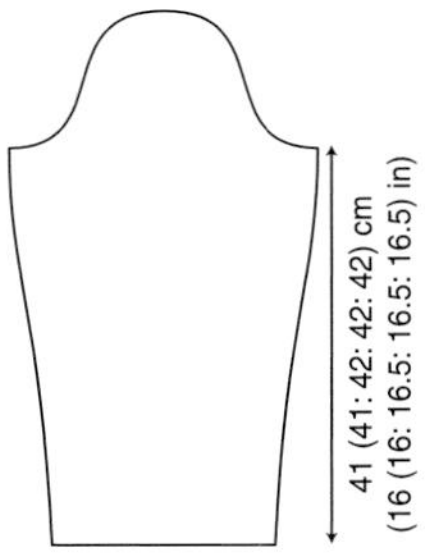
41 (41: 42: 42: 42) cm
(16 (16: 16.5: 16.5: 16.5) in)

Design number 4

Earth

KIM HARGREAVES

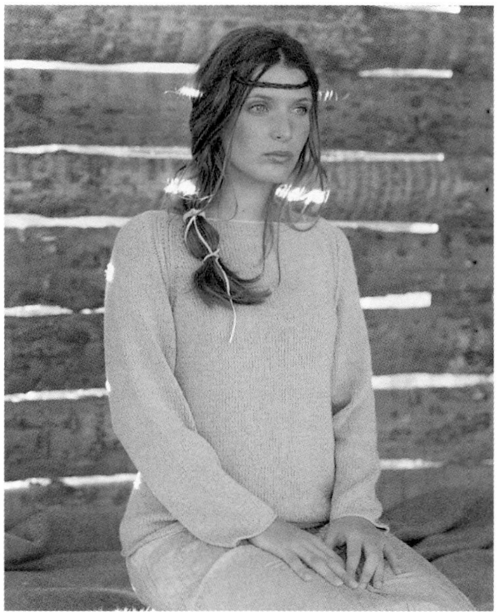

YARN

	XS	S	M	L	XL	
To fit bust	81	86	91	97	102	cm
	32	34	36	38	40	in
Rowan Linen Drape						
	10	10	11	11	12	x 50gm

(photographed in Reed 845)

NEEDLES
1 pair 3mm (no 11) (US 2/3) needles
1 pair 3¾mm (no 9) (US 5) needles

TENSION
23 sts and 30 rows to 10 cm measured over stocking stitch using 3¾mm (US 5) needles.

BACK and FRONT (both alike)
Cast on 104 (110: 116: 122: 128) sts using 3mm (US 2/3) needles.
Beg with a K row, work in st st as folls:
Work 8 rows.
Change to 3¾mm (US 5) needles.
Work 14 rows.
Row 23 (dec) (RS): K3, K2tog, K to last 5 sts, K2tog tbl, K3.
Work 5 rows.
Rep last 6 rows 4 times more and then row 23 again.
92 (98: 104: 110: 116) sts.
Work 15 rows.
Row 69 (inc) (RS): K3, M1, K to last 3 sts, M1, K3.
Work 7 rows.
Rep last 8 rows 4 times more and then row 69 again.
104 (110: 116: 122: 128) sts.
Cont straight until back measures 39 cm, ending with a WS row.

Shape raglan armholes

Cast off 6 sts at beg of next 2 rows.
92 (98: 104: 110: 116) sts.
Next row (RS): P2, K2, P1, P2tog, K to last 7 sts, P2tog tbl, P1, K2, P2.
Next row: K2, P2, K2, P to last 6 sts, K2, P2, K2.
Rep last 2 rows 9 (12: 17: 20: 25) times more.
72 (72: 68: 68: 64) sts.
Next row (RS): P2, K2, P1, P2tog, K to last 7 sts, P2tog tbl, P1, K2, P2.
Next row: K2, P2, K2, P to last 6 sts, K2, P2, K2.
Next row: P2, K2, P2, K to last 6 sts, P2, K2, P2.
Next row: K2, P2, K2, P to last 6 sts, K2, P2, K2.
Rep last 4 rows 8 (7: 5: 4: 2) times more.
Cast off rem 54 (56: 56: 58: 58) sts.

SLEEVES (both alike)
Cast on 52 (52: 54: 56: 56) sts using 3mm (US 2/3) needles.
Beg with a K row, work in st st as folls:
Work 10 rows.
Change to 3¾mm (US 5) needles.
Row 11 (RS): K3, M1, K to last 3 sts, M1, K3.
Working all increases as set by last row, cont as folls:
Inc 1 st at each end of every foll 8th row until there are 80 (82: 84: 86: 88) sts.
Cont straight until sleeve measures 45 (45: 46: 46: 46) cm, ending with a WS row.

Shape raglan

Cast off 6 sts at beg of next 2 rows.
68 (70: 72: 74: 76) sts.
Next row (RS): P2, K2, P1, P3tog, K to last 8 sts, P3tog tbl, P1, K2, P2.
Next row: K2, P2, K2, P to last 6 sts, K2, P2, K2.
Rep last 2 rows once more. 60 (62: 64: 66: 68) sts.
Next row (RS): P2, K2, P1, P2tog, K to last 7 sts, P2tog tbl, P1, K2, P2.
Next row: K2, P2, K2, P to last 6 sts, K2, P2, K2.
Rep last 2 rows 21 (22: 23: 24: 25) times more.
16 sts.
Next row (RS): P2, K2, P1, P2tog, K2, P2tog tbl, P1, K2, P2. 14 sts.
Next row: (K2, P2) 3 times, K2.
Next row: (P2, K2) 3 times, P2.
Next row: (K2, P2) 3 times, K2.
Next row: P2, K2, P1, P2tog, P2tog tbl, P1, K2, P2.
12 sts.
Next row: K2, P2, K4, P2, K2.
Next row: P2, K2, P4, K2, P2.
Next row: K2, P2, K4, P2, K2.
Cast off.

MAKING UP
PRESS all pieces as described on the information page. As there is no neckband on this garment, ensure all ends are sewn in neatly.
See information page for finishing instructions.

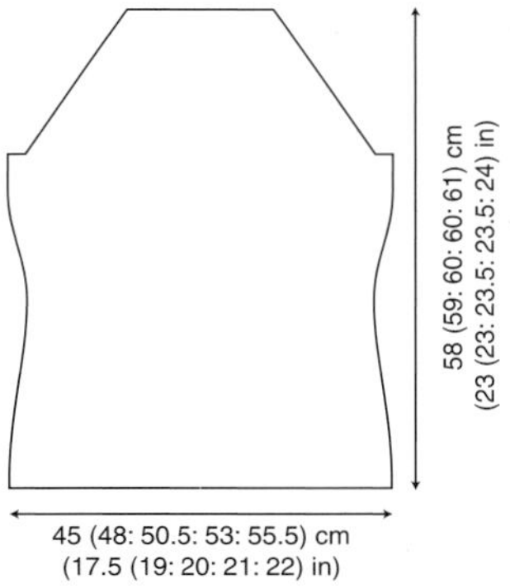
58 (59: 60: 60: 61) cm
(23 (23: 23.5: 23.5: 24) in)
45 (48: 50.5: 53: 55.5) cm
(17.5 (19: 20: 21: 22) in)

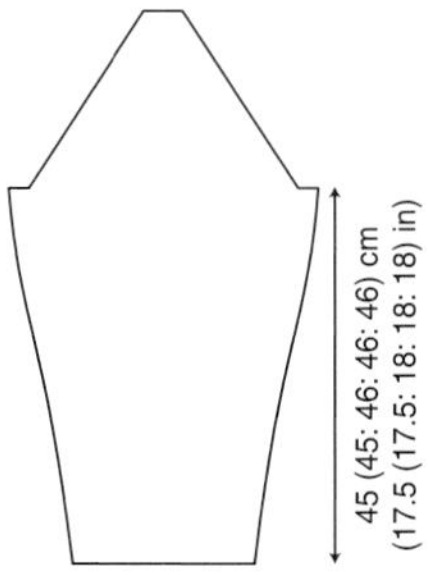
45 (45: 46: 46: 46) cm
(17.5 (17.5: 18: 18: 18) in)

Design number 5

Flourish

KIM HARGREAVES

YARN
Rowan Cotton Glace

		XS	S	M	L	XL	
To fit bust		81	86	91	97	102	cm
		32	34	36	38	40	in

Multi coloured cardigan

A Oyster	730	10	11	11	12	12 x 50gm
B Butter	795	1	1	1	1	1 x 50gm
C Terracotta	786	2	2	2	2	2 x 50gm
D Blood Orange	445	2	2	3	3	3 x 50gm
E Black	727	1	1	1	1	1 x 50gm

Alternative colourway (not photographed)

A Oyster	730	10	11	11	12	12 x 50gm
B Butter	795	1	1	1	1	1 x 50gm
C Bubbles	724	2	2	2	2	2 x 50gm
D Crushed Rose	793	2	2	3	3	3 x 50gm
E Black	727	1	1	1	1	1 x 50gm

One colour cardigan 8 8 9 9 10 x 50gm
(photographed in Glee 799)

NEEDLES
1 pair 2¾mm (no 12) (US 2) needles
1 pair 3¼mm (no 10) (US 3) needles

BUTTONS - 5

TENSION
23 sts and 32 rows to 10 cm measured over patterned
stocking stitch using 3¼mm (US 3) needles.

Multi coloured cardigan
BACK
Cast on 107 (113: 119: 125: 131) sts using 2¾mm
(US 2) needles and yarn C.
Break off yarn C and join in yarn A.
Knit 3 rows.
Row 4 (WS): P1 (0: 1: 0: 1), ★K1, P1, rep from ★ to
last 0 (1: 0: 1: 0) st, K0 (1: 0: 1: 0).
Row 5: As row 4.
These 2 rows form moss st.
Work a further 15 rows in moss st.
Change to 3¼mm (US 3) needles.
Using the **intarsia** technique described on the
information page and starting and ending rows as
indicated, cont in patt foll chart for back, which is
worked entirely in st st, as folls:
Work 2 rows.
Place markers on 26th (29th: 32nd: 35th: 38th) st in
from each end of row.
Row 3 (dec) (RS): K2tog, patt to within 1 st of
marked st, K3tog tbl, patt to within 1 st of second
marked st, K3tog, patt to last 2 sts, K2tog.
Work 7 rows.
Rep last 8 rows twice more and then row 3 (the dec
row) again. 83 (89: 95: 101: 107) sts.
Work 15 rows, ending with chart row 42.
Row 43 (inc) (RS): Inc in first st, ★patt to marked
st, M1, K marked st, M1, rep from ★ once more, patt
to last st, inc in last st.
Work 11 rows.
Rep last 12 rows twice more and then row 43 (the
inc row) again. 107 (113: 119: 125: 131) sts.
Work 13 (17: 17: 21: 21) rows, ending with chart
row 92 (96: 96: 100: 100).
(Work measures 35 (36: 36: 37: 37) cm.)
Shape armholes
Keeping chart correct, cast off 3 (4: 4: 5: 5) sts at beg
of next 2 rows. 101 (105: 111: 115: 121) sts.
Dec 1 st at each end of next 5 (5: 7: 7: 9) rows, then
on foll 6 (7: 7: 8: 8) alt rows. 79 (81: 83: 85: 87) sts.
Cont straight until chart row 156 (160: 164: 168: 170)
has been completed, ending with a WS row.
(Armhole measures 20 (20: 21: 21: 22) cm.)
Shape shoulders and back neck
Cast off 8 sts at beg of next 2 rows.
63 (65: 67: 69: 71) sts.
Next row (RS): Cast off 8 sts, patt until there are
11 (11: 12: 12: 13) sts on right needle and turn,
leaving rem sts on a holder.
Work each side of neck separately.
Cast off 4 sts at beg of next row.
Cast off rem 7 (7: 8: 8: 9) sts.
With RS facing, rejoin yarn to rem sts, cast off
centre 25 (27: 27: 29: 29) sts, patt to end.
Work to match first side, reversing shapings.

LEFT FRONT
Centre front panel
Cast on 28 sts using 2¾mm (US 2) needles and yarn C.
Break off yarn C and join in yarn A.
Knit 3 rows.
Row 4 (WS): ★K1, P1, rep from ★ to end.
This row sets position of moss st.
Row 5: P1, K1, pick up loop lying between needles
and P then K into back of this loop, moss st to end.
Work 5 rows.
Rep last 6 rows once more. 32 sts.
Break yarn and leave sts on a holder.

Side panel
Cast on 21 (24: 27: 30: 33) sts using 2¾mm (US 2)
needles and yarn C.
Break off yarn C and join in yarn A.
Knit 3 rows.
Row 4 (WS): ★P1, K1, rep from ★ to last 1 (0: 1: 0:
1) st, P1 (0: 1: 0: 1).
This row sets position of moss st.
Row 5: Moss st to last 2 sts, pick up loop lying
between needles and K then P into back of this
loop, K1, P1.
Work 5 rows.
Rep last 6 rows once more. 25 (28: 31: 34: 37) sts.
Join panels
Row 17 (RS): Moss st across first 24 (27: 30: 33: 36) sts
of side panel, (P1, K1) into next st, then moss st across
32 sts of centre front panel. 58 (61: 64: 67: 70) sts.
Work 2 rows.
Row 20 (WS): Moss st 6 sts and slip these sts onto
a holder for button band, M1, moss st to end.
53 (56: 59: 62: 65) sts.
Change to 3¼mm (US 3) needles.
Cont in patt foll chart for fronts as folls:
Work 2 rows.
Place marker on 26th (29th: 32nd: 35th: 38th) st in
from side seam.
Row 3 (dec) (RS): K2tog, patt to within 1 st of
marked st, K3tog tbl, patt to end.
Work 7 rows.
Rep last 8 rows twice more and then row 3 (the dec
row) again. 41 (44: 47: 50: 53) sts.
Work 15 rows, ending with chart row 42.
Row 43 (inc) (RS): Inc in first st, patt to marked st,
M1, K marked st, M1, patt to end.
Work 11 rows.
Rep last 12 rows twice more and then row 43 (the
inc row) again. 53 (56: 59: 62: 65) sts.
Work 13 (17: 17: 21: 21) rows, ending with chart
row 92 (96: 96: 100: 100). (Front matches back to
beg of armhole shaping.)
Shape armhole
Keeping chart correct, cast off 3 (4: 4: 5: 5) sts at beg
of next row. 50 (52: 55: 57: 60) sts.
Work 1 row.
Dec 1 st at armhole edge of next 5 (5: 7: 7: 8) rows,
then on foll 5 (3: 2: 0: 0) alt rows. 40 (44: 46: 50: 52) sts.
Work 1 (1: 1: 1: 0) row, ending with chart row 110.
Shape front slope
Dec 1 st at armhole edge of next and foll 0 (3: 4: 7: 8)
alt rows **and at same time** dec 1 st at neck edge
on next and every foll 6th row. 38 (38: 39: 39: 40) sts.
Dec 1 st at neck edge on every foll 6th row from
previous dec until 35 (35: 36: 36: 37) sts rem.
Work 6 (4: 8: 4: 6) rows, ending with chart row
135 (139: 143: 145: 147).
Shape neck
Cast off 3 sts at beg of next row. 32 (32: 33: 33: 34) sts.
Dec 1 st at neck edge of next 5 (5: 5: 3: 3) rows, then
on foll 3 (3: 3: 5: 5) alt rows, then on foll 4th row.
23 (23: 24: 24: 25) sts.
Work 5 rows, ending with chart row 156 (160: 164:
168: 170).
Shape shoulder
Cast off 8 sts at beg of next and foll alt row.
Work 1 row.
Cast off rem 7 (7: 8: 8: 9) sts.

RIGHT FRONT
Side panel
Cast on 21 (24: 27: 30: 33) sts using 2¾mm (US 2)
needles and yarn C.
Break off yarn C and join in yarn A.
Knit 3 rows.
Row 4 (WS): P1 (0: 1: 0: 1), ★K1, P1, rep from ★ to
end.
This row sets position of moss st.
Row 5: P1, K1, pick up loop lying between needles
and P then K into back of this loop, moss st to end.

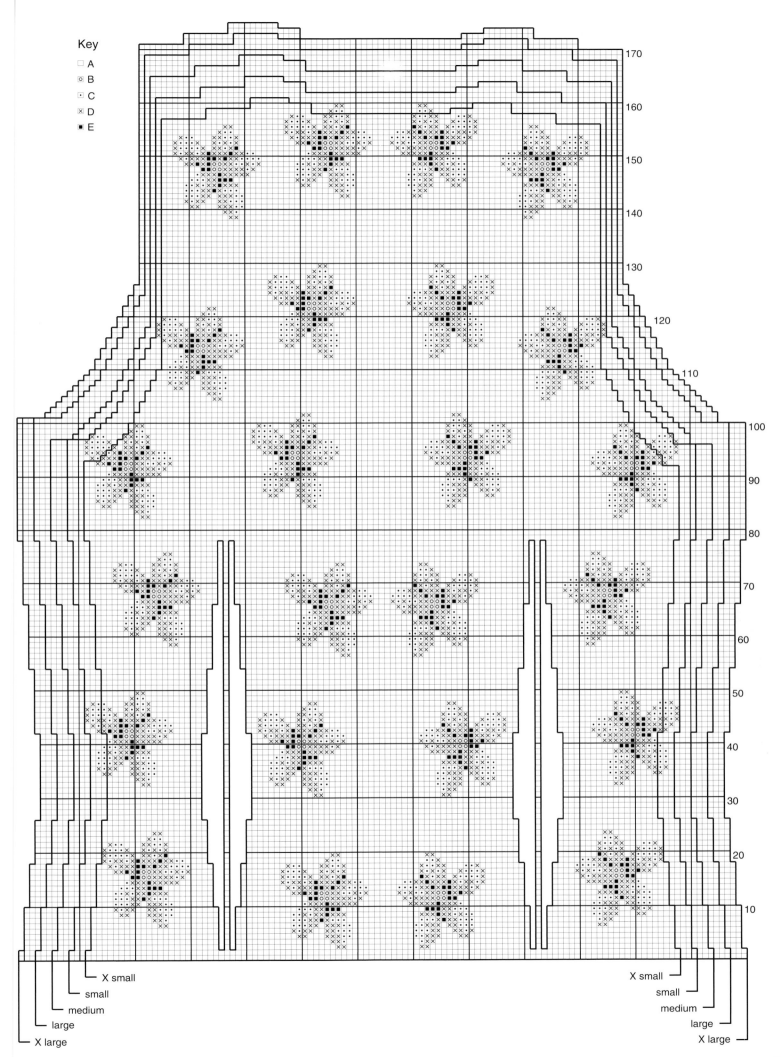

Key
☐ A
⊙ B
⊡ C
☒ D
■ E

170
160
150
140
130
120
110
100
90
80
70
60
50
40
30
20
10

X small
small
medium
large
X large

X small
small
medium
large
X large

73

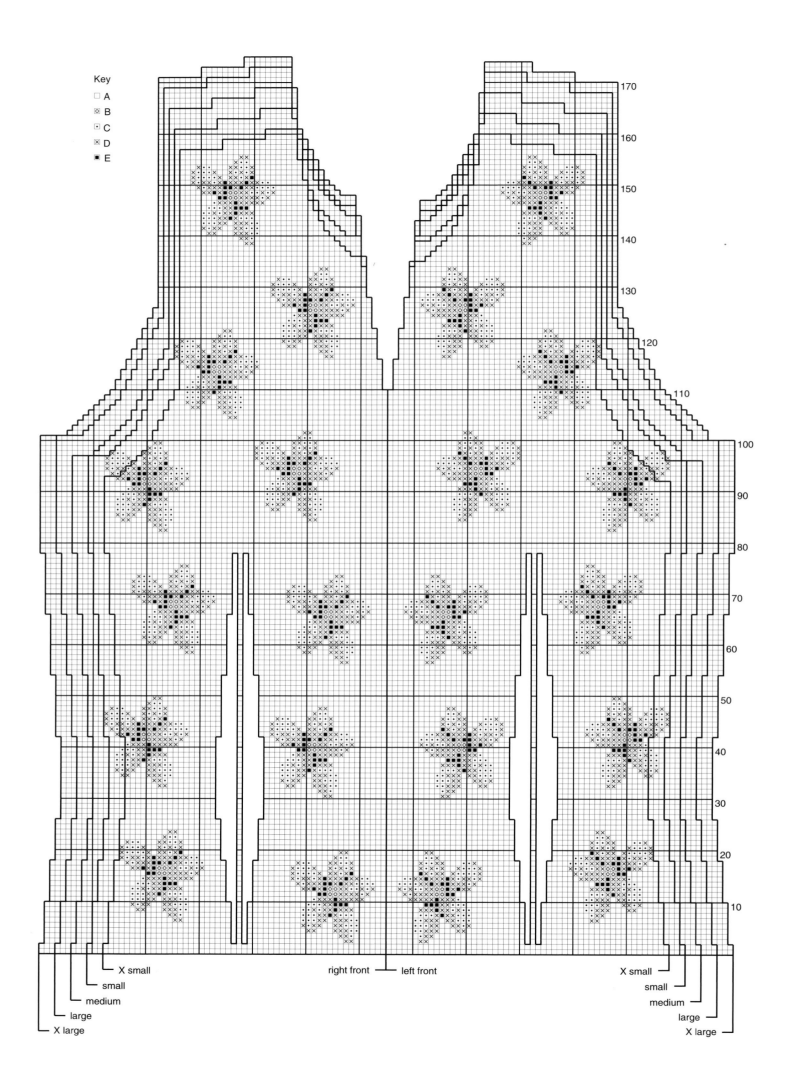

Key
☐ A
☉ B
⊡ C
☒ D
■ E

170

160

150

140

130

120

110

100

90

80

70

60

50

40

30

20

10

X small

small

medium

large

X large

right front — left front

X small

small

medium

large

X large

Work 5 rows.
Rep last 6 rows once more. 25 (28: 31: 34: 37) sts.
Break yarn and leave sts on a holder.

Centre front panel
Cast on 28 sts using 2¾mm (US 2) needles and yarn C.
Break off yarn C and join in yarn A.
Knit 3 rows.
Row 4 (WS): *P1, K1, rep from * to end.
This row sets position of moss st.
Row 5: Moss st to last 2 sts, pick up loop lying between needles and K then P into back of this loop, K1, P1.
Work 5 rows. Rep last 6 rows once more. 32 sts.

Join panels
Row 17 (RS): Moss st across first 31 sts of centre front panel, (P1, K1) into next st, then moss st across 25 (28: 31: 34: 37) sts of side panel.
58 (61: 64: 67: 70) sts.
Work 2 rows.
Row 20 (WS): Moss st to last 6 sts, M1 and turn, leaving rem 6 sts on a holder for buttonhole band.
53 (56: 59: 62: 65) sts.
Change to 3¼mm (US 3) needles.
Cont in patt foll chart for fronts as folls:
Work 2 rows.
Place marker on 26th (29th: 32nd: 35th: 38th) st in from side seam.
Row 3 (dec) (RS): Patt to within 1 st of marked st, K3tog, patt to last 2 sts, K2tog.
Complete to match left front, reversing shapings.

LEFT SLEEVE
Cast on 49 (49: 49: 53: 53) sts using 2¾mm (US 2) needles and yarn C.
Break off yarn C and join in yarn A.
Knit 3 rows.
Work 17 rows in moss st, inc 1 st at each end of 6th and foll 8th row. 53 (53: 53: 57: 57) sts.
Change to 3¼mm (US 3) needles.
Cont in patt foll chart for sleeve as folls:
Work 4 rows.
Inc 1 st at each end of next and every foll 8th row until there are 77 (79: 81: 83: 85) sts, taking inc sts into patt.
Cont straight until chart row 112 (112: 116: 116: 118) has been completed, ending with a WS row.

Shape top
Keeping chart correct, cast off 3 (4: 4: 5: 5) sts at beg of next 2 rows. 71 (71: 73: 73: 75) sts.
Dec 1 st at each end of next 5 rows, then on foll 3 alt rows, then on every foll 4th row until 45 (45: 47: 47: 49) sts rem.
Work 1 row.
Dec 1 st at each end of next and foll 2 (2: 3: 3: 4) alt rows, then on foll 3 rows. 33 sts.
Cast off 6 sts at beg of next 2 rows, ending with chart row 156 (156: 162: 162: 166).
Cast off rem 21 sts.

RIGHT SLEEVE
Work as given for left sleeve but reversing chart by reading odd numbered K rows from left to right, and even numbered P rows from right to left.

One colour cardigan
BACK and FRONTS
Work as given for multi coloured cardigan but using same colour throughout.

SLEEVES
Cast on 71 (73: 75: 77: 79) sts using 2¾mm (US 2) needles. Knit 3 rows.
Work 17 rows in moss st, inc 1 st at each end of 4th and every foll 6th row. 77 (79: 81: 83: 85) sts.
Change to 3¼mm (US 3) needles.
Beg with a K row, cont in st st until sleeve measures 9 cm, ending with a WS row.

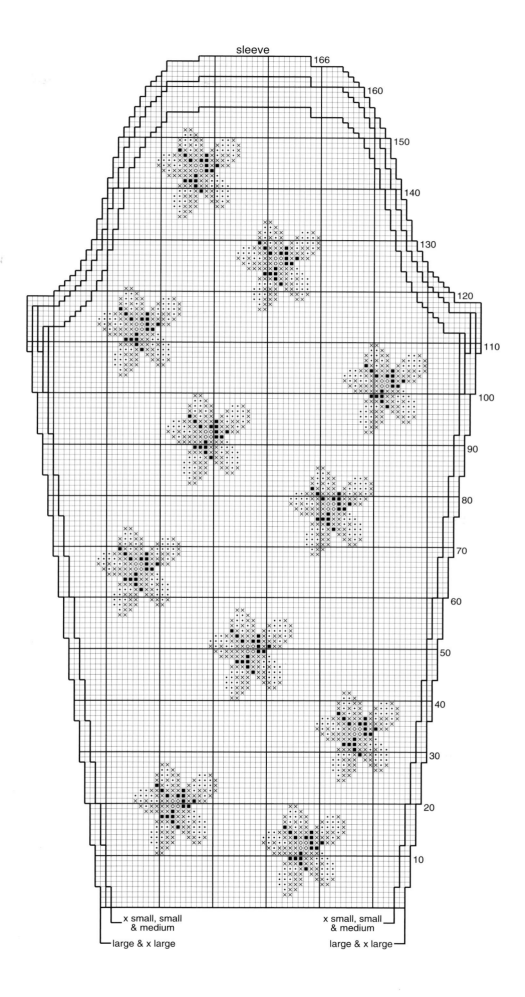

sleeve

x small, small & medium

large & x large

x small, small & medium

large & x large

Shape top

Cast off 3 (4: 4: 5: 5) sts at beg of next 2 rows.
71 (71: 73: 73: 75) sts.
Dec 1 st at each end of next 5 rows, then on foll
3 alt rows, then on every foll 4th row until 45 (45:
47: 47: 49) sts rem.
Work 1 row.
Dec 1 st at each end of next and foll 2 (2: 3: 3: 4) alt
rows, then on foll 3 rows, ending with a WS row. 33 sts.
Cast off 6 sts at beg of next 2 rows.
Cast off rem 21 sts.

MAKING UP

PRESS all pieces as described on the info page.
Multi coloured cardigan
Join shoulder seams using back stitch, or mattress
stitch if preferred.
Button band
Slip 6 sts left on holder for button band onto 2¾mm
(US 2) needles and rejoin yarn A with RS facing.
Cont in moss st as set until band, when slightly
stretched, fits up left front opening edge to start of
neck shaping, ending with a WS row.
Break yarn and leave sts on a holder.
Slip stitch band in place.
Mark positions for 5 buttons on this band – lowest
button level with beg of chart, top button 2 cm
below start of front slope shaping and rem 3 buttons
evenly spaced between.
Buttonhole band
Work as given for button band, rejoining yarn with
WS facing and with the addition of 5 buttonholes
to correspond with positions marked for buttons
worked as folls:
Buttonhole row (RS): Moss st 2 sts, yrn (to make
a buttonhole), work 2 tog, moss st 2 sts.
When band is completed, ending with a WS row, do
NOT break off yarn.
Slip stitch band in place.
Neckband
With RS facing, using 2¾mm (US 2) needles and
yarn A, moss st across 6 sts of buttonhole band, pick
up and knit 29 (29: 29: 31: 31) sts up right side of neck,
33 (35: 35: 37: 37) sts from back, 29 (29: 29: 31: 31) sts
down left side of neck, then moss st across 6 sts of
button band. 103 (105: 105: 111: 111) sts.
Work in moss st as set by front bands for 5 rows.
Cast off in moss st.
See information page for finishing instructions,
setting in sleeves using the set-in method.
One colour cardigan
Work as given for multi coloured cardigan but using
same colour throughout.

55 (56: 57: 58: 59) cm
(21.5 (22: 22.5: 23: 23) in)

46.5 (49: 51.5: 54.5: 57) cm
(18.5 (19.5: 20.5: 21.5: 22.5) in)

41 (41: 42: 42: 43) cm
(16 (16: 16.5: 16.5: 17) in)

9 cm (3.5 in)

Wicked

KIM HARGREAVES

YARN

Rowan 4 ply Cotton

			XS	S	M	L	XL	
To fit bust			81	86	91	97	102	cm
			32	34	36	38	40	in
A	Opaque	112	2	2	2	2	2	x 50gm
B	Allure	119	2	2	2	2	2	x 50gm
C	Ripple	121	2	2	2	2	2	x 50gm
D	Tear	116	2	2	2	2	2	x 50gm
E	Pool	124	2	2	2	2	2	x 50gm
F	Sage	123	2	2	2	3	3	x 50gm
G	Olive	118	1	1	1	2	2	x 50gm
H	Lemongrass	122	2	2	2	2	2	x 50gm

NEEDLES

1 pair 2¼mm (no 13) (US 1) needles
1 pair 3mm (no 11) (US 2/3) needles

BUTTONS - 7

TENSION

28 sts and 38 rows to 10 cm measured over pattern
using 3mm (US 2/3) needles.

Chart note: Some sections of chart show contrast
colours only. For these sections, work empty squares
of grid in background colour as indicated at side of
chart.

BACK

Cast on 130 (136: 144: 150: 158) sts using 2¼mm
(US 1) needles and yarn F.
Knit 4 rows.
Change to 3mm (US 2/3) needles.
Using the **fairisle** technique described on the
information page, starting and ending rows as
indicated, cont in patt foll chart for back, which is
worked entirely in st st, as folls:
Work 4 (6: 6: 8: 8) rows.
Dec 1 st at each end of next and every foll 4th row
until 108 (114: 122: 128: 136) sts rem.
Work 9 rows, ending with chart row
54 (56: 56: 58: 58).
Inc 1 st at each end of next and every foll 8th row
until there are 114 (120: 128: 134: 142) sts, then on

---

every foll 6th row until there are 130 (136: 144: 150:
158) sts, taking inc sts into patt.
Cont straight until chart row 128 (132: 132: 136: 136)
has been completed, ending with a WS row.
Shape armholes
Keeping chart correct, cast off 5 (6: 7: 8: 9) sts at beg
of next 2 rows.
120 (124: 130: 134: 140) sts.
Dec 1 st at each end of next 7 rows, then on every
foll alt row until 98 (100: 104: 106: 110) sts rem.
Cont straight until chart row 204 (208: 212: 216: 220)
has been completed, ending with a WS row.
Shape shoulders and back neck
Cast off 9 (9: 9: 9: 10) sts at beg of next 2 rows.
80 (82: 86: 88: 90) sts.
Next row (RS): Cast off 9 (9: 9: 9: 10) sts, patt until
there are 12 (12: 14: 14: 14) sts on right needle and
turn, leaving rem sts on a holder.
Work each side of neck separately.
Cast off 4 sts at beg of next row.
Cast off rem 8 (8: 10: 10: 10) sts.
With RS facing, rejoin yarn to rem sts, cast off
centre 38 (40: 40: 42: 42) sts, patt to end.
Work to match first side, reversing shapings.

LEFT FRONT

Cast on 66 (69: 73: 76: 80) sts using 2¼mm (US 1)
needles and yarn F.
Knit 4 rows.
Change to 3mm (US 2/3) needles.
Starting and ending rows as indicated, cont in patt
foll chart for left front as folls:
Work 4 (6: 6: 8: 8) rows.
Dec 1 st at beg of next and every foll 4th row until
55 (58: 62: 65: 69) sts rem.
Work 9 rows, ending with chart row
54 (56: 56: 58: 58).
Inc 1 st at beg of next and every foll 8th row until
there are 58 (61: 65: 68: 72) sts, then on every foll
6th row until there are 66 (69: 73: 76: 80) sts, taking
inc sts into patt.
Cont straight until chart row 128 (132: 132: 136: 136)
has been completed, ending with a WS row.
Shape armhole
Keeping chart correct, cast off 5 (6: 7: 8: 9) sts at beg
of next row.
61 (63: 66: 68: 71) sts.
Work 1 row.
Dec 1 st at armhole edge of next 7 rows, then on
every foll alt row until 50 (51: 53: 54: 56) sts rem.
Cont straight until chart row 181 (185: 189: 189: 193)
has been completed, ending with a RS row.
Shape neck
Cast off 12 (13: 13: 13: 13) sts at beg of next row,
then 4 sts at beg of foll alt row.
34 (34: 36: 37: 39) sts.
Dec 1 st at neck edge of next 3 rows, then on foll
3 (3: 3: 4: 4) alt rows, then on every foll 4th row
until 26 (26: 28: 28: 30) sts rem.
Cont straight until chart row 204 (208: 212: 216: 220)
has been completed, ending with a WS row.
Shape shoulder
Cast off 9 (9: 9: 9: 10) sts at beg of next and foll alt
row.
Work 1 row.
Cast off rem 8 (8: 10: 10: 10) sts.

RIGHT FRONT

Cast on 66 (69: 73: 76: 80) sts using 2¼mm (US 1)
needles and yarn F.
Knit 4 rows.
Change to 3mm (US 2/3) needles.
Starting and ending rows as indicated, cont in patt
foll chart for right front as folls:
Work 4 (6: 6: 8: 8) rows.
Dec 1 st at end of next and every foll 4th row until
55 (58: 62: 65: 69) sts rem.
Complete to match left front, reversing shapings.

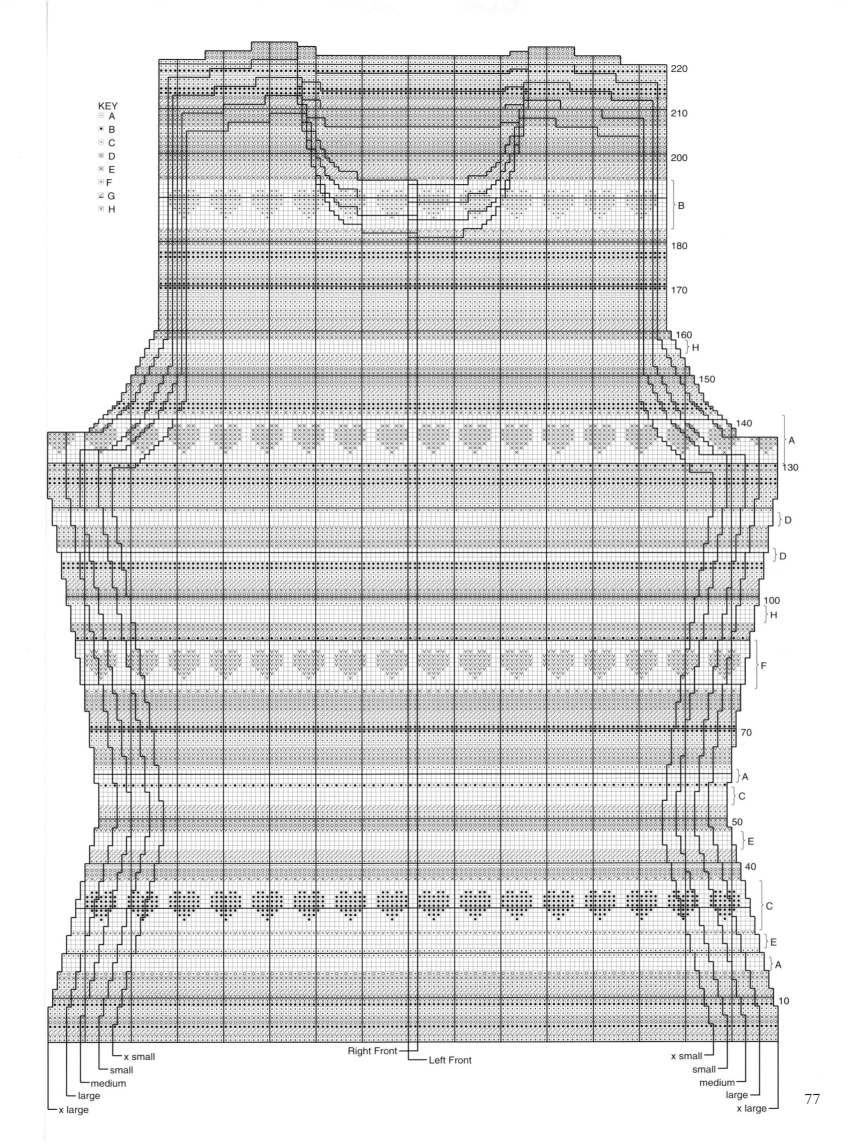

KEY
⊟ A
• B
⊡ C
◎ D
⊠ E
⊞ F
◩ G
☑ H

220
210
200
} B
180
170
160
} H
150
140
} A
130
} D
} D
100
} H
} F
70
} A
} C
50
} E
40
} C
} E
} A
10

Right Front — Left Front

x small
small
medium
large
x large

x small
small
medium
large
x large

SLEEVES (both alike)
Cast on 66 (66: 70: 70: 70) sts using 2¼mm (US 1)
needles and yarn F.
Knit 4 rows.
Change to 3mm (US 2/3) needles.
Cont in patt foll chart for sleeve, which is worked
entirely in st st, as folls:
Work 6 rows.
Inc 1 st at each end of next and every foll 8th row
until there are 98 (100: 102: 104: 106) sts, taking inc
sts into patt.
Cont straight until chart row 150 (150: 154: 154: 158)
has been completed, ending with a WS row.
Shape top
Keeping chart correct, cast off 5 (6: 7: 8: 9) sts at beg
of next 2 rows. 88 sts.
Dec 1 st at each end of next 3 rows, then on foll
3 (3: 2: 2: 1) alt rows, then on every foll 4th row
until 60 sts rem.
Work 1 row, ending with a WS row.
Dec 1 st at each end of next and foll 3 alt rows, then
on foll 3 rows, ending with a WS row. 46 sts.
Cast off 4 sts at beg of next 4 rows.
Cast off rem 30 sts.

MAKING UP
PRESS all pieces as described on the information
page.
Join shoulder seams using back stitch, or mattress
stitch if preferred.
Button band
With RS facing, using 2¼mm (US 1) needles and
yarn C, pick up and knit 134 (134: 140: 140: 140) sts
along left front opening edge.
★★Knit 3 rows.
Break off yarn C and join in yarn F.
Knit 1 row.
Cast off knitwise (on WS).★★
Buttonhole band
Work as given for button band, with the addition of
7 buttonholes worked in row 2 as folls:
Buttonhole row (RS): K4, ★yfwd, K2tog, K19 (19:
20: 20: 20), rep from ★ to last 4 sts, yfwd, K2tog, K2.
Neckband
With RS facing, using 2¼mm (US 1) needles and
yarn C, pick up and knit 40 (41: 41: 45: 45) sts up
right side of neck, 46 (48: 48: 50: 50) sts from back,
then 40 (41: 41: 45: 45) sts down left side of neck.
126 (130: 130: 140: 140) sts.
Work as given for button band from ★★ to ★★.
See information page for finishing instructions,
setting in sleeves using the set-in method.

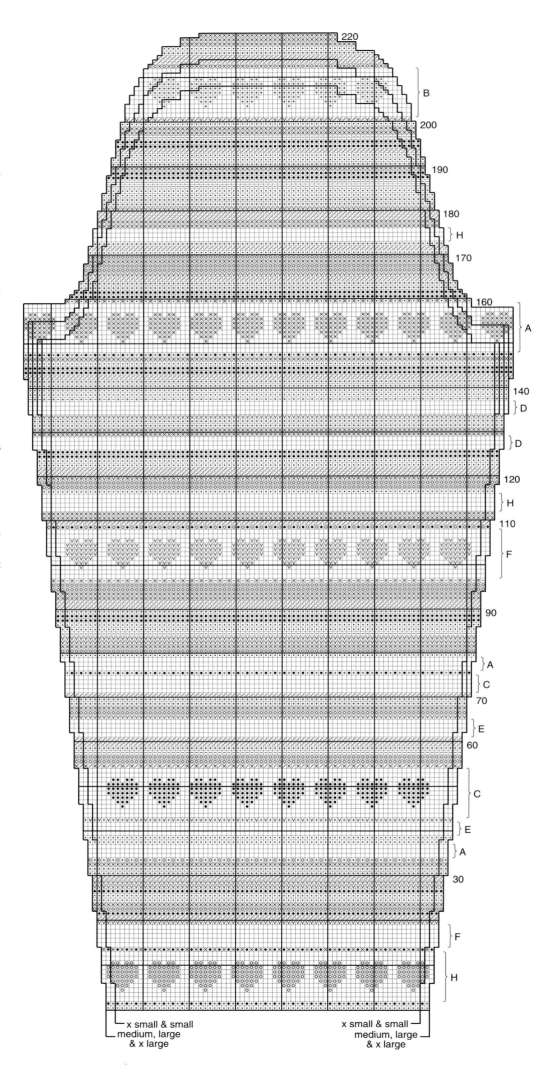

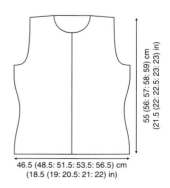

55 (56: 57: 58: 59) cm
(21.5 (22: 22.5: 23: 23) in)

46.5 (48.5: 51.5: 53.5: 56.5) cm
(18.5 (19: 20.5: 21: 22) in)

41 (41: 42: 42: 43) cm
(16 (16: 16.5: 16.5: 17) in)

x small & small
medium, large
& x large

x small & small
medium, large
& x large

Design number 7

Hunter

KIM HARGREAVES

YARN
Rowan Linen Drape

	ladies				mens			
	XS	S	M	L	XL	M	L	XL

To fit bust/chest

81	86	91	97	102	102	107	112 cm
32	34	36	38	40	40	42	44 in

Long stitch sweater

11	11	12	12	13	16	17	18	x 50gm

Long stitch border sweater

11	11	12	12	13	16	17	18	x 50gm

V neck sweater

11	11	12	12	13	15	16	17	x 50gm

(ladies long stitch sweater photographed in Natural 843 and V neck sweater in Bleached 840, mans long stitch border sweater in Pewter 841 and V neck sweater in Splash 847)

NEEDLES
1 pair 3mm (no 11) (US 2/3) needles
1 pair 3³⁄₄mm (no 9) (US 5) needles

TENSION
23 sts and 30 rows to 10 cm measured over stocking stitch using 3³⁄₄mm (US 5) needles.

Pattern note: The pattern is written for the 5 ladies sizes, followed by the mens sizes in **bold**.

Long stitch sweater
BACK
Cast on 111 (117: 123: 129: 135: **141: 147: 153**) sts using 3mm (US 2/3) needles.
Beg with a K row, work in st st as folls:
Work 8 rows.
Change to 3³⁄₄mm (US 5) needles.
Work a further 12 rows.
Cont in long st patt as folls:
Row 1 (RS): K to end, winding yarn round needle twice for each st.
Row 2: P to end, dropping extra loops.
Work in st st for 16 rows.
These 18 rows form long st patt.
★★Cont straight until back measures 27 (28: 28: 29: 29: **36: 37: 37**) cm, ending with a WS row.
Shape armholes
Cast off 4 sts at beg of next 2 rows.
103 (109: 115: 121: 127: **133: 139: 145**) sts.
Dec 1 st at each end of next 8 rows.
87 (93: 99: 105: 111: **117: 123: 129**) sts.
Cont straight until armhole measures 23 (23: 24: 24: 25: **26: 26: 27**) cm, ending with a WS row.
Shape shoulders and back neck
Ladies sizes only
Next row (RS): Cast off 5 (6: 7: 7: 8: **-**) sts, K until there are 12 (13: 15: 17: 19: **-**) sts on right needle and turn, leaving rem sts on a holder.
Work each side of neck separately.
Dec 1 st at beg of next row.
Cast off 5 (6: 7: 7: 8: **-**) sts at beg and dec 1 st at end of next row.
Work 1 row.
Mens sizes only
Cast off - (**10: 11: 11**) sts at beg of next 2 rows.
- (**97: 101: 107**) sts.
Next row (RS): Cast off - (**10: 11: 11**) sts, K until there are – (**13: 14: 16**) sts on right needle and turn, leaving rem sts on a holder.
Work each side of neck separately.
Cast off 4 sts at beg of next row.
All sizes
Cast off rem 5 (5: 6: 8: 9: **9: 10: 12**) sts.
With RS facing, rejoin yarn to rem sts, cast off centre 53 (55: 55: 57: 57: **51: 51: 53**) sts, K to end.
Complete to match first side, reversing shaping.

FRONT
Work as given for back until 8 (**6**) rows less have been worked than on back to start of shoulder shaping, ending with a WS row.
Shape neck
Next row (RS): K25 (27: 30: 32: 35: **37: 40: 42**) and turn, leaving rem sts on a holder.
Work each side of neck separately.
Cast off 4 sts at beg of next row.
21 (23: 26: 28: 31: **33: 36: 38**) sts.
Dec 1 st at neck edge of next 5 (**3**) rows.
16 (18: 21: 23: 26: **30: 33: 35**) sts.
Work 1 row, ending with a WS row.
Shape shoulder
Cast off 5 (6: 7: 7: 8: **10: 11: 11**) sts at beg and dec 1 st at end of next row.
10 (11: 13: 15: 17: **19: 21: 23**) sts.
Work 1 row.
Cast off 5 (6: 7: 7: 8: **10: 11: 11**) sts at beg of next row.
Work 1 row.
Cast off rem 5 (5: 6: 8: 9: **9: 10: 12**) sts.
With RS facing, rejoin yarn to rem sts, cast off centre 37 (39: 39: 41: 41: **43: 43: 45**) sts, K to end.
Complete to match first side, reversing shaping.

SLEEVES (both alike)
Cast on 59 (59: 61: 61: 63: **69: 69: 71**) sts using 3mm (US 2/3) needles.
Beg with a K row, work in st st as folls:
Work 8 rows.
Change to 3³⁄₄mm (US 5) needles.
Cont in st st, inc 1 st at each end of 3rd and foll 6th row. 63 (63: 65: 65: 67: **73: 73: 75**) sts.
Work a further 3 rows.
Cont in long st patt as folls:
Row 1 (RS): K to end, winding yarn round needle twice for each st.
Row 2: P to end, dropping extra loops.
This row sets position of 18 row long st patt as given for back.
Cont in patt, inc 1 st at each end of next and every foll 6th row to 89 (**109**) sts, then on every foll 4th row until there are 105 (105: 109: 109: 113: **117: 117: 121**) sts.
Cont straight until sleeve measures 46 (46: 47: 47: 47: **51: 51: 52**) cm, ending with a WS row.
Shape top
Cast off 4 sts at beg of next 2 rows.
97 (97: 101: 101: 105: **109: 109: 113**) sts.
Dec 1 st at each end of next and foll 5 alt rows.
Work 1 row.
Cast off rem 85 (85: 89: 89: 93: **97: 97: 101**) sts.

Long stitch border sweater
BACK
Cast on 111 (117: 123: 129: 135: **141: 147: 153**) sts using 3mm (US 2/3) needles.
Beg with a K row, work in st st as folls:
Work 8 rows.
Change to 3³⁄₄mm (US 5) needles.
Work a further 10 rows.
Work long st border as folls:
Row 1 (RS): K to end, winding yarn round needle twice for each st.
Row 2: P to end, dropping extra loops.
Work in st st for 8 rows.
Rep last 10 rows once more and then rows 1 and 2 again.
This completes long stitch border.
Beg with a K row, work in st st throughout and complete as given for back of long stitch sweater from ★★.

FRONT
Working first 40 rows in long st border as given for back and then completing front in st st, work as given for front of long stitch sweater.

SLEEVES (both alike)
Work as given for sleeves of long stitch sweater, working first 40 rows in long st border as given for back and then completing sleeves in st st.

V neck sweater
BACK
Beg with a K row and working in st st throughout, work as given for back of long stitch sweater until armhole measures 23 (23: 24: 24: 25: **26: 26: 27**) cm, ending with a WS row.
Shape shoulders and back neck
Cast off 8 (9: 10: 11: 12: **13: 14: 14**) sts at beg of next 2 rows.
71 (75: 79: 83: 87: **91: 95: 101**) sts.
Next row (RS): Cast off 8 (9: 10: 11: 12: **13: 14: 14**) sts, K until there are 13 (13: 14: 14: 15: **16: 17: 19**) sts on right needle and turn, leaving rem sts on a holder.
Work each side of neck separately.
Cast off 4 sts at beg of next row.
Cast off rem 9 (9: 10: 10: 11: **12: 13: 15**) sts.
With RS facing, rejoin yarn to rem sts, cast off centre 29 (31: 31: 33: 33: **33: 33: 35**) sts, K to end.
Complete to match first side, reversing shaping.

FRONT

Beg with a K row and working in st st throughout, work as given for back of long stitch sweater until armhole measures 8 (8: 8: 8: 9: **10: 10: 11**) cm, ending with a WS row.

Divide for neck
Next row (RS): K43 (46: 49: 52: 55: **58: 61: 64**) and turn, leaving rem sts on a holder.
Work each side of neck separately.
Work 1 row.
Dec 1 st at neck edge of next and every foll alt row until 25 (27: 30: 32: 35: **38: 41: 43**) sts rem.
Cont straight until front matches back to start of shoulder shaping, ending with a WS row.

Shape shoulder
Cast off 8 (9: 10: 11: 12: **13: 14: 14**) sts at beg of next and foll alt row.
Work 1 row.
Cast off rem 9 (9: 10: 10: 11: **12: 13: 15**) sts.
With RS facing, rejoin yarn to rem sts, K2tog, K to end.
Complete to match first side, reversing shaping.

SLEEVES (both alike)

Beg with a K row and working in st st throughout, work as given for sleeves of long stitch sweater.

MAKING UP

PRESS all pieces as described on the information page.
Join right shoulder seam using back stitch, or mattress stitch if preferred.

Long stitch and long stitch border sweaters
Neckband
With RS facing and using 3mm (US 2/3) needles, pick up and knit 15 (**13**) sts down left side of neck, 37 (39: 39: 41: 41: **43: 43: 45**) sts from front, 15 (**13**) sts up right side of neck, and 61 (63: 63: 65: 65: **59: 59: 61**) sts from back.
128 (132: 132: 136: 136: **128: 128: 132**) sts.
Beg with a K row, work 4 rows in rev st st.
Cast off knitwise (on WS).

V neck sweater
Neckband
With RS facing and using 3mm (US 2/3) needles, pick up and knit 40 sts down left side of neck, 40 sts up right side of neck, and 37 (39: 39: 41: 41: **41: 41: 43**) sts from back.
117 (119: 119: 121: 121: **121: 121: 123**) sts.
Beg with a K row, work 4 rows in rev st st.
Cast off knitwise (on WS).

All sweaters
See information page for finishing instructions, setting in sleeves using the shallow set-in method.

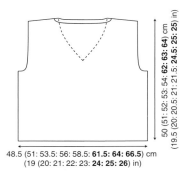

50 (51: 52: 53: 54: **62: 63: 64**) cm
(19.5 (20: 20.5: 21: 21.5: **24.5: 25: 25**) in)

48.5 (51: 53.5: 56: 58.5: **61.5: 64: 66.5**) cm
(19 (20: 21: 22: 23: **24: 25: 26**) in)

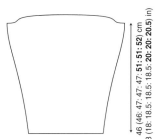

46 (46: 47: 47: 47: **51: 51: 52**) cm
(18 (18: 18.5: 18.5: 18.5: **20: 20: 20.5**) in)

Design number 8

Court House Steps

KAFFE FASSETT

YARN

Rowan 4 ply Cotton and Cotton Glace

			XS	S	M	L	XL	
To fit bust			81	86	91	97	102	cm
			32	34	36	38	40	in
A	4 ply	Bonny	104	1	1	1	1	1 x 50gm
B	4 ply	Vine	103	2	2	2	2	2 x 50gm
C	4 ply	Nightsky	115	2	2	2	2	2 x 50gm
D	4 ply	Vamp	117	1	1	2	2	2 x 50gm
E	Glace	Nghtshde	746	2	2	2	3	3 x 50gm
F	4 ply	Magenta	106	1	1	1	1	1 x 50gm
G	Glace	Poppy	741	2	2	2	2	2 x 50gm
H	Glace	Cr. Rose	793	2	2	2	2	2 x 50gm
J	Glace	Pepper	796	2	2	2	2	2 x 50gm
M	Glace	Bubbles	724	2	2	2	2	2 x 50gm
N	Glace	Dijon	739	2	2	2	2	2 x 50gm
P	Glace	Pear	780	1	1	1	1	1 x 50gm
R	Glace	Terracotta	786	2	2	2	2	2 x 50gm
S	Glace	Hyacinth	787	1	1	2	2	2 x 50gm
T	Glace	Bl.Orange	445	2	2	2	2	2 x 50gm

NEEDLES

1 pair 3mm (no 11) (US 2/3) needles
1 pair 3¼mm (no 10) (US 3) needles

TENSION

25 sts and 35 rows to 10 cm measured over patterned stocking stitch using 3¼mm (US 3) needles.

BACK and FRONT (both alike)

Cast on 130 (136: 142: 148: 154) sts using 3mm (US 2/3) needles and yarn E.
Row 1 (RS): Using yarn E, P3 (2: 1: 4: 3), *K4, P4, rep from * to last 7 (6: 5: 8: 7) sts, K4, P3 (2: 1: 4: 3).
Row 2: Using yarn B, K3 (2: 1: 4: 3), *P4, K4, rep from * to last 7 (6: 5: 8: 7) sts, P4, K3 (2: 1: 4: 3).
These 2 rows form rib.
Work a further 18 rows in rib using colours as folls:
Row 3: Using yarn B.
Rows 4 to 6: Using yarn T.
Rows 7 and 8: Using yarn D.
Row 9: Using yarn R.
Rows 10 and 11: Using yarn J.
Rows 12 and 13: Using yarn S.

Rows 14 to 16: Using yarn N.
Rows 17 and 18: Using yarn H.
Rows 19 and 20: Using yarn B.
Change to 3¼mm (US 3) needles.
Using the **intarsia** technique described on the information page and starting and ending rows as indicated, cont in patt foll chart, which is worked entirely in st st, as folls:
Work 86 (90: 90: 92: 92) rows, ending with a WS row.

Shape armholes
Keeping chart correct, cast off 5 sts at beg of next 2 rows.
120 (126: 132: 138: 144) sts.
Dec 1 st at each end of next 9 rows.
102 (108: 114: 120: 126) sts.
Cont straight until chart row 144 (148: 150: 152: 156) has been completed, ending with a WS row.
Change to 3mm (US 2/3) needles.
Row 1 (RS): Using yarn E, K1 (4: 3: 2: 1), *P4, K4, rep from * to last 5 (8: 7: 6: 5) sts, P4, K1 (4: 3: 2: 1).
Row 2: Using yarn B, P1 (4: 3: 2: 1), *K4, P4, rep from * to last 5 (8: 7: 6: 5) sts, K4, P1 (4: 3: 2: 1).
These 2 rows set position of rib.
Work a further 14 rows in rib using colours as folls:
Row 3: Using yarn B.
Rows 4 to 6: Using yarn T.
Rows 7 and 8: Using yarn D.
Row 9: Using yarn R.
Rows 10 and 11: Using yarn J.
Rows 12 and 13: Using yarn S.
Rows 14 to 16: Using yarn N.

Shape shoulders
Keeping rib correct, cont as folls:
Using yarn H, cast off 6 (7: 8: 9: 10) sts at beg of next 2 rows.
90 (94: 98: 102: 106) sts.
Using yarn B, cast off 6 (7: 8: 9: 10) sts at beg of next 2 rows.
Cast off rem 78 (80: 82: 84: 86) sts.

SLEEVES (both alike)

Cast on 70 (70: 74: 74: 78) sts using 3mm (US 2/3) needles and yarn E.
Row 1 (RS): Using yarn E, K1 (1: 3: 3: 1), *P4, K4, rep from * to last 5 (5: 7: 7: 5) sts, P4, K1 (1: 3: 3: 1).
Row 2: Using yarn B, P1 (1: 3: 3: 1), *K4, P4, rep from * to last 5 (5: 7: 7: 5) sts, K4, P1 (1: 3: 3: 1).
These 2 rows form rib.
Work a further 18 rows in rib using colours as given for back and front.
Change to 3¼mm (US 3) needles.
Using the **intarsia** technique described on the information page and starting and ending rows as indicated, cont in patt foll chart as folls:
Inc 1 st at each end of 3rd and every foll 6th row until there are 106 (106: 112: 112: 116) sts, taking inc sts into patt.
Cont straight until chart row 116 (116: 120: 120: 122) has been completed, ending with a WS row.

Shape top
Keeping chart correct, cast off 5 sts at beg of next 2 rows.
96 (96: 102: 102: 106) sts.
Dec 1 st at each end of next and foll 7 alt rows.
Work 1 row, ending with chart row 134 (134: 138: 138: 140).
Cast off rem 80 (80: 86: 86: 90) sts.

MAKING UP

PRESS all pieces as described on the information page.
Join both shoulder seams using back stitch, or mattress stitch if preferred, and leaving 31 (32: 33: 34: 34.5) cm open at centre of neck.
See information page for finishing instructions, setting in sleeves using the shallow set-in method.

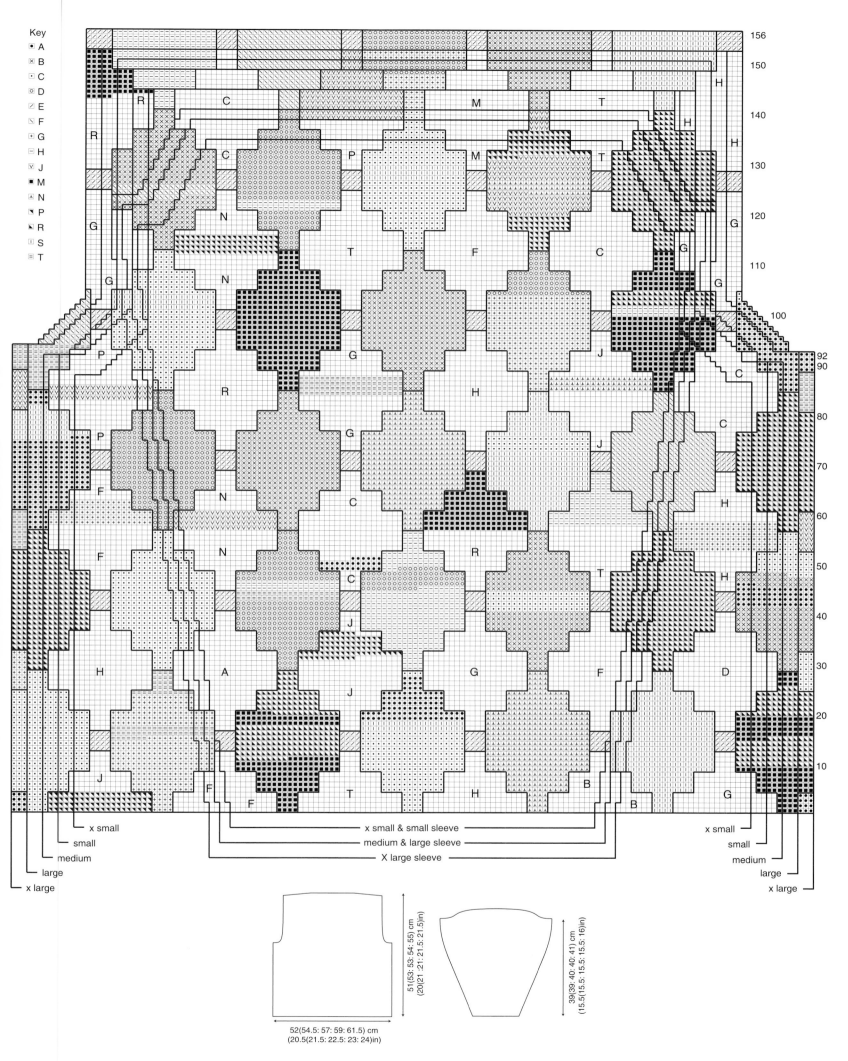

Design number 9

Frolic

KIM HARGREAVES

YARN

Rowan 4 ply Cotton

	XS	S	M	L	XL
To fit bust	81	86	91	97	102 cm
	32	34	36	38	40 in

Frill neck top   4   5   5   6   6 x 50gm
(photographed in Lemongrass 122)

Scoop neck top   4   4   4   5   5 x 50gm
(photographed in Bleached 113)

NEEDLES

1 pair 2¼mm (no 13) (US 1) needles
1 pair 3mm (no 11) (US 2/3) needles
1 2¼mm (no 13) (US 1) circular needle

TENSION

28 sts and 38 rows to 10 cm measured over flattened rib using 3mm (US 2/3) needles.

Frill neck top
FRONT and BACK (both alike)
Cast on 98 (106: 114: 122: 130) sts using 2¼mm (US 1) needles.
Row 1 (RS): K2, *P2, K2, rep from * to end.
Row 2: P2, *K2, P2, rep from * to end.
These 2 rows form rib.
Work a further 6 rows in rib.
Change to 3mm (US 2/3) needles.
Work 2 rows.
Dec 1 st at each end of next and every foll 6th row until 88 (96: 104: 112: 120) sts rem, then on every foll 8th row until 84 (92: 100: 108: 116) sts rem.
Work 15 rows, ending with a WS row.
Inc 1 st at each end of next and every foll 8th row until there are 92 (100: 108: 116: 124) sts, then on every foll 6th row until there are 106 (114: 122: 130: 138) sts, taking inc sts into rib.
Cont straight until work measures 37 cm, ending with a WS row.
Shape raglan armholes
Cast off 6 sts at beg of next 2 rows.
94 (102: 110: 118: 126) sts.
Next row (RS): P2, K2, P1, P2tog, rib to last 7 sts, P2tog tbl, P1, K2, P2.
Next row: K2, P2, K2 (1: 1: 1: 1), (K2tog tbl) 0 (1: 1: 1: 1) times, rib to last 6 (7: 7: 7: 7) sts, (K2tog) 0 (1: 1: 1: 1) times, K2 (1: 1: 1: 1), P2, K2.★★
Working all decreases as set by last 2 rows, cont as folls:
Dec 1 st at each end of next 1 (1: 7: 9: 15) rows, then on every foll alt row until 68 (72: 72: 76: 76) sts rem.
Work 1 row.
Cast off in rib.

SLEEVES (both alike)
Cast on 90 (90: 94: 94: 98) sts using 2¼mm (US 1) needles.
Work 2 rows in rib as given for back.
Change to 3mm (US 2/3) needles.
Shape raglan
Keeping rib correct, cast off 6 sts at beg of next 2 rows.
78 (78: 82: 82: 86) sts.★★★
Working all decreases in same way as given for back and front, dec 1 st at each end of next 5 rows, then on every foll alt row until 48 (46: 48: 46: 48) sts rem.
Work 1 row.
Cast off in rib.

Scoop neck top
FRONT and BACK (both alike)
Work as given for back and front of frill neck top to ★★.
Working all decreases as set by last 2 rows, cont as folls:
Dec 1 st at each end of next 1 (1: 7: 9: 15) rows, then on every foll alt row until 72 (76: 76: 80: 80) sts rem.
Work 1 row, ending with a WS row.
Shape neck
Next row (RS): P2, K2, P1, P2tog, rib 13 and turn, leaving rem sts on a holder.
Work each side of neck separately.
Cast off 2 sts at beg of next row. 17 sts.
Dec 1 st at neck edge of next 3 rows, then on foll 2 alt rows **and at same time** dec 1 st at raglan edge of next and every foll alt row. 8 sts.
Work 1 row.
Next row (RS): P2, K2, P1, P3tog.
Next row: K2, P2, K2.
Cast off rem 6 sts.
With RS facing, rejoin yarn to rem sts, cast off centre 32 (36: 36: 40: 40) sts, rib to last 7 sts, P2tog tbl, P1, K2, P2.
Work 1 row.
Next row (RS): Cast off 3 sts, rib to last 7 sts, P2tog tbl, P1, K2, P2. 15 sts.

Dec 1 st at neck edge of next 2 rows, then on foll 2 alt rows **and at same time** dec 1 st at raglan edge of 2nd and every foll alt row. 8 sts.
Work 1 row.
Next row (RS): P3tog tbl, P1, K2, P2.
Next row: K2, P2, K2.
Cast off rem 6 sts.

SLEEVES (both alike)
Work as given for sleeves of frill neck top to ★★★.
Working all decreases in same way as given for back and front, dec 1 st at each end of next 5 rows, then on every foll alt row until 40 (38: 40: 38: 40) sts rem.
Work 1 row.
Cast off in rib.

MAKING UP
PRESS all pieces as described on the information page.
Join both front and right back raglan seams using back stitch, or mattress stitch if preferred.

Frill neck top
Neckband
With RS facing and using 2¼mm (US 1) circular needle, pick up and knit 47 (45: 47: 45: 47) sts from left sleeve, 66 (70: 70: 74: 74) sts from front, 46 (44: 46: 44: 46) sts from right sleeve, and 67 (71: 71: 75: 75) sts from back.
226 (230: 234: 238: 242) sts.
Working backwards and forwards in rows, cont as folls:
Row 1 (WS): K2, *P2, K2, rep from * to end.
This row sets position of rib as given for back.
Work a further 4 rows in rib.
Row 6 (RS): K1, *M1, K1, rep from * to end.
Row 7: P1, *M1 purlwise, P1, rep from * to end.
Cast off knitwise.

Scoop neck top
Neckband
With RS facing and using 2¼mm (US 1) needles, pick up and knit 39 (37: 39: 37: 39) sts from left sleeve, 58 (62: 62: 66: 66) sts from front, 38 (36: 38: 36: 38) sts from right sleeve, and 59 (63: 63: 67: 67) sts from back.
194 (198: 202: 206: 210) sts.
Row 1 (WS): K2, *P2, K2, rep from * to end.
This row sets position of rib as given for back.
Work a further 4 rows in rib.
Cast off in rib.

Both tops
See information page for finishing instructions.

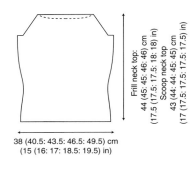

Frill neck top:
44 (45: 45: 46: 46) cm
(17.5 (17.5: 17.5: 18: 18) in)
Scoop neck top
43 (44: 44: 45: 45) cm
(17 (17.5: 17.5: 17.5: 17.5) in)

38 (40.5: 43.5: 46.5: 49.5) cm
(15 (16: 17: 18.5: 19.5) in)

0.5cm (0.25 in)

Design number 10

Spellbound

KIM HARGREAVES

YARN
Rowan All Seasons Cotton

	XS	S	M	L	XL	
To fit bust	81	86	91	97	102	cm
	32	34	36	38	40	in

Polo neck sweater 15 15 16 17 18 x 50gm
(photographed in Jersey 191)

Crew neck sweater 14 15 15 16 17 x 50gm
(photograhed in Bleached 182 and Carnation 186)

NEEDLES
1 pair 4½mm (no 7) (US 7) needles
1 pair 5mm (no 6) (US 8) needles
2 double-pointed 4½mm (no 7) (US 7) needles

TENSION
17 sts and 24 rows to 10 cm measured over stocking
stitch using 5mm (US 8) needles.

SPECIAL ABBREVIATIONS
Right dec = sl 1, K1, psso, slip st now on right
needle back onto left needle, lift 2nd st on left
needle over this st and then slip this st back onto
right needle
Left dec = sl 1, K2tog, psso

Polo neck sweater
BACK and FRONT (both alike)
Cast on 96 (100: 104: 108: 112) sts using 4½mm
(US 7) needles.
Row 1 (RS): (K1, P1) 4 times, K2 (4: 2: 4: 2), *P4,
K4, rep from * to last 14 (16: 14: 16: 14) sts, P4,
K2 (4: 2: 4: 2), (P1, K1) 4 times.
Row 2: (K1, P1) 4 times, P2 (4: 2: 4: 2), *K4, P4, rep
from * to last 14 (16: 14: 16: 14) sts, K4, P2 (4: 2: 4: 2),
(P1, K1) 4 times.
Rep last 2 rows 4 times more.
Change to 5mm (US 8) needles.
Row 1 (RS): (K1, P1) 4 times, K to last 8 sts, (P1, K1)
4 times.
Row 2: (K1, P1) 4 times, P to last 8 sts, (P1, K1)
4 times.
These 2 rows set the sts – first and last 8 sts worked
in moss st with all other sts worked in st st.
Keeping patt correct as set, cont as folls:
Work a further 16 rows.
Next row (eyelet row) (RS): K1, P1, K1, yfwd,
K2tog, P1, K1, P1, K to last 8 sts, P1, K1, P1, K2tog,
yfwd, K1, P1, K1.
Work 9 rows.
Rep last 10 rows 6 times more and then first of
these rows (the eyelet row) again.
Cont straight until back measures 46 cm, ending
with a WS row.
Shape raglan armholes
Cast off 6 sts at beg of next 2 rows.
84 (88: 92: 96: 100) sts.**
Next row (RS): P2, K to last 2 sts, P2.
Next row: K2, P to last 2 sts, K2.
Next row: P2, right dec, K to last 5 sts, left dec, P2.
Next row: K2, P to last 2 sts, K2.
Rep last 4 rows 7 (6: 8: 10: 12) times more.
52 (60: 56: 52: 48) sts.
Next row (RS): P2, K to last 2 sts, P2.
Next row: K2, P to last 2 sts, K2.
Next row: P2, K to last 2 sts, P2.
Next row: K2, P to last 2 sts, K2.
Next row: P2, right dec, K to last 5 sts, left dec, P2.
Next row: K2, P to last 2 sts, K2.
Rep last 6 rows 2 (3: 2: 1: 0) times more.
Cast off rem 40 (44: 44: 44: 44) sts.

SLEEVES (both alike)
Cast on 60 (60: 62: 64: 64) sts using 4½mm (US 7)
needles.
Row 1 (RS): P0 (0: 1: 2: 2), *K4, P4, rep from * to
last 4 (4: 5: 6: 6) sts, K4, P0 (0: 1: 2: 2).
Row 2: K0 (0: 1: 2: 2), *P4, K4, rep from * to last
4 (4: 5: 6: 6) sts, P4, K0 (0: 1: 2: 2).
Rep last 2 rows 4 times more.
Change to 5mm (US 8) needles.
Beg with a K row, cont in st st as folls:
Work 6 (4: 4: 4: 2) rows.
Next row (RS): K3, M1, K to last 3 sts, M1, K3.
Working all increases as set by last row, inc 1 st at each
end of every foll 16th (14th: 14th: 14th: 12th) row
until there are 64 (64: 70: 72: 76) sts, then on every
foll 14th (12th: 12th: 12th: 10th) row until there are
72 (74: 76: 78: 80) sts.
Cont straight until sleeve measures 42 (42: 43: 43:
43) cm, ending with a WS row.
Shape raglan
Cast off 6 sts at beg of next 2 rows.
60 (62: 64: 66: 68) sts.
Next row (RS): P2, K to last 2 sts, P2.
Next row: K2, P to last 2 sts, K2.
Next row: P2, right dec, K to last 5 sts, left dec, P2.

Next row: K2, P to last 2 sts, K2.****
Rep last 4 rows 4 (3: 5: 4: 6) times more.
40 (46: 40: 46: 40) sts.
Next row (RS): P2, K to last 2 sts, P2.
Next row: K2, P to last 2 sts, K2.
Next row: P2, K to last 2 sts, P2.
Next row: K2, P to last 2 sts, K2.
Next row: P2, right dec, K to last 5 sts, left dec, P2.
Next row: K2, P to last 2 sts, K2.
Rep last 6 rows 4 (5: 4: 5: 4) times more.
Cast off rem 20 (22: 20: 22: 20) sts.

Crew neck sweater
BACK
Work as given for back of polo neck sweater to **.
84 (88: 92: 96: 100) sts.
Extra small, small and large sizes only
Next row (RS): P2, K to last 2 sts, P2.
Next row: K2, P to last 2 sts, K2.
Extra small size only
Next row (RS): P2, right dec, K to last 5 sts, left
dec, P2.
Next row: K2, P to last 2 sts, K2.
Next row: P2, K to last 2 sts, P2.
Next row: K2, P to last 2 sts, K2.
Rep last 2 rows once more.
All sizes
Next row (RS): P2, right dec, K to last 5 sts, left
dec, P2.
Next row: K2, P to last 2 sts, K2.
Next row: P2, K to last 2 sts, P2.
Next row: K2, P to last 2 sts, K2.***
Rep last 4 rows 11 (13: 14: 14: 15) times more.
Cast off rem 32 (32: 32: 36: 36) sts.

FRONT
Work as given for back to ***.
Rep last 4 rows 8 (10: 11: 11: 12) times more.
44 (44: 44: 48: 48) sts.
Shape neck
Next row (RS): P2, right dec, K4 and turn, leaving
rem sts on a holder.
Next row: P2tog, P3, K2.
Next row: P2, K4.
Next row: P2tog, P2, K2.
Next row: P2, right dec.
Next row: K2tog, K1.
Next row: P2tog and fasten off.
With RS facing, rejoin yarn to rem sts, cast off
centre 26 (26: 26: 30: 30) sts, K to last 5 sts, left dec,
P2. 7 sts.
Next row: K2, P3, P2tog.
Next row: K4, P2.
Next row: K2, P2, P2tog.
Next row: Left dec, P2.
Next row: K1, K2tog.
Next row: P2tog and fasten off.

SLEEVES (both alike)
Work as given for sleeves of polo neck sweater to
****.
Rep last 4 rows 9 (8: 10: 9: 11) times more.
20 (26: 20: 26: 20) sts.
Next row (RS): P2, K to last 2 sts, P2.
Next row: K2, P to last 2 sts, K2.
Next row: P2, K to last 2 sts, P2.
Next row: K2, P to last 2 sts, K2.
Next row: P2, right dec, K to last 5 sts, left dec, P2.
Next row: K2, P to last 2 sts, K2.
Rep last 6 rows 0 (1: 0: 1: 0) times more and then
first 4 of these rows again. 16 (18: 16: 18: 16) sts.
Left sleeve only
Next row: P2, right dec, K to last 5 sts, left dec, P2.
Next row: Cast off 3 sts, P to last 2 sts, K2.
Next row: P2, K to end.
Rep last 2 rows once more. 6 (8: 6: 8: 6) sts.
Next row: Cast off 3 (4: 3: 4: 3) sts, P to last 2 sts,
K2.

Right sleeve only
Next row: Cast off 5 sts, K to last 5 sts, left dec, P2.
Next row: K2, P to last 2 sts, K2.
Next row: Cast off 3 sts, K to last 2 sts, P2.
Next row: K2, P to last 2 sts, K2.
Next row: Cast off 3 (4: 3: 4: 3) sts, K to last 2 sts, P2. 3 (4: 3: 4: 3) sts
Next row: K2, P to end.
Both sleeves
Cast off rem 3 (4: 3: 4: 3) sts.

MAKING UP
PRESS all pieces as described on the info page.
Polo neck sweater
Join both front and right back raglan seams using back stitch, or mattress stitch if preferred.
Neckband
With RS facing and using 4¹/₂mm (US 7) needles, pick up and knit 20 sts from top of left sleeve, 40 (44: 44: 44: 44) sts from front, 20 sts from top of right sleeve, and 40 (44: 44: 44: 44) sts from back. 120 (128: 128: 128: 128) sts.
Row 1 (WS): ★K4, P4, rep from ★ to end.
Rep this row for 18 cm. Cast off in rib.
Crew neck sweater
Join both front and right back raglan seams using back stitch, or mattress stitch if preferred.
Neckband
With RS facing and using 4¹/₂mm (US 7) needles, pick up and knit 13 sts from top of left sleeve, 40 (40: 40: 44: 44) sts from front, 13 sts from top of right sleeve, and 30 (30: 30: 34: 34) sts from back. 96 (96: 96: 104: 104) sts.
Row 1 (WS): ★K4, P4, rep from ★ to end.
Rep this row for 10 cm. Cast off in rib.
Both sweaters
Side ties (make 2)
Using double pointed 4¹/₂mm (US 7) needles, cast on 3 sts.
Next row (RS): K3 – all 3 sts now on right needle, ★slip sts to opposite end of needle and transfer this needle to left hand, without turning work and taking yarn quite tightly across back of work, K same 3 sts again – all 3 sts now on right needle again, rep from ★ until tie is 2 m long.
Next row: K3tog and fasten off.
With centre of each tie at underarm, thread ties in and out of eyelet holes along side seams, knotting ends at lower edge.
See information page for finishing instructions.

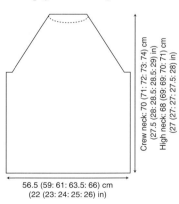

56.5 (59: 61: 63.5: 66) cm
(22 (23: 24: 25: 26) in)

Crew neck: 70 (71: 72: 73: 74) cm
(27.5 (28: 28.5: 28.5: 29) in)
High neck: 68 (69: 69: 70: 71) cm
(27 (27: 27: 27.5: 28) in)

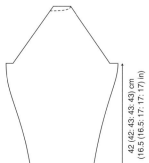

42 (42: 43: 43: 43) cm
(16.5 (16.5: 17: 17: 17) in)

Design number 11

Brocade

KAFFE FASSETT

YARN
Rowan Wool Cotton

		XS	S	M	L	XL	
To fit bust			81	86	91	97	102 cm
			32	34	36	38	40 in
A Rich	911	8	9	9	9	10 x 50gm
B Pinky	902	4	5	5	5	5 x 50gm
C Amazon	905	1	1	1	1	1 x 50gm
D Deepest Olive	907	2	2	2	2	2 x 50gm

NEEDLES
1 pair 3¹/₄mm (no 10) (US 3) needles
1 pair 3³/₄mm (no 9) (US 5) needles
1 pair 4mm (no 8) (US 6) needles

BUTTONS - 7

TENSION
25 sts and 29 rows to 10 cm measured over patterned stocking stitch using 4mm (US 6) needles.

BACK
Cast on 120 (126: 132: 138: 144) sts using 3¹/₄mm (US 3) needles and yarn D.
Purl 4 rows.
Change to 3³/₄mm (US 5) needles.
Using the **fairisle** technique described on the information page and starting and ending rows as indicated, cont in patt foll lower section of body chart, which is worked entirely in st st, as folls:
Row 1 (RS): Using yarn D P4, work next 112 (118: 124: 130: 136) sts as given for row 1 of chart, using yarn D P4.
Row 2: Using yarn D P4, work next 112 (118: 124: 130: 136) sts as given for row 2 of chart, using yarn D P4.
These 2 rows set the sts.
Keeping sts correct as set, work a further 10 rows, ending with chart row 12.
Change to 4mm (US 6) needles.
Using the **intarsia** technique described on the information page and starting and ending rows as indicated, cont in patt foll main section of body chart, which is worked entirely in st st, as folls:
Work 76 (78: 78: 80: 80) rows.

Shape armholes
Keeping chart correct, cast off 3 (4: 4: 5: 5) sts at beg of next 2 rows.
114 (118: 124: 128: 134) sts.
Dec 1 st at each end of next 5 (5: 7: 7: 9) rows, then on foll 3 (4: 4: 5: 5) alt rows, then on every foll 4th row until 94 (96: 98: 100: 102) sts rem.
Cont straight until chart row 134 (136: 140: 142: 144) has been completed, ending with a WS row.
Shape shoulders and back neck
Cast off 9 sts at beg of next 2 rows.
76 (78: 80: 82: 84) sts.
Next row (RS): Cast off 9 sts, patt until there are 12 (12: 13: 13: 14) sts on right needle and turn, leaving rem sts on a holder.
Work each side of neck separately.
Cast off 4 sts at beg of next row.
Cast off rem 8 (8: 9: 9: 10) sts.
With RS facing, rejoin yarn to rem sts, cast off centre 34 (36: 36: 38: 38) sts, patt to end.
Work to match first side, reversing shapings.

LEFT FRONT
Cast on 60 (63: 66: 69: 72) sts using 3¹/₄mm (US 3) needles and yarn D.
Purl 4 rows.
Change to 3³/₄mm (US 5) needles.
Cont in patt foll lower section of body chart as folls:
Row 1 (RS): Using yarn D P4, work next 52 (55: 58: 61: 64) sts as given for row 1 of chart, using yarn D P4.
Row 2: Using yarn D P4, work next 52 (55: 58: 61: 64) sts as given for row 2 of chart, using yarn D P4.
These 2 rows set the sts.
Keeping sts correct as set, work a further 10 rows, ending with chart row 12.
Change to 4mm (US 6) needles.
Cont in patt foll main section of body chart as folls:
Work 76 (78: 78: 80: 80) rows.
Shape armhole
Keeping chart correct, cast off 3 (4: 4: 5: 5) sts at beg of next row. 57 (59: 62: 64: 67) sts.
Work 1 row.
Dec 1 st at armhole edge of next 5 (5: 7: 7: 9) rows, then on foll 3 (4: 4: 5: 5) alt rows, then on every foll 4th row until 47 (48: 49: 50: 51) sts rem.
Cont straight until chart row 115 (117: 121: 121: 123) has been completed, ending with a RS row.
Shape neck
Keeping chart correct, cast off 6 (7: 7: 7: 7) sts at beg of next row and 4 sts at beg of foll alt row.
37 (37: 38: 39: 40) sts.
Dec 1 st at neck edge of next 7 rows, then on foll 4 (4: 4: 5: 5) alt rows.
26 (26: 27: 27: 28) sts.
Work 1 row, ending with chart row 134 (136: 140: 142: 144).
Shape shoulder
Cast off 9 sts at beg of next and foll alt row.
Work 1 row.
Cast off rem 8 (8: 9: 9: 10) sts.

RIGHT FRONT
Work as given for left front, reversing shapings.

SLEEVES (both alike)
Cast on 54 (54: 54: 58: 58) sts using 3¹/₄mm (US 3) needles and yarn D.
Purl 4 rows.
Change to 3³/₄mm (US 5) needles.
Cont in patt foll chart for sleeves as folls:
Work 12 rows.
Change to 4mm (US 6) needles.
Inc 1 st at each end of 3rd and every foll 6th row until there are 84 (86: 88: 90: 92) sts, taking inc sts into patt.
Cont straight until chart row 116 (116: 118: 118: 122) has been completed, ending with a WS row.

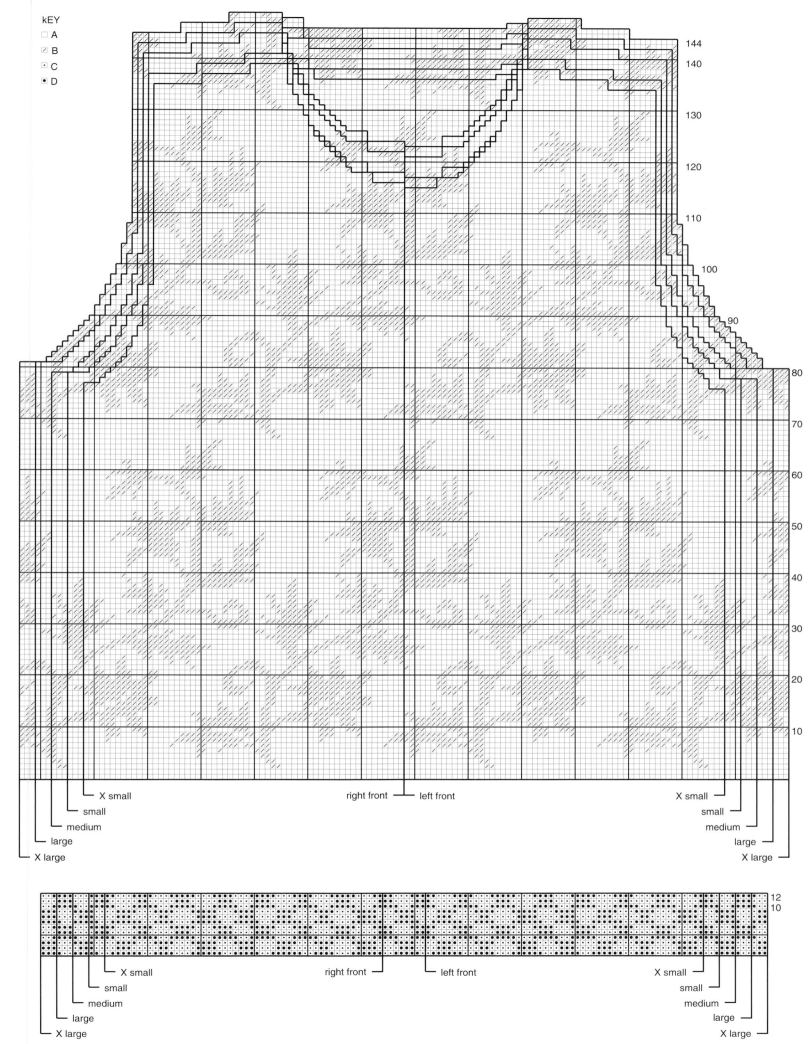

kEY
A
B
C
D

144
140
130
120
110
100
90
80
70
60
50
40
30
20
10

X small
small
medium
large
X large

right front — left front

X small
small
medium
large
X large

12
10

X small
small
medium
large
X large

right front — left front

X small
small
medium
large
X large

85

Shape top

Keeping chart correct, cast off 3 (4: 4: 5: 5) sts at beg of next 2 rows. 78 (78: 80: 80: 82) sts.

Dec 1 st at each end of next 5 rows, then on foll 3 alt rows, then on every foll 4th row until 56 (56: 58: 58: 60) sts rem.

Work 1 row.

Dec 1 st at each end of next and foll 4 (4: 5: 5: 6) alt rows, then on foll 7 rows. 32 sts.

Cast off 4 sts at beg of next 2 rows, ending with chart row 160 (160: 164: 164: 170).

Cast off rem 24 sts.

MAKING UP

PRESS all pieces as described on the information page.

Join shoulder seams using back stitch, or mattress stitch if preferred.

Button band

With RS facing, using 3¼mm (US 3) needles and yarn A, pick up and knit 97 (97: 103: 103: 103) sts along left front opening edge between neck shaping and top of lower edge border.

Row 1 (WS): K1, *P1, K1, rep from * to end.

Row 2: As row 1.

These 2 rows form moss st.

Work a further 2 rows in moss st.

Cast off in moss st.

Buttonhole band

Work as given for button band, with the addition of 7 buttonholes worked in row 2 as folls:

Buttonhole row (RS): Moss st 3 sts, *yrn (to make a buttonhole), work 2 tog, moss st 13 (13: 14: 14: 14) sts, rep from * to last 4 sts, yrn (to make 7th buttonhole), work 2 tog, moss st 2 sts.

Collar

Cast on 109 (113: 113: 121: 121) sts using 3¼mm (US 3) needles and yarn A.

Work in moss st as given for button band for 8 cm.

Cast off in moss st.

Sew cast-on edge of collar to neck edge, positioning ends of collar halfway across top of bands.

See information page for finishing instructions, setting in sleeves using the set-in method.

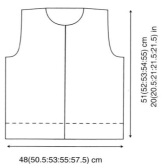

51(52:53:54:55) cm
20(20.5:21:21.5:21.5) in

48(50.5:53:55:57.5) cm
19(20:21:21.5:22.5) in

41(41:42:42:43) cm
16(16:16.5:16.5:17) in

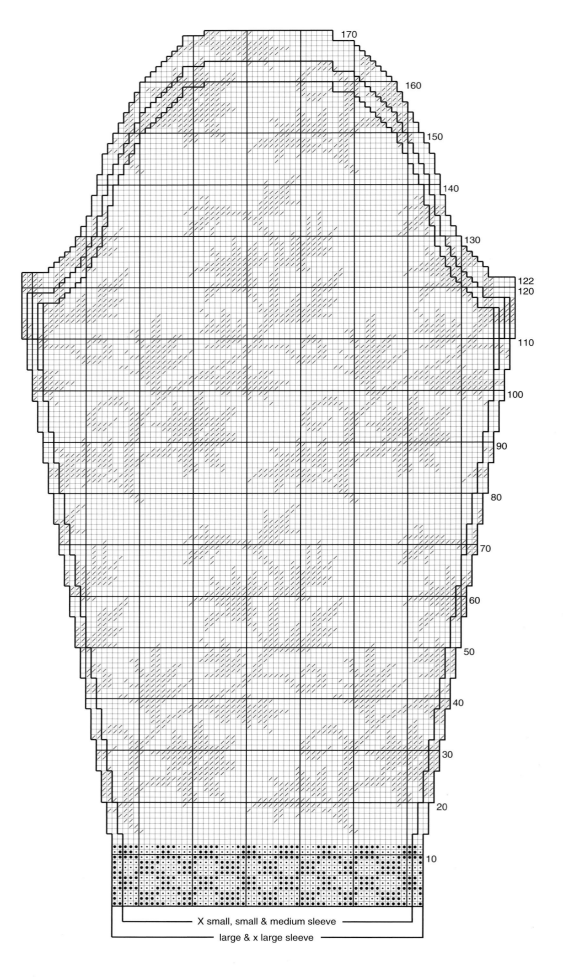

X small, small & medium sleeve

large & x large sleeve

Design number 12

Ursula

KIM HARGREAVES

YARN

One size to fit bust	81-91	cm
	32-36	in

Rowan 4 ply Cotton 2 x 50gm
(photographed in Blaze 105 and Sage 123)
Lightweight washable fabric for lining (optional)

HOOK & NEEDLES

1 3.00mm (no 10) (US D3) crochet hook
2 double-pointed 2¾mm (no 12) (US 2) needles

TENSION

23 sts and 12 rows to 10 cm measured over treble pattern using 3.00mm (US D3) hook.

CROCHET ABBREVIATIONS

Ch = chain; **dc** = double crochet; **htr** = half treble; **sp** = space; **tr** = treble; **tr2tog** = *yrh and insert hook into next st, yrh and draw loop through, yrh and draw through 2 loops, rep from * once more, yrh and draw through all 3 loops on hook (1 st decreased);

tr3tog = *yrh and insert hook into next st, yrh and draw loop through, yrh and draw through 2 loops, rep from * twice more, yrh and draw through all 4 loops on hook (2 sts decreased); **yrh** = yarn round hook.

BIKINI TOP (make two)

Make 36 ch using 3.00mm (US D3) hook.
Row 1 (RS): 1 dc into 3rd ch from hook, 1 dc into each ch to end, turn. 35 sts.
Row 2: 3 ch (counts as 1 htr and 1 ch), miss last 2 dc of previous row, *1 htr into next dc, 1 ch, miss 1 dc, rep from * to end, 1 htr into 2 ch loop at beg of previous row, turn.
Row 3: 1 ch (does NOT count as st), 1 dc into htr at end of previous row, *1 dc into next ch sp, 1 dc into next htr, rep from * to end, working last dc into 2nd of 3 ch at beg of previous row, turn.
Cont in tr patt as folls:
Row 4: 3 ch (counts as first tr), miss dc at end of previous row, 1 tr into next dc, tr2tog over next 2 dc, 1 tr into each of next 27 dc, tr2tog over next 2 dc, 1 tr into each of last 2 dc, turn. 33 sts.
Row 5: 3 ch (counts as first tr), miss tr at end of previous row, 1 tr into next tr, tr2tog over next 2 sts, 1 tr into each tr to last 4 sts, tr2tog over next 2 sts, 1 tr into next tr, 1 tr into top of 3 ch at beg of previous row, turn.
Rep row 5, 12 times more. 7 sts.
Row 18: 3 ch (counts as first tr), miss tr at end of previous row, 1 tr into each st to end, working last tr into top of 3 ch at beg of previous row, turn.
Row 19: 3 ch (counts as first tr), miss tr at end of previous row, 1 tr into next tr, tr3tog over next 3 tr, 1 tr into next tr, 1 tr into top of 3 ch at beg of previous row, turn. 5 sts.
Row 20: As row 18.
Row 21: 3 ch (counts as first tr), miss tr at end of previous row, tr3tog over next 3 tr, 1 tr into top of 3 ch at beg of previous row, turn. 3 sts.
Row 22: As row 18.
Row 23: 3 ch (does NOT count as st), miss tr at end of previous row, tr2tog over next 2 sts.
Fasten off.

Edging

With RS facing and using 3.00mm (US D3) hook, rejoin yarn at beg of row 1 and work 1 row of dc evenly up row-end edge, over fasten-off point and down other row-end edge to end of row 1, working 2 dc into each row end, several dc into fasten-off point so edge is a smooth curve and ensuring an odd number of sts are worked. Turn.
Row 2: 3 ch (counts as 1 htr and 1 ch), miss last 2 dc of previous row, *1 htr into next dc, 1 ch, miss 1 dc, rep from * to end, 1 htr into dc at beg of previous row, turn.
Row 3: 1 ch, 1 dc into htr at end of previous row, *1 dc into next ch sp, 1 dc into next htr, rep from * to end, working last dc into 2nd of 3 ch at beg of previous row. Fasten off.

BIKINI BOTTOM

Make 48 ch using 3.00mm (US D3) hook.
Work rows 1 to 3 as given for bikini top, dec 1 st at centre of row 3. 46 sts.
Cont in tr patt as folls:
Row 4: 3 ch (counts as first tr), miss dc at end of previous row, 1 tr into next dc, tr2tog over next 2 dc, 1 tr into each of next 38 sts, tr2tog over next 2 dc, 1 tr into each of last 2 dc, turn. 44 sts.
Row 5: 3 ch (counts as first tr), miss tr at end of previous row, 1 tr into next tr, tr2tog over next 2 sts, 1 tr into each tr to last 4 sts, tr2tog over next 2 sts, 1 tr into next tr, 1 tr into top of 3 ch at beg of previous row, turn.
Rep row 5, 15 times more. 12 sts.
Row 21: 3 ch (counts as first tr), miss tr at end of previous row, 1 tr into each st to end, working last tr into top of 3 ch at beg of previous row, turn.

Row 22: As row 5. 10 sts.
Rows 23 to 27: As row 21.
Row 28: 3 ch (counts as first tr), miss tr at end of previous row, 1 tr into next tr, 2 tr into next tr, 1 tr into each tr to last 3 sts, 2 tr into next tr, 1 tr into next tr, 1 tr into top of 3 ch at beg of previous row, turn. 12 sts.
Row 29: As row 21.
Rows 30 and 31: As rows 28 and 29. 14 sts.
Rows 32 to 37: As row 28. 26 sts.
Place markers at base of both ends of last row (ie at top of ends of row 36).
Row 38: 3 ch (counts as first tr), miss tr at end of previous row, 1 tr into next tr, 3 tr into next tr, 1 tr into each tr to last 3 sts, 3 tr into next tr, 1 tr into next tr, 1 tr into top of 3 ch at beg of previous row, turn. 30 sts.
Rows 39 and 40: As row 28. 34 sts.
Row 41: As row 38. 38 sts.
Rows 42 and 43: As row 28. 42 sts.
Row 44: As row 38. 46 sts.
Rows 45 to 51: As row 28. 60 sts.
Row 52: As row 21.
Row 53: As row 28. 62 sts.
Place markers at base of both ends of last row (ie at top of ends of row 52).
Row 54: As row 21.
Row 55: As row 28. 64 sts.
Rows 56 and 57: As row 21.
Row 58: As row 28. 66 sts.
Rows 59 and 60: As row 21.
Row 61: As row 28. 68 sts.
Rows 62 and 63: As row 21, inc 1 st at centre of last row. 69 sts. Fasten off.

Edging

With RS facing and using 3.00mm (US D3) hook, rejoin yarn at beg of row 1 and work 1 row of dc evenly up row-end edge, across top of last row and down other row-end edge to end of row 1, working 2 dc into each row end, 1 dc into each tr across row 63 and several dc into corners so edge lays flat and ensuring an odd number of sts are worked. Turn.
Row 2: 3 ch (counts as 1 htr and 1 ch), miss last 2 dc of previous row, *1 htr into next dc, 1 ch, miss 1 dc, rep from * to end, replacing (1 htr into next dc, 1 ch, miss 1 dc, 1 htr into next dc, 1 ch, miss 1 dc) between markers with (1 htr into next dc, 1 ch, miss 2 dc, 1 htr into next dc, 1 ch, miss 1 dc) to pull edge in neatly and ending with 1 htr into dc at beg of previous row, turn.
Row 3: 1 ch, 1 dc into htr at end of previous row, *1 dc into next ch sp, 1 dc into next htr, rep from * to end, working last dc into 2nd of 3 ch at beg of previous row. Fasten off.

MAKING UP

PRESS all pieces as described on the info page.
Ties
Cast on 4 sts using double-pointed 2¾mm (US 2) needles.
Next row (RS): K4, all 4 sts now on right needle, *slip sts to opposite end of needle and transfer this needle to left hand, without turning work and taking yarn quite tightly across back of work, K same 4 sts again – all 4 sts now on right needle again, rep from * until tie is 120 cm long.
Next row: K4tog and fasten off.
Thread this tie through holes across lower edge of bikini top pieces.
Make another 2 ties, each 50 cm long, and attach these to top corners of bikini top.
Make another 2 ties, each 100 cm long, and thread these through holes across top of bikini bottom.
Lining (optional)
We chose to line the bikini bottoms. Cut a piece of fabric same size as crochet section and fold in raw edges along all sides. Slip stitch lining in place to WS of crochet.

Marcia

DEBBIE ABRAHAMS

YARN
Rowan Cotton Glace

			S–M	M–L	
To fit bust			81–91	91–102cm	
			32–36	36–40	in
A	Oyster	730	10	11	x 50gm
B	Pepper	796	2	2	x 50gm
C	Terracotta	786	1	2	x 50gm
D	Reef	801	2	2	x 50gm
E	Fizz	722	2	2	x 50gm
F	Crushed Rose	793	2	2	x 50gm

NEEDLES
1 pair 2¾mm (no 12) (US 2) needles
1 pair 3¼mm (no 10) (US 3) needles

BUTTONS – 3

BEADS – approx 500 (600) beads (for knitted pieces) (See page 117 for details).
2 large beads (for ends of tie).

TENSION
23 sts and 32 rows to 10 cm measured over stocking stitch using 3¼mm (US 3) needles.

Beading note: Thread beads onto yarns before beginning. To place beads within knitting, "bead 1" as folls: slip next st purlwise with yarn at RS of work, slide bead along yarn so that it sits on RS of work in front of st just slipped, and then take yarn back to WS of work. Do not place a bead on end sts of rows.

BACK
Cast on 121 (143) sts using 2¾mm (US 2) needles and yarn A.
Break off yarn A and join in yarn B.
Row 1 (RS): K1, *P1, K1, rep from * to end.
Row 2: As row 1.
These 2 rows form moss st.
Work a further 6 rows in moss st, inc 1 st at centre of last row. 122 (144) sts.
Change to 3¼mm (US 3) needles.
Using the **intarsia** technique described on the information page and starting and ending rows as

indicated, cont in patt foll chart as folls:
Row 1 (RS): Moss st 6 sts using yarn B, work next 110 (132) sts as row 1 of chart, moss st 6 sts using yarn B.
Row 2: Moss st 6 sts using yarn B, work next 110 (132) sts as row 2 of chart, moss st 6 sts using yarn B.
These 2 rows set the sts – first and last 6 sts still worked in moss st with central sts worked foll chart.
Cont as set until chart row 45 has been completed, ending with a RS row.
Now work all 122 (144) sts foll chart until chart row 105 has been completed, ending with a RS row.
Break off all contrasts and cont using yarn A only.
Purl 5 rows.
Next row (RS): Knit.
Next row (eyelet row): P3 (2), *P2tog, yrn, P4, rep from * to last 5 (4) sts, P2tog, yrn, P3 (2).
Knit 4 rows.
Beg with a K row, now work in st st throughout as folls:
Cont straight until back measures 44 cm, ending with a WS row.
Shape armholes
Cast off 6 (8) sts at beg of next 2 rows. 110 (128) sts.
Dec 1 st at each end of next 7 (9) rows, then on foll 3 (5) alt rows. 90 (100) sts.
Cont straight until armhole measures 21 (22) cm, ending with a WS row.
Shape shoulders and back neck
Cast off 8 (9) sts at beg of next 2 rows. 74 (82) sts.
Next row (RS): Cast off 8 (9) sts, K until there are 12 (14) sts on right needle and turn, leaving rem sts on a holder. Work each side of neck separately.
Cast off 4 sts at beg of next row.
Cast off rem 8 (10) sts.
With RS facing, rejoin yarn to rem sts, cast off centre 34 (36) sts, K to end.
Work to match first side, reversing shapings.

LEFT FRONT
Cast on 61 (72) sts using 2¾mm (US 2) needles and yarn A.
Break off yarn A and join in yarn B.
Work 8 rows in moss st.
Change to 3¼mm (US 3) needles.
Cont in patt foll chart as folls:
Row 1 (RS): Moss st 6 sts using yarn B, work last 55 (66) sts as row 1 of chart.
Row 2: Work first 55 (66) sts as row 2 of chart, moss st 6 sts using yarn B.
These 2 rows set the sts – side edge 6 sts still worked in moss st with centre sts worked foll chart.
Cont as set until chart row 45 has been completed, ending with a RS row.
Now work all 61 (72) sts foll chart until chart row 105 has been completed, ending with a RS row.
Break off all contrasts and cont using yarn A only.
Purl 5 rows.
Next row (RS): Knit.
Next row (eyelet row): P2, *P2tog, yrn, P4, rep from * to last 5 (4) sts, P2tog, yrn, P3 (2).
Knit 4 rows.
Beg with a K row, now work in st st throughout as folls:
Cont straight until left front matches back to beg of armhole shaping, ending with a WS row.
Shape armhole
Cast off 6 (8) sts at beg of next row. 55 (64) sts.
Work 1 row.
Dec 1 st at armhole edge of next 7 (8) rows. 48 (56) sts.
Work 1 (0) row, ending with a WS row.
Shape neck
Dec 1 st at both ends of next and foll 2 (5) alt rows. 42 (44) sts.
Work 1 row, ending with a WS row.
Dec 1 st at neck edge of next and foll 12 (10) alt rows, then on every foll 4th row until 24 (28) sts rem.
Cont straight until left front matches back to start of shoulder shaping, ending with a WS row.

Shape shoulder
Cast off 8 (9) sts at beg of next and foll alt row.
Work 1 row.
Cast off rem 8 (10) sts.

RIGHT FRONT
Cast on 61 (72) sts using 2¾mm (US 2) needles and yarn A.
Break off yarn A and join in yarn B.
Work 8 rows in moss st.
Change to 3¼mm (US 3) needles.
Cont in patt foll chart as folls:
Row 1 (RS): Work first 55 (66) sts as row 1 of chart, moss st 6 sts using yarn B.
Row 2: Moss st 6 sts using yarn B, work last 55 (66) sts as row 2 of chart.
These 2 rows set the sts – side edge 6 sts still worked in moss st with centre sts worked foll chart.
Cont as set until chart row 45 has been completed, ending with a RS row.
Now work all 61 (72) sts foll chart until chart row 105 has been completed, ending with a RS row.
Break off all contrasts and cont using yarn A only.
Purl 5 rows.
Next row (RS): Knit.
Next row (eyelet row): P2 (1), *P2tog, yrn, P4, rep from * to last 5 sts, P2tog, yrn, P3.
Knit 4 rows.
Beg with a K row, now work in st st and complete to match left front, reversing shapings.

SLEEVES (both alike)
Cast on 75 (77) sts using 2¾mm (US 2) needles and yarn B.
Break off yarn B and join in yarn A.
Work in moss st as given for back for 8 rows, inc 1 st at centre of last row. 76 (78) sts.
Change to 3¼mm (US 3) needles.
Beg with a K row, cont in st st as folls:
Dec 1 st at each end of 7th and every foll 8th row until 62 (64) sts rem.
Cont straight until sleeve measures 24 cm, ending with a WS row.
Inc 1 st at each end of next and every foll 6th row until there are 80 (84) sts.
Cont straight until sleeve measures 45 (46) cm, ending with a WS row.
Shape top
Cast off 6 (8) sts at beg of next 2 rows. 68 sts.
Dec 1 st at each end of next 3 rows, then on foll 2 alt rows, then on every foll 4th row until 48 (46) sts rem.
Work 1 row, ending with a WS row.
Dec 1 st at each end of next and foll 2 (1) alt rows, then on foll 9 rows, ending with a WS row. 24 sts.
Cast off 4 sts at beg of next 2 rows.
Cast off rem 16 sts.

MAKING UP
PRESS all pieces as described on the info page.
Join both shoulder seams using back stitch, or mattress stitch if preferred.
Buttonhole band
Mark positions for 3 buttonholes along right front opening edge – top buttonhole to come 1.5 cm down from beg of front neck shaping, and other 2 buttonholes to be evenly spaced between this buttonhole and eyelet row.
With RS facing, 2¾mm (US 2) needles and yarn A, pick up and knit 112 sts up right front opening edge to beg of front neck shaping, 50 (53) sts up front neck to shoulder and 21 (22) sts across to centre back neck.
183 (187) sts.
Work in moss st as given for back for 1 row.
Row 2 (buttonhole row) (RS): Moss st to first marker, *yrn (to make a buttonhole), work 2 tog, moss st to next marker, rep from * once more, yrn (to make 3rd buttonhole), work 2 tog, moss st to end.

Work 1 row in moss st.
Break off yarn A and join in yarn B.
Row 4 (RS): Knit.
Cast off knitwise.
Button band
With RS facing, 2¾mm (US 2) needles and yarn A, starting at centre back neck, pick up and knit 21 (22) sts across back neck to shoulder, 50 (53) sts down front neck to beg of front neck shaping, and 112 sts down left front opening edge to cast-on edge. 183 (187) sts.
Work in moss st as given for back for 3 rows.
Break off yarn A and join in yarn B.

Row 4 (RS): Knit.
Cast off knitwise.
Join ends of bands at centre back neck.
Using yarn B, make a twisted cord 140 cm long and thread through eyelet row. Attach large beads to ends of cord. Embroider flowers onto plain blocks of chart using photograph as a guide.
See information page for finishing instructions, setting in sleeves using the set-in method.

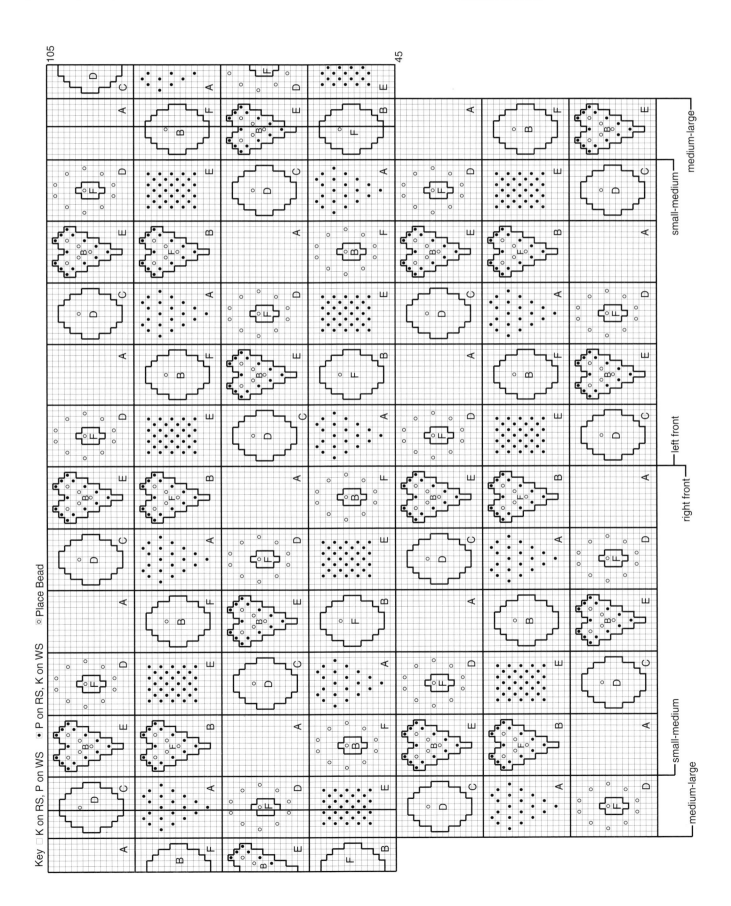

Design number 14

Tiger Lily

CAROL MELDRUM

YARN
Rowan Cotton Glace
Ladies version

			XS	S	M	L	XL	
To fit bust			81	86	91	97	102	cm
			32	34	36	38	40	in
A	Hyacinth	787	10	11	11	12	12	x 50gm
B	Steel	798	1	1	1	1	1	x 50gm
C	Mint	748	1	1	1	1	1	x 50gm
D	Bud	800	1	1	1	1	1	x 50gm
E	Bubbles	724	1	1	1	1	1	x 50gm
F	Nightshade	746	3	3	3	3	3	x 50gm

Childrens version

To fit age			8–12 years	
A	Steel	798	11	x 50gm
B	Pixie	723	3	x 50gm
C	Bud	800	1	x 50gm

Small amounts of same yarn in Bubbles 724 and
Lagoon 797 for embroidery

NEEDLES
1 pair 2¾mm (no 12) (US 2/3) needles
1 pair 3¼mm (no 10) (US 3) needles

TENSION
23 sts and 32 rows to 10 cm measured over stocking
stitch using 3¼mm (US 3) needles.

Ladies version
BACK
Cast on 125 (131: 137: 143: 149) sts using 2¾mm
(US 2) needles and yarn F.
Work in garter st for 6 rows.
Change to 3¼mm (US 3) needles.
Next row (RS): Knit.
Next row: K4, P to last 4 sts, K4.
Rep last 2 rows 12 times more.
Break off yarn F and join in yarn A.★★
Beg with a K row, cont in st st throughout as folls:
Cont straight until back measures 49 (50: 50: 51: 51) cm,
ending with a WS row.
Shape armholes
Cast off 4 (5: 5: 6: 6) sts at beg of next 2 rows.
117 (121: 127: 131: 137) sts.
Break off yarn A and join in yarn B.
Dec 1 st at each end of next 8 rows.
101 (105: 111: 115: 121) sts.
Break off yarn B and join in yarn F.
Using the **fairisle** technique described on the
information page and starting and ending rows as
indicated, cont in patt from chart, which is worked
entirely in st st, as folls:
Dec 1 st at each end of next 1 (1: 3: 3: 5) rows, then
on every foll alt row until 89 (91: 93: 95: 97) sts
rem.
Cont straight until armhole measures 21 (21: 22: 22:
23) cm, ending with a WS row.
Shape shoulders and back neck
Cast off 7 (7: 8: 8: 8) sts at beg of next 2 rows.
75 (77: 77: 79: 81) sts.
Next row (RS): Cast off 7 (7: 8: 8: 8) sts, patt until
there are 12 (12: 11: 11: 12) sts on right needle and
turn, leaving rem sts on a holder.
Work each side of neck separately.
Cast off 4 sts at beg of next row.
Cast off rem 8 (8: 7: 7: 8) sts.
With RS facing, rejoin yarn to rem sts, cast off
centre 37 (39: 39: 41: 41) sts, patt to end.
Work to match first side, reversing shapings.

FRONT
Work as given for back to ★★.
Beg with a K row, cont in st st throughout as folls:
Cont straight until front measures 29 (30: 30: 31: 31) cm,
ending with a RS row.
Place motif
Row 1 (WS): Using yarn A P44 (47: 50: 53: 56),
using yarn E P37, using yarn A P44 (47: 50: 53: 56).
Row 2: Using yarn A K44 (47: 50: 53: 56), using
yarn E K37, using yarn A K44 (47: 50: 53: 56).
Rows 3 to 42: As rows 1 and 2, 20 times.
Row 43: As row 1.
Break off yarn E and cont using yarn A only.
Cont straight until front matches back to beg of
armhole shaping, ending with a WS row.
Shape armholes
Cast off 4 (5: 5: 6: 6) sts at beg of next 2 rows.
117 (121: 127: 131: 137) sts.
Break off yarn A and join in yarn B.
Dec 1 st at each end of next 6 rows.
105 (109: 115: 119: 125) sts.
Divide for front opening
Next row (RS): K2tog, K50 (52: 55: 57: 60) and
turn, leaving rem sts on a holder.
Work each side of neck separately.
Dec 1 st at armhole edge of next row.
50 (52: 55: 57: 60) sts.
Break off yarn B and join in yarn F.

Starting and ending rows as indicated, cont in patt
from chart as folls:
Dec 1 st at armhole edge of next 1 (1: 3: 3: 5) rows,
then on every foll alt row until 44 (45: 46: 47: 48) sts
rem.
Cont straight until 19 (19: 19: 21: 21) rows less have
been worked than on back to start of shoulder
shaping, ending with a RS row.
Shape neck
Cast off 9 (10: 10: 10: 10) sts at beg of next row, then
6 sts at beg of foll alt row. 29 (29: 30: 31: 32) sts.
Dec 1 st at neck edge of next 3 rows, then on foll
3 (3: 3: 4: 4) alt rows, then on foll 4th row.
22 (22: 23: 23: 24) sts.
Work 3 rows, ending with a WS row.
Shape shoulder
Cast off 7 (7: 8: 8: 8) sts at beg of next and foll alt
row.
Work 1 row.
Cast off rem 8 (8: 7: 7: 8) sts.
With RS facing, rejoin yarn to rem sts, cast off
centre st, patt to last 2 sts, K2tog.
Work to match first side, reversing shapings.

SLEEVES (both alike)
Cast on 69 (71: 73: 75: 77) sts using 2¾mm (US 2)
needles and yarn F.
Work in garter st for 6 rows.
Change to 3¼mm (US 3) needles.
Beg with a K row, cont in st st throughout as folls:
Work 10 rows.
Break off yarn F and join in yarn A.
Work 2 rows, ending with a WS row.
Dec 1 st at each end of next row.
67 (69: 71: 73: 75) sts.
Work 7 rows.
Place motif
Row 1 (RS): Using yarn A K27 (28: 29: 30: 31),
using yarn E K13, using yarn A K27 (28: 29: 30: 31).
Row 2: Using yarn A P27 (28: 29: 30: 31), using
yarn E P13, using yarn A P27 (28: 29: 30: 31).
These 2 rows set the sts.
Keeping sts correct as now set, work 16 rows, dec 1 st
at each end of next and foll 10th row.
63 (65: 67: 69: 71) sts.
Break off yarn E and cont using yarn A only.
Work 4 rows.
Dec 1 st at each end of next and foll 10th row.
59 (61: 63: 65: 67) sts.
Work 21 rows, ending with a WS row.
Inc 1 st at each end of next and every foll 10th row
until there are 73 (75: 77: 79: 81) sts.
Cont straight until sleeve measures 45 (45: 45: 46:
46) cm, ending with a WS row.
Shape top
Cast off 4 (5: 5: 6: 6) sts at beg of next 2 rows.
65 (65: 67: 67: 69) sts.
Dec 1 st at each end of next 3 rows, then on foll
3 alt rows, then on every foll 4th row until
41 (41: 43: 43: 45) sts rem.
Work 1 row, ending with a WS row.
Dec 1 st at each end of next and foll 3 (3: 4: 4: 5) alt
rows, then on foll 3 rows. 27 sts.
Cast off 4 sts at beg of next 2 rows.
Cast off rem 19 sts.

MAKING UP
PRESS all pieces as described on the information
page.
Front opening edging
With RS facing, 2¾mm (US 2) needles and yarn A,
pick up and knit 30 (30: 32: 32: 34) sts down left
side of front opening, then 30 (30: 32: 32: 34) sts up
right side of front opening. 60 (60: 64: 64: 68) sts.
Knit 2 rows.
Cast off knitwise (on WS).
Join both shoulder seams using back stitch or
mattress stitch if preferred.

Neckband

With RS facing, 2¾mm (US 2) needles and yarn A, starting and ending at cast-off edges of front opening edging, pick up and knit 36 (37: 37: 40: 40) sts up right side of neck, 45 (47: 47: 49: 49) sts from back, then 36 (37: 37: 40: 40) sts down left side of neck. 117 (121: 121: 129: 129) sts.
Knit 2 rows.
Cast off knitwise (on WS).
See information page for finishing instructions, setting in sleeves using the set-in method and leaving side seams open for first 32 rows. Following diagram and using back stitch and french knots, embroider design around sleeve and front motifs.

Childrens version

BACK

Cast on 129 sts using 2¾mm (US 2) needles and yarn B.
Work in garter st for 6 rows.
Change to 3¼mm (US 3) needles.
Next row (RS): Knit.
Next row: K4, P to last 4 sts, K4.
Rep last 2 rows 12 times more.
Break off yarn B and join in yarn A.
Beg with a K row, cont in st st throughout as folls:
Cont straight until back measures 35 cm, ending with a WS row.
Shape armholes
Cast off 6 sts at beg of next 2 rows. 117 sts.
Cont straight until armhole measures 23 cm, ending with a WS row.
Shape shoulders and back neck
Cast off 13 sts at beg of next 2 rows. 91 sts.
Next row (RS): Cast off 13 sts, K until there are 16 sts on right needle and turn, leaving rem sts on a holder.
Work each side of neck separately.
Cast off 4 sts at beg of next row.
Cast off rem 12 sts.
With RS facing, rejoin yarn to rem sts, cast off centre 33 sts, K to end.
Work to match first side, reversing shapings.

FRONT

Work as given for back until 27 rows less have been worked than on back to beg of armhole shaping, ending with a RS row.
Place motif
Row 1 (WS): Using yarn A P46, using yarn C P37, using yarn A P46.
Row 2: Using yarn A K46, using yarn C K37, using yarn A K46.
These 2 rows set the sts.
Keeping sts correct as set, work a further 25 rows, ending with a WS row.

Shape armholes

Keeping sts correct as set, cast off 6 sts at beg of next 2 rows. 117 sts.
Work a further 14 rows using colours as set.
Break off yarn C and cont using yarn A only.
Cont straight until 16 rows less have been worked than on back to start of shoulder shaping, ending with a WS row.
Shape neck
Next row (RS): K49 and turn, leaving rem sts on a holder.
Work each side of neck separately.
Cast off 4 sts at beg of next row. 45 sts.
Dec 1 st at neck edge of next 3 rows, then on foll 4 alt rows. 38 sts.
Work 3 rows, ending with a WS row.
Shape shoulder
Cast off 13 sts at beg of next and foll alt row.
Work 1 row.
Cast off rem 12 sts.
With RS facing, rejoin yarn to rem sts, cast off centre 19 sts, K to end.
Work to match first side, reversing shapings.

SLEEVES (both alike)

Cast on 55 sts using 2¾mm (US 2) needles and yarn B.
Work in garter st for 6 rows.
Change to 3¼mm (US 3) needles.
Beg with a K row, cont in st st throughout as folls:
Work 10 rows, inc 1 st at each end of 5th of these rows. 57 sts.
Break off yarn B and join in yarn A.
Inc 1 st at each end of next and foll 6th row. 61 sts.
Work 3 rows, ending with a WS row.
Place motif
Row 1 (RS): Using yarn A K24, using yarn C K13, using yarn A K24.
Row 2: Using yarn A P24, using yarn C P13, using yarn A P24.
These 2 rows set the sts.
Keeping sts correct as now set, work a further 16 rows, inc 1 st at each end of next and every foll 4th row. 69 sts.
Break off yarn C and cont using yarn A only.
Inc 1 st at each end of next and every foll 4th row until there are 107 sts.
Cont straight until sleeve measures 41 cm, ending with a WS row.
Cast off.

MAKING UP

PRESS all pieces as described on the info page.
Join both shoulder seams using back stitch.
Neckband
With RS facing, 2¾mm (US 2) needles and yarn A, pick up and knit 20 sts down left side of neck, 19 sts

from front, 20 sts up right side of neck, then 41 sts from back. 100 sts.
Knit 2 rows.
Cast off knitwise (on WS).
See information page for finishing instructions, setting in sleeves using the square set-in method and leaving side seams open for first 32 rows. Following diagram and using back stitch and french knots, embroider design around sleeve and front motifs.

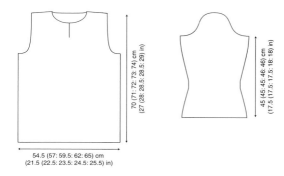

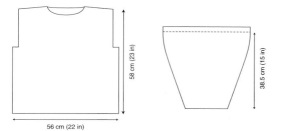

Yoke chart

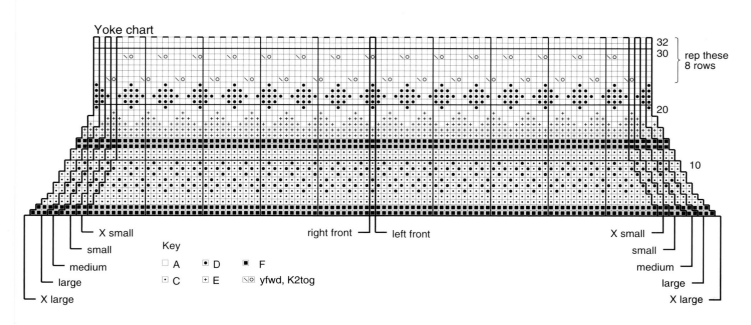

32
30 } rep these 8 rows

20

10

X small
small
medium
large
X large

right front — left front

X small
small
medium
large
X large

Key

☐ A   ◉ D   ▪ F
· C   ⊞ E   ⊠ yfwd, K2tog

91

Design number 15

Hope

KIM HARGREAVES

YARN

	XS	S	M	L	XL	
To fit bust	81	86	91	97	102	cm
	32	34	36	38	40	in

Rowan All Seasons Cotton

| | 10 | 11 | 12 | 12 | 13 | x 50gm |

(photographed in Bleached 182)

NEEDLES

1 pair 4½mm (no 7) (US 7) needles
1 pair 5mm (no 6) (US 8) needles
Cable needle

TENSION

17 sts and 24 rows to 10 cm measured over stocking stitch using 5mm (US 8) needles.

SPECIAL ABBREVIATIONS

Cr3R = Cross 3 right Slip next st onto cn and leave at back of work, K2, then P1 from cn
Cr3L = Cross 3 left Slip next 2 sts onto cn and leave at front of work, P1, then K2 from cn
C3B = Cable 3 back Slip next st onto cn and leave at back of work, K2, then K1 from cn
C3F = Cable 3 front Slip next 2 sts onto cn and leave at front of work, K1, then K2 from cn
C6B = Cable 6 back Slip next 3 sts onto cn and leave at back of work, K3, then K3 from cn
C6F = Cable 6 front Slip next 3 sts onto cn and leave at front of work, K3, then K3 from cn

BACK

Cast on 86 (92: 98: 104: 110) sts using 4½mm (US 7) needles.
Row 1 (RS): P3 (0: 3: 0: 3), K2, (P4, K2) 5 (6: 6: 7: 7) times, P2, K12, P2, (K2, P4) 5 (6: 6: 7: 7) times, K2, P3 (0: 3: 0: 3).
Row 2: K3 (0: 3: 0: 3), P2, (K4, P2) 5 (6: 6: 7: 7) times, K2, P12, K2, (P2, K4) 5 (6: 6: 7: 7) times, P2, K3 (0: 3: 0: 3).
Rep these 2 rows 6 times more.
Change to 5mm (US 8) needles.
Starting and ending rows as indicated and repeating the patt rows as detailed throughout, cont in patt from chart as folls:
Inc 1 st at each end of next and every foll 8th row until there are 98 (104: 110: 116: 122) sts, taking inc sts into patt.
Cont straight until back measures 27 (28: 28: 29: 29) cm, ending with a WS row.
Shape armholes
Keeping patt correct, cast off 3 (4: 4: 5: 5) sts at beg of next 2 rows. 92 (96: 102: 106: 112) sts.
Dec 1 st at each end of next 5 (5: 7: 7: 9) rows, then on foll 4 (5: 5: 6: 6) alt rows. 74 (76: 78: 80: 82) sts.
Cont straight until armhole measures 20 (20: 21: 21: 22) cm, ending with a WS row.
Shape shoulders and back neck
Cast off 6 (7: 7: 7: 8) sts at beg of next 2 rows.
62 (62: 64: 66: 66) sts.
Next row (RS): Cast off 6 (7: 7: 7: 8) sts, patt until there are 11 (10: 11: 12: 11) sts on right needle and turn, leaving rem sts on a holder.
Work each side of neck separately.
Cast off 4 sts at beg of next row.
Cast off rem 7 (6: 7: 8: 7) sts.
With RS facing, slip centre 28 sts onto a holder, rejoin yarn to rem sts, patt to end.
Work to match first side, reversing shapings.

FRONT

Work as given for back until 14 rows less have been worked than on back to start of shoulder shaping, ending with a WS row.
Shape neck
Next row (RS): Patt 26 (27: 28: 29: 30) sts and turn, leaving rem sts on a holder.
Work each side of neck separately.
Dec 1 st at neck edge of next 4 rows, then on foll 3 alt rows. 19 (20: 21: 22: 23) sts.
Work 3 rows, ending with a WS row.
Shape shoulder
Cast off 6 (7: 7: 7: 8) sts at beg of next and foll alt row.
Work 1 row. Cast off rem 7 (6: 7: 8: 7) sts.
With RS facing, slip centre 22 sts onto a holder, rejoin yarn to rem sts, patt to end.
Work to match first side, reversing shapings.

LEFT SLEEVE

Cast on 54 (54: 56: 58: 58) sts using 4½mm (US 7) needles.
Row 1 (RS): P2 (2: 3: 4: 4), ★K2, P4, rep from ★ to last 4 (4: 5: 6: 6) sts, K2, P2 (2: 3: 4: 4).
Row 2: K2 (2: 3: 4: 4), ★P2, K4, rep from ★ to last 4 (4: 5: 6: 6) sts, P2, K2 (2: 3: 4: 4).
Rep these 2 rows 6 times more.
Change to 5mm (US 8) needles.
Starting and ending rows as indicated and repeating the 12 patt rows throughout, cont in patt from chart as folls: Inc 1 st at each end of 3rd and every foll 10th row to 70 (64: 68: 70: 62) sts, then on every foll – (8th: 8th: 8th: 8th) row until there are – (72: 74: 76: 78) sts, taking inc sts into patt.
Cont straight until left sleeve measures 41 (41: 42: 42: 42) cm, ending with a WS row.
Shape top
Keeping patt correct, cast off 3 (4: 4: 5: 5) sts at beg of next 2 rows. 64 (64: 66: 66: 68) sts.

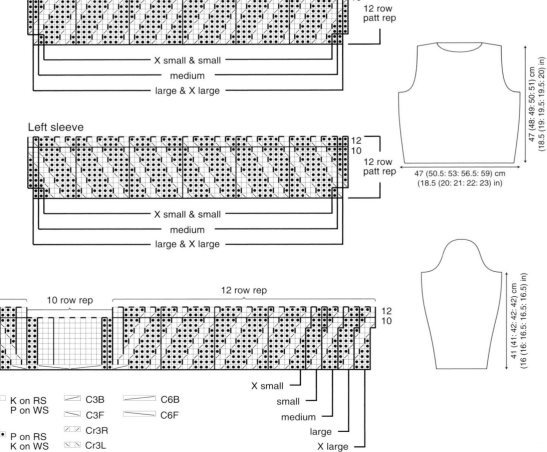

Right sleeve

12
10

12 row patt rep

X small & small
medium
large & X large

Left sleeve

12
10

12 row patt rep

X small & small
medium
large & X large

47 (48: 49: 50: 51) cm
(18.5 (19: 19.5: 19.5: 20) in)

47 (50.5: 53: 56.5: 59) cm
(18.5 (20: 21: 22: 23) in)

Back & front

12 row rep   10 row rep   12 row rep

12
10

X small
small
medium
large
X large

X small
small
medium
large
X large

41 (41: 42: 42: 42) cm
(16 (16: 16.5: 16.5: 16.5) in)

Key

	K on RS / P on WS		C3B		C6B
			C3F		C6F
	P on RS / K on WS		Cr3R		
			Cr3L		

Dec 1 st at each end of next 5 rows, then on foll 2 alt rows, then on every foll 4th row until 44 (44: 46: 46: 48) sts rem. Work 1 row.
Dec 1 st at each end of next and foll 1 (1: 2: 2: 3) alt rows, then on foll 5 rows, ending with a WS row. 30 sts.
Cast off 4 sts at beg of next 2 rows.
Cast off rem 22 sts.

RIGHT SLEEVE

Work as given for left sleeve, foll chart for right sleeve.

MAKING UP

PRESS all pieces as described on the info page. Join right shoulder seam using back stitch, or mattress stitch if preferred.

Neckband

With RS facing and using 4½mm (US 7) needles, pick up and knit 20 sts down left side of neck, patt across 22 sts from front holder, pick up and knit 19 sts up right side of front neck, and 6 sts from right side of back neck, patt across 28 sts from back holder, then pick up and knit 7 sts from left side of back neck. 102 sts.

Row 1 (WS): P1, (K2, P2) 3 times, K2, P12, K2, (P2, K2) 9 times, P12, (K2, P2) 6 times, P1.
This row sets position of rib with centre front and back sts still worked as cable.
Keeping cable correct, work 16 rows.
Cast off, dec 6 sts across top of each cable.
See information page for finishing instructions, setting in sleeves using the set-in method.

Design number 16

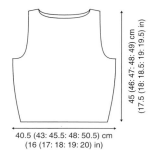

Tune

KIM HARGREAVES

YARN

Rowan 4 ply Cotton

	XS	S	M	L	XL	
To fit bust	81	86	91	97	102	cm
	32	34	36	38	40	in

Wider stripe vest

		XS	S	M	L	XL	
A	Pool	124	3	4	4	5	5	x 50gm
B	Ripple	121	2	2	2	2	2	x 50gm

Narrower stripe vest

A	Marine	102	3	3	3	3	3	x 50gm
B	Bleached	113	2	2	3	3	3	x 50gm

NEEDLES

1 pair 2¼mm (no 13) (US 1) needles
1 pair 3mm (no 11) (US 2/3) needles

TENSION

28 sts and 38 rows to 10 cm measured over stocking stitch using 3mm (US 2/3) needles.

Wider stripe vest

BACK

Cast on 100 (107: 114: 121: 128) sts using 2¼mm (US 1) needles and yarn A. Knit 4 rows.
Change to 3mm (US 2/3) needles and, beg with a K row, work in striped st st as folls:
Rows 1 and 2: Using yarn B.
Rows 3 to 6: Using yarn A.
These 6 rows form stripe patt.
Keeping patt correct, inc 1 st at each end of 13th row **from beg of stripes and every foll 12th row until there are 114 (121: 128: 135: 142) sts.
Cont straight until back measures 25 (26: 26: 27: 27) cm, ending with a WS row.
Shape armholes
Cast off 4 (5: 5: 6: 6) sts at beg of next 2 rows.
106 (111: 118: 123: 130) sts.
Dec 1 st at each end of next 9 (9: 11: 11: 13) rows, then on foll 3 (4: 4: 5: 5) alt rows. 82 (85: 88: 91: 94) sts.
Cont straight until armhole measures approx 11 cm, ending after 2 rows using yarn B.
Break off yarn B and cont in st st using yarn A only.
Cont straight until armhole measures 19 (19: 20: 20: 21) cm, ending with a WS row.
Shape back neck
Next row (RS): K17 (18: 19: 20: 21) and turn, leaving rem sts on a holder.
Work each side of neck separately.
Cast off 5 sts at beg of next row. 12 (13: 14: 15: 16) sts.
Dec 1 st at neck edge of next 2 rows.
10 (11: 12: 13: 14) sts.
Shape shoulder
Cast off 3 (3: 3: 4: 4) sts at beg and dec 1 st at end of next row.
Work 1 row. Rep last 2 rows once more.
Cast off rem 2 (3: 4: 3: 4) sts.
With RS facing, rejoin yarn to rem sts, cast off centre 48 (49: 50: 51: 52) sts, K to end.
Work to match first side, reversing shapings.

FRONT

Work as given for back until 6 rows less have been worked than on back to start of back neck shaping (this is 10 rows down from shoulder shaping), ending with a WS row.
Shape neck
Next row (RS): K20 (21: 22: 23: 24) and turn, leaving rem sts on a holder.
Work each side of neck separately.
Cast off 5 sts at beg of next row. 15 (16: 17: 18: 19) sts.
Dec 1 st at neck edge of next 5 rows, then on foll alt row. 9 (10: 11: 12: 13) sts.
Work 1 row, ending with a WS row.

Shape shoulder

Cast off 3 (3: 3: 4: 4) sts at beg and dec 1 st at end of next row.
Work 1 row.
Cast off 3 (3: 3: 4: 4) sts at beg of next row.
Work 1 row.
Cast off rem 2 (3: 4: 3: 4) sts.
With RS facing, rejoin yarn to rem sts, cast off centre 42 (43: 44: 45: 46) sts, K to end.
Work to match first side, reversing shapings.

Narrower stripe vest

BACK

Cast on 100 (107: 114: 121: 128) sts using 2¼mm (US 1) needles and yarn A.
Knit 4 rows.
Change to 3mm (US 2/3) needles and, beg with a K row, work in striped st st as folls:
Rows 1 and 2: Using yarn B.
Rows 3 and 4: Using yarn A.
These 4 rows form stripe patt.
Working in stripes **throughout**, complete as given for back of wider stripe vest from **.

FRONT

Work as given for front of wider stripe vest, working in narrower stripes throughout.

MAKING UP

PRESS all pieces as described on the information page.
Join right shoulder seam using back stitch, or mattress stitch if preferred.
Neckband
With RS facing, using 2¼mm (US 1) needles and yarn A, pick up and knit 18 sts down left side of front neck, 42 (43: 44: 45: 46) sts from front, 18 sts up right side of front neck, 12 sts down right side of back neck, 48 (49: 50: 51: 52) sts from back, and 12 sts up left side of back neck. 150 (152: 154: 156: 158) sts.
*Row 1 (WS): Knit.
Row 2: Purl.
Rows 3 and 4: As rows 1 and 2.
Cast off knitwise (on WS).
Join left shoulder and neckband seam using back stitch, or mattress stitch if preferred.
Armhole borders (both alike)
With RS facing, using 2¼mm (US 1) needles and yarn A, pick up and knit 138 (140: 146: 148: 154) sts evenly around armhole edge.
Work from * to * as given for neckband.
See information page for finishing instructions.

40.5 (43: 45.5: 48: 50.5) cm
(16 (17: 18: 19: 20) in)

45 (46: 47: 48: 49) cm
(17.5 (18: 18.5: 19: 19.5) in)

Mia

DEBBIE BLISS

YARN
Rowan Cotton Glace

		XS	S	M	L	XL	
To fit bust		81	86	91	97	102	cm
		32	34	36	38	40	in
A Mint	748	7	7	8	8	9	x 50gm
B Ecru	725	2	2	2	2	2	x 50gm
C Pear	780	1	1	1	1	1	x 50gm
D Lagoon	797	4	4	4	5	5	x 50gm
E Bubbles	724	1	1	1	1	1	x 50gm
F Candy Floss	747	1	1	2	2	2	x 50gm
G Butter	795	1	1	1	1	1	x 50gm
H Sky	749	1	1	1	1	1	x 50gm

NEEDLES
1 pair 2¾mm (no 12) (US 2) needles
1 pair 3¼mm (no 10) (US 3) needles

BUTTONS
5

TENSION
27 sts and 30 rows to 10 cm measured over patterned stocking stitch using 3¼mm (US 3) needles.

BACK
Cast on 123 (129: 137: 143: 151) sts using 2¾mm (US 2) needles and yarn A.
Row 1 (RS): K1 (0: 0: 1: 1), *P1, K1, rep from * to last 0 (1: 1: 0: 0) st, P0 (1: 1: 0: 0).
Row 2: As row 1.
These 2 rows form moss st.
Work a further 14 rows in moss st, shaping side seams by dec 1 st at each end of 5th (9th: 9th: 9th: 9th) row and every foll 4th row.
117 (125: 133: 139: 147) sts.
Change to 3¼mm (US 3) needles.
Using the **fairisle** technique described on the information page, starting and ending rows as indicated and repeating the 64 row repeat throughout, cont in patt foll chart for body, which is worked entirely in st st, as folls:
Dec 1 st at each end of 3rd (next: next: next: next) and every foll 4th row until 107 (113: 121: 127: 135) sts.

Work 11 rows.
Inc 1 st at each end of next and every foll 6th row until there are 123 (129: 137: 143: 151) sts, taking inc sts into patt.
Cont straight until back measures 32 (33: 33: 34: 34) cm, ending with a WS row.
Shape armholes
Keeping patt correct, cast off 3 (4: 4: 5: 5) sts at beg of next 2 rows.
117 (121: 129: 133: 141) sts.
Dec 1 st at each end of next 7 (7: 9: 9: 11) rows, then on foll 4 (5: 5: 6: 6) alt rows.
95 (97: 101: 103: 107) sts.
Cont straight until armhole measures 20 (20: 21: 21: 22) cm, ending with a WS row.
Shape shoulders and back neck
Keeping patt correct, cast off 9 (9: 10: 10: 11) sts at beg of next 2 rows.
77 (79: 81: 83: 85) sts.
Next row (RS): Cast off 9 (9: 10: 10: 11) sts, patt until there are 14 sts on right needle and turn, leaving rem sts on a holder.
Work each side of neck separately.
Cast off 4 sts at beg of next row.
Cast off rem 10 sts.
With RS facing, rejoin yarn to rem sts, cast off centre 31 (33: 33: 35: 35) sts, patt to end.
Work to match first side, reversing shapings.

LEFT FRONT
Cast on 67 (70: 74: 77: 81) sts using 2¾mm (US 2) needles and yarn A.
Row 1 (RS): K1 (0: 0: 1: 1), *P1, K1, rep from * to end.
Row 2: *K1, P1, rep from * to last 1 (0: 0: 1: 1) st, K1 (0: 0: 1: 1).
These 2 rows form moss st.
Work a further 13 rows in moss st, shaping side seam by dec 1 st at beg of 5th (9th: 9th: 9th: 9th) row and every foll 4th row.
64 (68: 72: 75: 79) sts.
Row 16 (WS): Moss st 8 sts and slip these sts onto a holder for button band, M1, moss st to end.
57 (61: 65: 68: 72) sts.
Change to 3¼mm (US 3) needles.
Cont in patt foll chart as folls:
Dec 1 st at beg of 3rd (next: next: next: next) and every foll 4th row until 52 (55: 59: 62: 66) sts.
Work 11 rows.
Inc 1 st at beg of next and every foll 6th row until there are 60 (63: 67: 70: 74) sts, taking inc sts into patt.
Cont straight until left front matches back to beg of armhole shaping, ending with a WS row.
Shape armhole
Keeping patt correct, cast off 3 (4: 4: 5: 5) sts at beg of next row.
57 (59: 63: 65: 69) sts.
Work 1 row.
Dec 1 st at armhole edge of next 7 (7: 9: 9: 11) rows, then on foll 4 (5: 5: 6: 6) alt rows.
46 (47: 49: 50: 52) sts.
Cont straight until 21 (21: 21: 23: 23) rows less have been worked than on back to start of shoulder shaping, ending with a RS row.
Shape neck
Keeping patt correct, cast off 6 (7: 7: 7: 7) sts at beg of next row and 4 sts at beg of foll alt row.
36 (36: 38: 39: 41) sts.
Dec 1 st at neck edge of next 4 rows, then on foll 3 (3: 3: 4: 4) alt rows, then on foll 4th row.
28 (28: 30: 30: 32) sts.
Work 4 rows, ending with a WS row.
Shape shoulder
Keeping patt correct, cast off 9 (9: 10: 10: 11) sts at beg of next and foll alt row.
Work 1 row.
Cast off rem 10 sts.

RIGHT FRONT
Cast on 67 (70: 74: 77: 81) sts using 2¾mm (US 2) needles and yarn A.
Row 1 (RS): *K1, P1, rep from * to last 1 (0: 0: 1: 1) st, K1 (0: 0: 1: 1).
Row 2: K1 (0: 0: 1: 1), *P1, K1, rep from * to end.
These 2 rows form moss st.
Work a further 13 rows in moss st, shaping side seam by dec 1 st at end of 5th (9th: 9th: 9th: 9th) row and every foll 4th row.
64 (68: 72: 75: 79) sts.
Row 16 (WS): Moss st to last 8 sts, M1 and turn, leaving last 8 sts on a holder for buttonhole band.
57 (61: 65: 68: 72) sts.
Change to 3¼mm (US 3) needles.
Cont in patt foll chart as folls:
Dec 1 st at end of 3rd (next: next: next: next) and every foll 4th row until 52 (55: 59: 62: 66) sts.
Complete to match left front, reversing shapings.

SLEEVES (both alike)
Cast on 59 (59: 61: 63: 63) sts using 2¾mm (US 2) needles and yarn A.
Row 1 (RS): K1, *P1, K1, rep from * to end.
Row 2: As row 1.
These 2 rows form moss st.
Work in moss st for a further 14 rows, inc 1 st at each end of 9th of these rows.
61 (61: 63: 65: 65) sts.
Change to 3¼mm (US 3) needles.
Cont in patt foll chart for sleeve as folls:
Inc 1 st at each end of 3rd (3rd: next: next: next) and every foll 8th (6th: 6th: 6th: 6th) row to 65 (93: 93: 97: 89) sts, then on every foll 6th (-: 4th: 4th: 4th) row until there are 91 (-: 97: 99: 103) sts, taking inc sts into patt.
Cont straight until sleeve measures approx 42 (43: 43: 44: 44) cm from cast-on edge, ending with same WS patt row as on body.
Shape top
Keeping patt correct, cast off 3 (4: 4: 5: 5) sts at beg of next 2 rows.
85 (85: 89: 89: 93) sts.
Dec 1 st at each end of next 5 rows, then on foll 3 alt rows, then on every foll 4th row until 61 (61: 67: 67: 73) sts rem.
Work 1 row.
Dec 1 st at each end of next and foll 1 (1: 4: 4: 7) alt rows, then on foll 5 rows. 47 sts.
Cast off 6 sts at beg of next 4 rows.
Cast off rem 23 sts.

MAKING UP
PRESS all pieces as described on the information page.
Join both shoulder seams using back stitch, or mattress stitch if preferred.
Button band
Slip 8 sts left on holder for button band onto 2¾mm (US 2) needles and rejoin yarn A with RS facing.
Cont in moss st as set until band, when slightly stretched, fits up left front opening edge to neck shaping, ending with a WS row.
Cast off.
Slip stitch band in place.
Mark positions for 5 buttons on this band – lowest button to come immediately after moss st at lower edge, top button 1.5 cm below neck shaping and rem 3 buttons evenly spaced between.
Buttonhole band
Work as given for button band, rejoining yarn with WS facing and with the addition of 5 buttonholes to correspond with positions marked for buttons worked as folls:
Buttonhole row (RS): K1, P1, K2tog, yfwd, (K1, P1) twice.
Slip stitch band in place.

Neckband

With RS facing, 2¾mm (US 2) needles and yarn A,
starting and ending halfway across top of front
bands, pick up and knit 29 (30: 30: 33: 33) sts up
right side of neck, 39 (41: 41: 43: 43) sts from back,
and 29 (30: 30: 33: 33) sts down left side of neck.
97 (101: 101: 109: 109) sts.
Work in moss st as given for sleeves for 10 rows.
Cast off in moss st.
See information page for finishing instructions,
setting in sleeves using the set-in method.

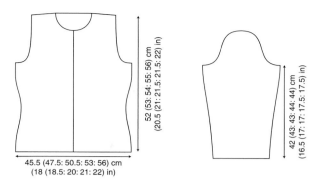

52 (53: 54: 55: 56) cm
(20.5 (21: 21.5: 21.5: 22) in)

45.5 (47.5: 50.5: 53: 56) cm
(18 (18.5: 20: 21: 22) in)

42 (43: 43: 44: 44) cm
(16.5 (17: 17: 17.5: 17.5) in)

Body Chart

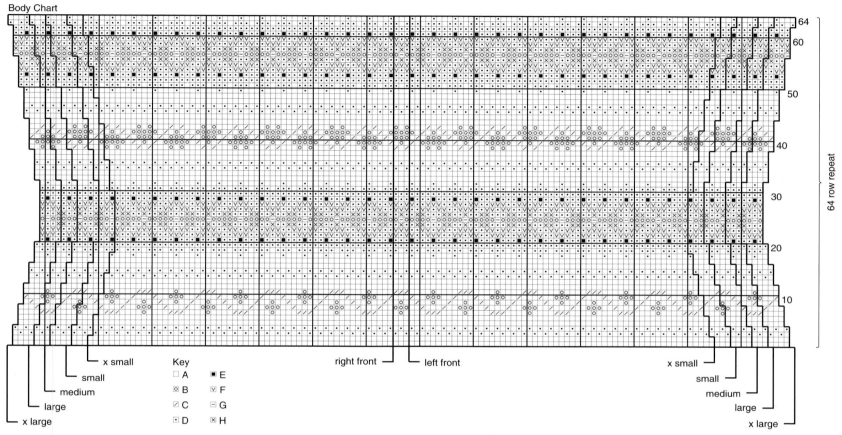

64 row repeat

x small
small
medium
large
x large

x small
small
medium
large
x large

right front — — left front

Key

□ A		■ E	
⊙ B		☑ F	
☑ C		⊟ G	
⊡ D		☒ H	

Sleeve Chart

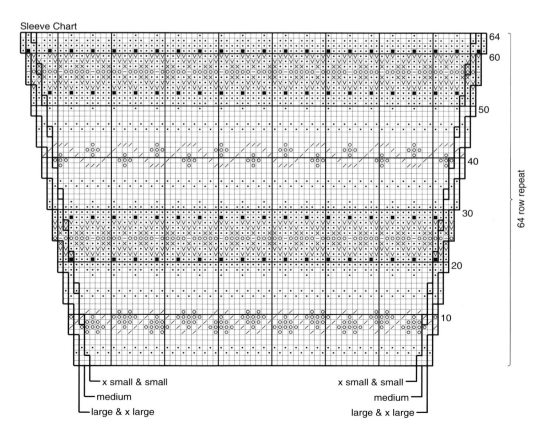

64 row repeat

x small & small
medium
large & x large

x small & small
medium
large & x large

Core

KIM HARGREAVES

YARN

	XS	S	M	L	XL	
To fit bust	81	86	91	97	102	cm
	32	34	36	38	40	in

Rowan Handknit DK Cotton

| | 12 | 13 | 13 | 14 | 14 | x 50gm |

(photographed in Sugar 303)

Rowan Denim | 13 | 14 | 15 | 15 | 16 | x 50gm

(photographed in Memphis 229)

NEEDLES

1 pair 3¼mm (no 10) (US 3) needles
1 pair 4mm (no 8) (US 6) needles

BUTTONS - 9

TENSION

Handknit DK Cotton: 20 sts and 28 rows to 10 cm measured over stocking stitch using 4mm (US 6) needles.

Denim: Before washing 20 sts and 28 rows to 10 cm measured over stocking stitch using 4mm (US 6) needles.

Tension note: Denim will shrink in length when washed for the first time. Allowances have been made in this pattern for shrinkage (see size diagram for after washing measurements).

Pattern note: Pattern is written for Handknit DK Cotton with alterations for Denim given in **bold** afterwards in brackets. Where no bold figures are given, instructions are same for both yarns unless stated otherwise.

BACK

Cast on 81 (85: 91: 95: 101) sts using 3¼mm (US 3) needles.
Row 1 (RS): K1, *P1, K1, rep from * to end.
Row 2: As row 1.
These 2 rows form moss st.
Work a further 8 rows in moss st, ending with a WS row.
Change to 4mm (US 6) needles.
Next row (RS): P21 (22: 24: 25: 27), K2, P1, K33 (35: 37: 39: 41), P1, K2, P21 (22: 24: 25: 27).
Next row: K21 (22: 24: 25: 27), P2, K1, P33 (35: 37: 39: 41), K1, P2, K21 (22: 24: 25: 27).
These 2 rows set the sts.
Keeping patt correct as set, cont as folls:
Work a further 4 (6: 6: 6: 6) rows for Handknit DK Cotton, **or 6 (8: 8: 8: 8) rows for Denim.**
Next row (RS) (inc): P21 (22: 24: 25: 27), K2, P1, M1, K33 (35: 37: 39: 41), M1, P1, K2, P21 (22: 24: 25: 27). 83 (87: 93: 97: 103) sts.
Next row: K21 (22: 24: 25: 27), P2, K1, P35 (37: 39: 41: 43), K1, P2, K21 (22: 24: 25: 27).
Working all increases as set by last 2 rows, inc 1 st at either side of centre panel on every foll 8th (**10th**) row until there are 97 (101: 107: 111: 117) sts, taking inc sts into st st.
Cont straight until back measures 28 (29: 29: 30: 30) cm for Handknit DK Cotton, **or 32.5 (34: 34: 35: 35) cm for Denim**, ending with a WS row.
Shape armholes
Keeping patt correct, cast off 4 sts at beg of next 2 rows. 89 (93: 99: 103: 109) sts.
Dec 1 st at each end of next 7 (7: 9: 9: 11) rows, then on foll alt row. 73 (77: 79: 83: 85) sts.
Work 1 row, ending with a WS row.
Next row (RS): P2tog, P to last 2 sts, P2tog.
Next row: Knit.
Beg with a K row, now cont in st st as folls:
Dec 1 st at each end of next and foll 1 (2: 2: 3: 3) alt rows. 67 (69: 71: 73: 75) sts.
Cont straight until armhole measures 21 (21: 22: 22: 23) cm for Handknit DK Cotton, **or 24.5 (24.5: 25.5: 25.5: 27) cm for Denim**, ending with a WS row.
Shape shoulders and back neck
Cast off 6 (6: 7: 7: 7) sts at beg of next 2 rows. 55 (57: 57: 59: 61) sts.
Next row (RS): Cast off 6 (6: 7: 7: 7) sts, K until there are 11 (11: 10: 10: 11) sts on right needle and turn, leaving rem sts on a holder.
Work each side of neck separately.
Cast off 4 sts at beg of next row.
Cast off rem 7 (7: 6: 6: 7) sts.
With RS facing, rejoin yarn to rem sts, cast off centre 21 (23: 23: 25: 25) sts, K to end.
Work to match first side, reversing shapings.

LEFT FRONT

Cast on 47 (49: 52: 54: 57) sts using 3¼mm (US 3) needles.
Row 1 (RS): *K1, P1, rep from * to last 1 (1: 0: 0: 1) st, K1 (1: 0: 0: 1).

Row 2: K1 (1: 0: 0: 1), *P1, K1, rep from * to end.
These 2 rows form moss st.
Work a further 7 rows in moss st, ending with a RS row.
Row 10 (WS): Moss st 7 and slip these 7 sts onto a holder for button band, M1, moss st to end. 41 (43: 46: 48: 51) sts.
Change to 4mm (US 6) needles.
Next row (RS): P21 (22: 24: 25: 27), K2, P1, moss st 7, P1, K2, P7 (8: 9: 10: 11).
Next row: K7 (8: 9: 10: 11), P2, K1, moss st 7, K1, P2, K21 (22: 24: 25: 27).
These 2 rows set the sts.
Keeping sts correct as now set, cont as folls:
Work a further 12 (14: 14: 14: 14) rows for Handknit DK Cotton, **or 16 (18: 18: 18: 18) rows for Denim.**
Next row (RS) (inc): P21 (22: 24: 25: 27), K2, P1, M1, moss st 7, M1, P1, K2, P7 (8: 9: 10: 11).
Next row: K7 (8: 9: 10: 11), P2, K1, moss st 9, K1, P2, K21 (22: 24: 25: 27).
Working all increases as set by last 2 rows, inc 1 st at either side of moss st panel on every foll 16th (**20th**) row until there are 49 (51: 54: 56: 59) sts, taking inc sts into moss st.
Cont straight until left front matches back to beg of armhole shaping, ending with a WS row.
Shape armhole
Keeping patt correct, cast off 4 sts at beg of next row. 45 (47: 50: 52: 55) sts.
Work 1 row.
Dec 1 st at armhole edge of next 7 (7: 9: 9: 11) rows, then on foll alt row.
37 (39: 40: 42: 43) sts.
Work 1 row, ending with a WS row.
Next row (RS): P2tog, P to end.
Next row: Knit.
Beg with a K row, now cont in st st as folls:
Dec 1 st at armhole edge of next and foll 1 (2: 2: 3: 3) alt rows. 34 (35: 36: 37: 38) sts.
Cont straight until 21 (21: 21: 23: 23) rows for Handknit DK Cotton, **or 25 (25: 25: 27: 27) rows for Denim**, less have been worked than on back to start of shoulder shaping, ending with a RS row.
Shape neck
Cast off 5 (6: 6: 6: 6) sts at beg of next row. 29 (29: 30: 31: 32) sts.
Dec 1 st at neck edge of next 5 rows, then on foll 4 (4: 4: 5: 5) alt rows for Handknit DK Cotton, **or 3 (3: 3: 4: 4) alt rows for Denim**, then every foll 4th row until 19 (19: 20: 20: 21) sts rem.
Work 3 (**5**) rows, ending with a WS row.
Shape shoulder
Cast off 6 (6: 7: 7: 7) sts at beg of next and foll alt row.
Work 1 row.
Cast off rem 7 (7: 6: 6: 7) sts.

RIGHT FRONT

Cast on 47 (49: 52: 54: 57) sts using 3¼mm (US 3) needles.
Row 1 (RS): K1 (1: 0: 0: 1), *P1, K1, rep from * to end.
Row 2: *K1, P1, rep from * to last 1 (1: 0: 0: 1) st, K1 (1: 0: 0: 1).
These 2 rows form moss st.
Work a further 7 rows in moss st, ending with a RS row.
Row 10 (WS): Moss st to last 7 sts, M1 and turn, leaving last 7 sts on a holder for buttonhole band. 41 (43: 46: 48: 51) sts.
Change to 4mm (US 6) needles.
Next row (RS): P7 (8: 9: 10: 11), K2, P1, moss st 7, P1, K2, P21 (22: 24: 25: 27).
Next row: K21 (22: 24: 25: 27), P2, K1, moss st 7, K1, P2, K7 (8: 9: 10: 11).
These 2 rows set the sts.
Complete to match left front, reversing shapings.

LEFT SLEEVE

Sleeve front

Cast on 38 (38: 39: 40: 40) sts using 4mm (US 6) needles.

Row 1 (RS): (K1, P1) twice, K to end.

Row 2: P to last 5 sts, K1, (P1, K1) twice.

Rep last 2 rows 9 times more, inc 1 st at end of 9th (**11th**) of these rows.

39 (39: 40: 41: 41) sts.

Break yarn and leave sts on a holder.

Sleeve back

Cast on 14 (14: 15: 16: 16) sts using 4mm (US 6) needles.

Row 1 (RS): K to last 4 sts, (P1, K1) twice.

Row 2: K1, (P1, K1) twice, P to end.

Rep last 2 rows 9 times more, inc 1 st at beg of 9th (**11th**) of these rows. 15 (15: 16: 17: 17) sts.

Join sections

Handknit DK Cotton version

Next row (RS): Inc in first st of sleeve back, K to last 5 sts of this section then, with WS of sleeve front against RS of sleeve back, K tog first st of sleeve front with next st of sleeve back, K tog next 4 sts of sleeve front with rem 4 sts of sleeve back, K to last st of sleeve front, inc in last st.

51 (51: 53: 55: 55) sts.

Denim version

Next row (RS): K to last 5 sts of sleeve back then, with WS of sleeve front against RS of sleeve back, K tog first st of sleeve front with next st of sleeve back, K tog next 4 sts of sleeve front with rem 4 sts of sleeve back, K to end of sleeve front.

49 (49: 51: 53: 53) sts.

Both versions

Beg with a P row, cont in st st, inc 1 st at each end of every foll 10th (**12th**) row from previous inc until there are 55 (67: 67: 69: 65) sts for Handknit DK Cotton, **or 53 (67: 67: 69: 63) sts for Denim**, then on every foll 12th (-: 12th: 12th: 8th) row for Handknit DK Cotton, **or 14th (-: 14th: 14th: 10th) row for Denim**, until there are 65 (-: 69: 71: 73) sts.

Cont straight until sleeve measures 40 (40: 41: 41: 41) cm for Handknit DK Cotton, **or 46.5 (46.5: 48: 48: 48) cm for Denim**, ending with a WS row.

Shape top

Cast off 4 sts at beg of next 2 rows.

57 (59: 61: 63: 65) sts.

Dec 1 st at each end of next 5 rows, then on foll 3 alt rows.

Work 3 rows.

Dec 1 st at each end of next and every foll 4th row until 33 (37: 39: 43: 45) sts rem for Handknit DK Cotton, **or 29 (31: 33: 35: 37) sts rem for Denim**.

Work 1 row.

Dec 1 st at each end of next and foll alt row until 27 sts rem.

Dec 1 st at each end of next 3 rows, ending with a WS row. 21 sts.

Cast off 4 sts at beg of next 2 rows.

Cast off rem 13 sts.

RIGHT SLEEVE

Sleeve back

Cast on 14 (14: 15: 16: 16) sts using 4mm (US 6) needles.

Row 1 (RS): (K1, P1) twice, K to end.

Row 2: P to last 5 sts, K1, (P1, K1) twice.

Rep last 2 rows 9 times more, inc 1 st at end of 9th (**11th**) of these rows. 39 (39: 40: 41: 41) sts.

Break yarn and leave sts on a holder.

Sleeve front

Cast on 38 (38: 39: 40: 40) sts using 4mm (US 6) needles.

Row 1 (RS): K to last 4 sts, (P1, K1) twice.

Row 2: K1, (P1, K1) twice, P to end.

Rep last 2 rows 9 times more, inc 1 st at beg of 9th (**11th**) of these rows. 15 (15: 16: 17: 17) sts.

Join sections

Handknit DK Cotton version

Next row (RS): Inc in first st of sleeve front, K to last 5 sts of this section then, with WS of sleeve front against RS of sleeve back, K tog next st of sleeve front with first st of sleeve back, K tog rem 4 sts of sleeve front with next 4 sts of sleeve back, K to last st of sleeve back, inc in last st.

51 (51: 53: 55: 55) sts.

Denim version

Next row (RS): K to last 5 sts of sleeve front then, with RS of sleeve back against WS of sleeve front, K tog next st of sleeve front with first st of sleeve back, K tog rem 4 sts of sleeve front with next 4 sts of sleeve back, K to end of sleeve back.

49 (49: 51: 53: 53) sts.

Both versions

Complete as given for left sleeve.

MAKING UP

Handknit DK Cotton version

PRESS all pieces as described on the information page.

Denim version

Do not press.

Both versions

Join both shoulder seams using back stitch, or mattress stitch if preferred.

Button band

Slip 7 sts left on holder for button band onto 3¼mm (US 3) needles and rejoin yarn with RS facing.

Cont in moss st as set until band, when slightly stretched, fits up left front to neck shaping, ending with a WS row.

Cast off.

Slip stitch band in place.

Mark positions for 5 buttons on this band – lowest button to come in 3rd row of band, top button 1.5 cm below neck shaping and rem 3 buttons evenly spaced between.

Buttonhole band

Work as given for button band, rejoining yarn with WS facing and with the addition of 5 buttonholes to correspond with positions marked for buttons worked as folls:

Buttonhole row (RS): Moss st 2, cast off 2 sts, moss st to end and back, casting on 2 sts over those cast off on previous row.

Slip stitch band in place.

Collar

Cast on 83 (87: 87: 95: 95) sts using 3¼mm (US 3) needles.

Row 1 (RS): K3, (P1, K1) to last 4 sts, P1, K3.

Row 2: K1, P2, K2, (P1, K1) to last 4 sts, K1, P2, K1.

These 2 rows set the sts.

Keeping sts correct as set, cont as folls:

Row 3 (RS): K3, P1, M1, moss st to last 4 sts, M1, P1, K3.

85 (89: 89: 97: 97) sts.

Row 4: K1, P2, K1, moss st to last 4 sts, K1, P2, K1.

Row 5: K3, P1, moss st to last 4 sts, P1, K3.

Row 6: K1, P2, K1, M1, moss st to last 4 sts, M1, K1, P2, K1.

87 (91: 91: 99: 99) sts.

Row 7: As row 5.

Row 8: As row 4.

Rep rows 3 to 8, 2 (**3**) times more, and then rows 3 to 6 (**4**) again. 99 (103: 103: 111: 111) sts for Handknit DK Cotton, **or 101 (105: 105: 113: 113) sts for Denim**.

Cast off in patt.

Left cuff

Cast on 47 (47: 49: 51: 51) sts using 3¼mm (US 3) needles.

Work in moss st as given for back for 6 rows.

Row 7 (buttonhole row) (RS): Moss st 2, cast off 2 sts, moss st to end.

Row 8: Moss st to end, casting on 2 sts over those cast off on previous row.

Work a further 8 rows in moss st.

Cast off in moss st.

Right cuff

Work as given for left cuff, reversing position of buttonhole as folls:

Row 7 (buttonhole row) (RS): Moss st to last 4 sts, cast off 2 sts, moss st to end.

Pocket flaps (make 2)

Cast on 25 sts using 3¼mm (US 3) needles.

Row 1 (RS): K3, P1, moss st to last 4 sts, P1, K3.

Row 2: K1, P2, K1, moss st to last 4 sts, K1, P2, K1.

These 2 rows set the sts.

Keeping sts correct as set, cont as folls:

Rep last 2 rows 5 (**6**) times more.

Next row (RS): K3, P1, P2tog, moss st to last 6 sts, P2tog, P1, K3.

Next row: K1, P2, K1, K2tog, moss st to last 6 sts, K2tog, K1, P2, K1. 21 sts.

Rep last 2 rows twice more and then first of these 2 rows again. 11 sts.

Next row (WS): K1, P2, K1, sl 1, K2tog, psso, K1, P2, K1.

Next row: K3, sl 1, P2tog, psso, K3.

Next row: K1, P1, sl 1, P2tog, psso, P1, K1.

Next row: K1, sl 1, K2tog, psso, K1.

Next row: Sl 1, K2tog, psso.

Fasten off.

After all knitting is complete, machine wash all Denim pieces as described on ball band before sewing together.

Sew cast-on edge of collar to neck edge, positioning ends of collar halfway across top of front bands. Join sleeve seams then, with RS facing, sew cast edge of cuff to lower edge of sleeve using back stitch. Fold cuff down. Sew pocket flaps in place at top of front moss st panels as in photograph.

See information page for finishing instructions, setting in sleeves using the set-in method. Sew buttons to front bands and cuffs to correspond with buttonholes, and through all layers to secure pocket flaps in place.

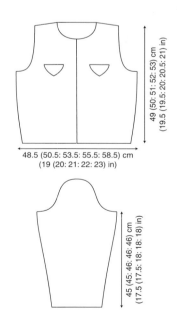

49 (50: 51: 52: 53) cm
(19.5 (19.5: 20: 20.5: 21) in)

48.5 (50.5: 53.5: 55.5: 58.5) cm
(19 (20: 21: 22: 23) in)

45 (45: 46: 46: 46) cm
(17.5 (17.5: 18: 18: 18) in)

As this design from Rowan Magazine Number 21 has been so popular and because it is still a fashionable shape, we have decided to up-date the pattern to include a Handknit D.K. Cotton option.

Design number 19

Raewyn

DEBBIE BLISS

YARN
Rowan Handknit DK Cotton

			Children's
4-6	6-8	8-10	years

To fit chest

64	69	76	cm
25	27	30	in

Handknit DK Cotton

10	12	15	x	50gm

Denim

12	14	17	x	50gm

(photographed in Handknit DK in Chime 204)

	Ladies			Mens	
S	M	L	S	M	L

To fit chest/bust

84	91	99	99	107	114cm
33	36	39	39	42	45in

Handknit DK Cotton

20	21	22	22	23	24 x 50gm

Denim

22	24	25	24	25	27 x 50gm

(ladies photographed in Denim in Memphis 229, mans in Handknit DK in Zing 300)

NEEDLES
1 pair 3¼mm (no 10) (US 3) needles
1 pair 4mm (no 8) (US 6) needles
Cable needle

TENSION
Handknit DK Cotton: 20 sts and 28 rows to 10 cm measured over stocking stitch using 4mm (US 6) needles.
Denim: Before washing 20 sts and 28 rows to 10 cm measured over stocking stitch using 4mm (US 6) needles.
Tension note: Denim will shrink in length when washed for the first time. Allowances have been made in this pattern for shrinkage (see size diagram for after washing measurements).

Pattern note: The pattern is written for the 3 childrens sizes, followed by the 3 ladies sizes in **bold**, followed by the 3 mens sizes.

Shaping note: To keep cast-off edges neat and to avoid them stretching too much, it is advisable to work 2 sts tog over tops of cables when casting off. Stitch counts given do NOT take into account these decreases.

SPECIAL ABBREVIATIONS
Tw3R = Slip next st onto cn and leave at back of work, K2, then P1 from cn
Tw3L = Slip next 2 sts onto cn and leave at front of work, P1, then K2 from cn
Tw3RB = Slip next st onto cn and leave at back of work, (K1 tbl) twice, then P1 from cn
Tw3LB = Slip next 2 sts onto cn and leave at front of work, P1, then (K1 tbl) twice from cn
C4F = Slip next 2 sts onto cn and leave at front of work, K2, then K2 from cn
C4B = Slip next 2 sts onto cn and leave at back of work, K2, then K2 from cn
C4FB = Slip next 2 sts onto cn and leave at front of work, (K1 tbl) twice, then (K1 tbl) twice from cn
Tw5R = Slip next 2 sts onto cn and leave at front of work, K2, P1, then K2 from cn
MB = Make bobble as folls: P1, pick up loop lying between needles and (K1, P1) twice into this loop, turn and P4, turn and K4tog, P1, then pass bobble st over this P st

BACK
Childrens and mens sizes only
Cast on 92 (100: 108: –: 132: 140: 148) sts using 3¼mm (US 3) needles.
Row 1 (RS): *K1, P1, rep from * to end.
Row 2: *P1, K1, rep from * to end.
Rep last 2 rows 2 (–: 3) times more.
Change to 4mm (US 6) needles.
Ladies sizes only
Cast on – (**118: 124: 132:** –) sts using 4mm (US 6) needles.
All sizes
Handknit DK Cotton version
Beg with a K row, cont in st st until back measures 21 (24: 27: **35: 36: 37:** 31: 32: 33) cm from cast-on edge, ending with a WS row.
Denim version
Beg with a K row, cont in st st until back measures 24.5 (28: 31.5: **41: 42: 43:** 36: 37.5: 38.5) cm from cast-on edge, ending with a WS row.
Both versions
Next row (RS): *K1, P1, rep from * to end.
Next row: *P1, K1, rep from * to end.
These 2 rows form moss st.
Work a further 1 row in moss st.

Childrens sizes only
Next row (WS): Moss st 8 (12: 16), inc once in each of next 2 sts, moss st 9, inc in next st, moss st 4, inc once in each of next 2 sts, moss st 7, inc once in each of next 2 sts, (moss st 10, inc once in each of next 2 sts) twice, moss st 7, inc once in each of next 2 sts, moss st 4, inc in next st, moss st 9, inc once in each of next 2 sts, moss st 8 (12: 16). 108 (116: 124) sts.
Ladies and mens sizes only
Next row (WS): Moss st – (**2: 5: 9:** 9: 13: 17), inc once in each of next 2 sts, moss st 7, inc in next st, moss st 1, inc in next st, moss st 7, inc once in each of next 2 sts, moss st 9, inc in next st, moss st 4, inc once in each of next 2 sts, moss st 7, (inc once in each of next 2 sts, moss st 10) twice, inc once in each of next 2 sts, moss st 7, inc once in each of next 2 sts, moss st 4, inc in next st, moss st 9, inc once in each of next 2 sts, moss st 7, inc in next st, moss st 1, inc in next st, moss st 7, inc once in each of next 2 sts, moss st – (**2: 5: 9:** 9: 13: 17).
(**142: 148: 156:** 156: 164: 172) sts.
All sizes
Starting and ending rows as indicated and repeating the patt rows throughout, cont in patt from chart as folls:
Next row (RS): Moss st 6 (10: 14: **0: 3: 7:** 7: 11: 15), work next 96 (**142: 142**) sts as row 1 of chart, moss st 6 (10: 14: **0: 3: 7:** 7: 11: 15).
This row sets position of chart with edge sts worked in moss st.
Handknit DK Cotton version
Cont straight until back measures 45 (51: 57: **70: 71: 72:** 66: 67: 68) cm from cast-on edge, ending with a WS row.
Denim version
Cont straight until back measures 52.5 (59.5: 66.5: **81.5: 83: 84:** 77: 78: 79.5) cm from cast-on edge, ending with a WS row.
Both versions
Shape shoulders and back neck
Keeping chart correct, cast off 13 (14: 15: **16: 17: 18:** 18: 20: 21) sts at beg of next 2 rows.
82 (88: 94: **110: 114: 120:** 120: 124: 130) sts.
Next row (RS): Cast off 13 (14: 15: **16: 17: 18:** 18: 20: 21) sts, patt until there are 16 (17: 18: **20: 21: 23:** 23: 23: 25) sts on right needle and turn, leaving rem sts on a holder.
Work each side of neck separately.
Cast off 4 sts at beg of next row.
Cast off rem 12 (13: 14: **16: 17: 19:** 19: 19: 21) sts.
With RS facing, rejoin yarn to rem sts, cast off centre 24 (26: 28: **38:** 38) sts, patt to end.
Work to match first side, reversing shapings.

FRONT

Handknit DK Cotton version

Work as given for back until 14 (**16**: 18) rows less have been worked than on back to start of shoulder shaping, ending with a WS row.

Denim version

Work as given for back until 16 (**20**: 22) rows less have been worked than on back to start of shoulder shaping, ending with a WS row.

Both versions
Shape neck

Next row (RS): Patt 46 (49: 52: **61: 64: 68**: 68: 72: 76) sts and turn, leaving rem sts on a holder.
Work each side of neck separately.

Ladies and mens sizes only

Cast off – (**4**: 4) sts at beg of next row.
– (**57: 60: 64**: 64: 68: 72) sts.

All sizes

Dec 1 st at neck edge of next 5 (**7**: 7) rows, then on foll 3 (**2**: 2) alt rows.
38 (41: 44: **48: 51: 55**: 55: 59: 63) sts.
Cont straight until front matches back to start of shoulder shaping, ending at side edge.

Shape shoulder

Keeping chart correct, cast off 13 (14: 15: **16: 17: 18**: 18: 20: 21) sts at beg of next and foll alt row.
Work 1 row.
Cast off rem 12 (13: 14: **16: 17: 19**: 19: 19: 21) sts.
With RS facing, rejoin yarn to rem sts, cast off centre 16 (18: 20: **20: 20**) sts, patt to end.
Work to match first side, reversing shapings.

SLEEVES (both alike)

Cast on 42 (44: 46: **50**: 54) sts using 3¼mm (US 3) needles.
Work in moss st as given for back for 8 (**2**: 8) rows, ending with a WS row.

Ladies sizes only

Row 3 (RS): Moss st 4, ★MB, moss st 8, rep from ★ to last 6 sts, MB, moss st 4.
Work a further 3 rows in moss st, end with a WS row.

All sizes

Change to 4mm (US 6) needles.
Beg with a K row, cont in st st as folls:

Handknit DK Cotton version

Inc 1 st at each end of 5th (**next:** 7th) and every foll 4th (**6th:** 6th) row until there are 64 (72: 78: **76**: 82) sts.
Work 1 (**5**: 3) rows, ending with a WS row.
Work in moss st for 3 rows, inc 1 st at each end of 3rd (**1st:** 3rd) of these rows. 66 (74: 80: **78**: 84) sts.
Next row (WS): Moss st 0 (0: 2: **1**: 4), (inc once in each of next 2 sts) 0 (0: 1: **1**: 1) times, moss st 6 (10: 9: **9**: 9), inc in next st, moss st 4, inc once in each of next 2 sts, moss st 7, (inc once in each of next 2 sts, moss st 10) twice, inc once in each of next 2 sts, moss st 7, inc once in each of next 2 sts, moss st 4, inc in next st, moss st 6 (10: 9: **9**: 9), (inc once in each of next 2 sts) 0 (0: 1: **1**: 1) times, moss st 0 (0: 2: **1**: 4). 78 (86: 96: **94**: 100) sts.
Starting and ending rows as indicated and repeating the patt rows throughout, cont in patt foll chart for sleeve as folls:
Inc 1 st at each end of 3rd (**3rd:** 5th) and every foll

6th (**4th:** 4th) row until there are 88 (96: 108: **114**: 118) sts, taking inc sts into patt.
Cont straight until sleeve measures 33 (38: 43: **49**: 55) cm, ending with a WS row.

Denim version

Inc 1 st at each end of 5th (**next:** 7th) and every foll 6th (**6th:** 6th) row until there are 60 (66: 72: **80**: 86) sts.
Work 5 (3: 1: **5**: 5) rows, ending with a WS row.
Work in moss st for 3 rows, inc 1 st at each end of 1st (3rd: 3rd: **1st:** 1st) of these rows.
62 (68: 74: **82**: 88) sts.

45 (51: 57: **73: 74: 75**: 66: 67: 68) cm
(17.5 (20: 22.5: **28.5: 29: 29.5**: 26: 26.5: 27) in

46 (50: 54: **58: 62: 66**: 66: 70: 74) cm
(18 (19.5: 21.5: **23: 24.5: 26**: 26: 27.5: 29) in

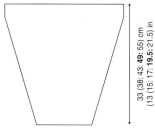

33 (38: 43: **49**: 55) cm
(13 (15: 17: **19.5**: 21.5) in

Yoke chart

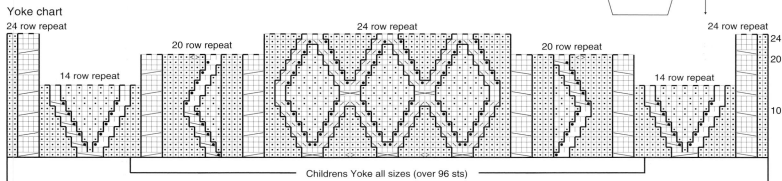

24 row repeat
20 row repeat
14 row repeat
24 row repeat
20 row repeat
14 row repeat
24 row repeat

24
20
10

Childrens Yoke all sizes (over 96 sts)
Adults Yoke all sizes (over 142 sts)

Key

□	K on RS, P on WS
⊡	P on RS, K on WS
	Tw3R
	Tw3L
	Tw3RB
	Tw3LB
	C4F
	C4B
	C4FB
	Tw5
	MB

Sleeve chart

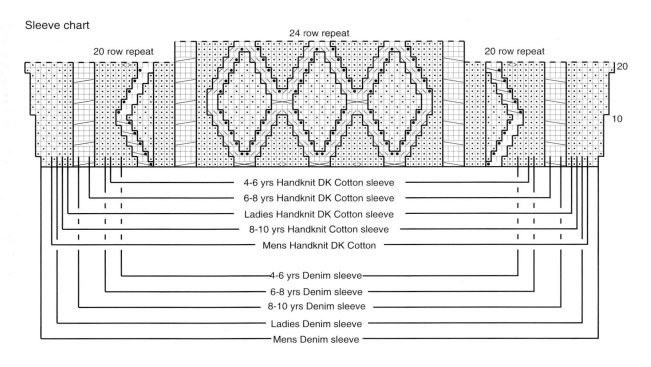

20 row repeat
24 row repeat
20 row repeat

20
10

4-6 yrs Handknit DK Cotton sleeve
6-8 yrs Handknit DK Cotton sleeve
Ladies Handknit DK Cotton sleeve
8-10 yrs Handknit Cotton sleeve
Mens Handknit DK Cotton
4-6 yrs Denim sleeve
6-8 yrs Denim sleeve
8-10 yrs Denim sleeve
Ladies Denim sleeve
Mens Denim sleeve

Next row (WS): Moss st 0 (**3**: 6), (inc once in each of next 2 sts) 0 (0: 1: **1**: 1) times, moss st 4 (7: 8: **9**: 9), inc in next st, moss st 4, inc once in each of next 2 sts, moss st 7, (inc once in each of next 2 sts, moss st 10) twice, inc once in each of next 2 sts, moss st 7, inc once in each of next 2 sts, moss st 4, inc in next st, moss st 4 (7: 8: **9**: 9), (inc once in each of next 2 sts) 0 (0: 1: **1**: 1) times, moss st 0 (**3**: 6). 74 (80: 90: **98**: 104) sts.
Starting and ending rows as indicated and repeating the patt rows throughout, cont in patt foll chart for sleeve as folls:
Inc 1 st at each end of 3rd and every foll 4th (**6th**: 8th) row until there are 88 (96: 108: **114**: 118) sts, taking inc sts into patt.
Cont straight until sleeve measures 38.5 (44.5: 50: **57**: 64) cm, ending with a WS row.
Both versions
Cast off in patt.

MAKING UP
Handknit DK Cotton version
PRESS all pieces as described on the info page.
Denim version
Do not press.
Both versions
Join right shoulder seam using back stitch, or mattress stitch if preferred.
Neckband
With RS facing and using 3¼mm (US 3) needles, pick up and knit 17 (**24**: 24) sts down left side of neck, 16 (18: 20: **20**: 20) sts from front, 17 (**24**: 24) sts up right side of neck, and 32 (34: 36: **46**: 46) sts from back. 82 (86: 90: **114**: 114) sts.
Childrens and mens sizes only
Row 1 (WS): P2, ★K2, P2, rep from ★ to end.
Row 2: K2, ★P2, K2, rep from ★ to end.
These 2 rows form rib.
Work in rib for a further 3 (-: 5) rows, ending with a WS row.
Beg with a K row, work in st st for 6 rows.
Ladies sizes only
Work in moss st as given for back for 1 row.
Row 2 (RS): Moss st 6, ★MB, moss st 8, rep from ★ to last 8 sts, MB, moss st 6.
Work a further 3 rows in moss st.
All sizes
Cast off.
Ladies sizes only
Hem edging
With RS facing and using 3¼mm (US 3) needles, pick up and knit - (**121**: 121: 132: -) sts across cast-on edge of back.
Row 1 (WS): K1, ★P1, K1, rep from ★ to end.
This row sets position of moss st.
Work a further 2 rows in moss st, end with a WS row.
★★Keeping moss st correct, cont as folls:
Next row (RS): Moss st 11 and turn.
Work on this set of 11 sts only for first point.
Work 5 rows, dec 1 st at each end of 2nd and foll alt row. 7 sts.
Next row: Work 2 tog, moss st 1, (K1, P1) twice into next st, turn and P4, turn and K4, turn and (P2tog) twice, turn and K2tog, moss st 1, work 2 tog. 5 sts.
Work 3 rows, dec 1 st at each end of 2nd of these rows. 3 sts.
Next row: Sl 1, work 2 tog, psso.
Fasten off.
Return to rem sts and rejoin yarn with RS facing.
★★★
Rep from ★★ to ★★★ until all sts have been worked.
Work edging across cast-on edge of front in same way.
All sizes
After all knitting is complete, machine wash all Denim pieces as described on ball band before sewing together.
See information page for finishing instructions, setting in sleeves using the straight cast-off method.

Design number 20

Charm

KIM HARGREAVES

YARN
Rowan 4 ply Cotton

	XS	S	M	L	XL	
To fit bust	81	86	91	97	102	cm
	32	34	36	38	40	in
Cardigan (photographed in Ripple 121)	7	7	7	8	8	x 50gm
Sweater (photographed in Opaque 112)	7	7	7	8	8	x 50gm

NEEDLES
1 pair 2¾mm (no 12) (US 2/3) needles
1 pair 3mm (no 11) (US 2/3) needles

FASTENERS – 2 hook & eye fasteners

BEADS - (optional)
approx 8,000 (8,500: 9,000: 9,000: 9,500) small glass beads

TENSION
28 sts and 38 rows to 10 cm measured over pattern using 3mm (US 2/3) needles.

Beading note: When working with beads, thread approx 500 beads onto yarn before beginning. Work until all of these beads have been used then break yarn and thread on another 500 beads.

Pattern note: This lace pattern is pretty enough to be effective when knitted without beads.

Cardigan
BACK
Using 2¾mm (US 2/3) needles and thumb method, work beaded cast on as folls: cast on 1 st leaving beads at ball side of this st, ★bring a bead up to within 1.5 cm of needle and cast on another st making sure that the bead is on top of the st and needle, then slip bead round to back of st so that it will sit on the RS of the work, rep from ★ until 121 (127: 133: 139: 145) sts are on right needle, cast on 1 st without a bead. 122 (128: 134: 140: 146) sts.
Knit 1 row, ensuring all beads are sitting at front (RS) of work.
Knit a further 3 rows.
Change to 3mm (US 2/3) needles and lace patt as folls:
Row 1 (RS): K1, ★bring bead up to needle, yfwd, K2, K2tog, K2, rep from ★ to last st, K1.
Row 2: P1, ★P5, slide bead along to sit next to st just worked and then purl the yfwd of the previous row, rep from ★ to last st, P1.
Row 3: K1, ★K2, K2tog, K2, bring bead up to needle, yfwd, rep from ★ to last st, K1.
Row 4: P1, ★move bead away from last st and purl the yfwd of previous row (bead sits between this P st and next st), P5, rep from ★ to last st, P1.
These 4 rows form patt.
Cont in patt, inc 1 st at each end of 5th and every foll 12th row until there are 134 (140: 146: 152: 158) sts, taking inc sts into patt.
Cont straight until back measures 27 (28: 28: 29: 29) cm, ending with a WS row.
Shape armholes
Keeping patt correct, cast off 5 (6: 6: 7: 7) sts at beg of next 2 rows. 124 (128: 134: 138: 144) sts.
Dec 1 st at each end of next 9 (9: 11: 11: 13) rows, then on foll 2 (3: 3: 4: 4) alt rows.
102 (104: 106: 108: 110) sts.
Cont straight until armhole measures 20 (20: 21: 21: 22) cm, ending with a WS row.
Shape shoulders and back neck
Keeping patt correct, cast off 11 sts at beg of next 2 rows. 80 (82: 84: 86: 88) sts.
Next row (RS): Cast off 11 sts, patt until there are 14 (14: 15: 15: 16) sts on right needle and turn, leaving rem sts on a holder.
Work each side of neck separately.
Cast off 4 sts at beg of next row.
Cast off rem 10 (10: 11: 11: 12) sts.
With RS facing, rejoin yarn to rem sts, cast off centre 30 (32: 32: 34: 34) sts, patt to end.
Work to match first side, reversing shapings.

LEFT FRONT
Using 2¾mm (US 2/3) needles, work beaded cast on as given for back, casting on 59 (62: 65: 68: 71) sts (omitting beads from first and last cast on sts).
Knit 1 row, ensuring all beads are sitting at front (RS) of work.
Knit a further 3 rows.
Change to 3mm (US 2/3) needles and work in lace patt as folls:
Row 1 (RS): K1, ★bring bead up to needle, yfwd, K2, K2tog, K2, rep from ★ to last 4 (1: 4: 1: 4) sts, (bring bead up to needle, yfwd, K2, K2tog) 1 (0: 1: 0: 1) times, K0 (1: 0: 1: 0).

Row 2: P3 (1: 3: 1: 3), (slide bead along to sit next to st just worked and then purl the yfwd of the previous row) 1 (0: 1: 0: 1) times, ★P5, slide bead along to sit next to st just worked and then purl the yfwd of the previous row, rep from ★ to last st, K1.
Row 3: K1, ★K2, K2tog, K2, bring bead up to needle, yfwd, rep from ★ to last 4 (1: 4: 1: 4) sts, K4 (1: 4: 1: 4).
Row 4: P4 (1: 4: 1: 4), ★move bead away from last st and purl the yfwd of previous row (bead sits between this P st and next st), P5, rep from ★ to last st, K1.
These 4 rows form patt.
Cont in patt, inc 1 st at beg of 5th and every foll 12th row until there are 65 (68: 71: 74: 77) sts, taking inc sts into patt.
Cont straight until left front matches back to beg of armhole shaping, ending with a WS row.
Shape armhole
Keeping patt correct, cast off 5 (6: 6: 7: 7) sts at beg of next row. 60 (62: 65: 67: 70) sts.
Work 1 row.
Dec 1 st at armhole edge of next 9 (9: 11: 11: 13) rows, then on foll 2 (3: 3: 4: 4) alt rows.
49 (50: 51: 52: 53) sts.
Cont straight until 27 (27: 27: 29: 29) rows less have been worked than on back to start of shoulder shaping, ending with a RS row.
Shape neck
Keeping patt correct, cast off 7 (8: 8: 8: 8) sts at beg of next row. 42 (42: 43: 44: 45) sts.
Dec 1 st at neck edge of next 5 rows, then on foll 3 (3: 3: 4: 4) alt rows, then on every foll 4th row until 32 (32: 33: 33: 34) sts rem.
Work 7 rows, ending with a WS row.
Shape shoulder
Keeping patt correct, cast off 11 sts at beg of next and foll alt row.
Work 1 row.
Cast off rem 10 (10: 11: 11: 12) sts.

RIGHT FRONT
Using 2¾mm (US 2/3) needles, work beaded cast on as given for back, casting on 59 (62: 65: 68: 71) sts (omitting beads from first and last cast on sts).
Knit 1 row, ensuring all beads are sitting at front (RS) of work.
Knit a further 3 rows.
Change to 3mm (US 2/3) needles and work in lace patt as folls:
Row 1 (RS): K4 (1: 4: 1: 4), ★bring bead up to needle, yfwd, K2, K2tog, K2, rep from ★ to last st, K1.
Row 2: P1, ★P5, slide bead along to sit next to st just worked and then purl the yfwd of the previous row, rep from ★ to last 4 (1: 4: 1: 4) sts, P4 (1: 4: 1: 4).
Row 3: (K2tog, K2, bring bead up to needle, yfwd) 1 (0: 1: 0: 1) times, K0 (1: 0: 1: 0), ★K2, K2tog, K2, bring bead up to needle, yfwd, rep from ★ to last st, K1.
Row 4: P1, ★move bead away from last st and purl the yfwd of previous row (bead sits between this P st and next st), P5, rep from ★ to last 4 (1: 4: 1: 4) sts, (move bead away from last st and purl the yfwd of previous row) 1 (0: 1: 0: 1) times, P3 (1: 3: 1: 3).
These 4 rows form patt.
Cont in patt, inc 1 st at end of 5th and every foll 12th row until there are 65 (68: 71: 74: 77) sts, taking inc sts into patt.
Complete to match left front, reversing shapings.

SLEEVES (both alike)
Using 2¾mm (US 2/3) needles, work beaded cast on as given for back, casting on 62 (62: 62: 68: 68) sts (omitting beads from first and last cast on sts).
Knit 1 row, ensuring all beads are sitting at front (RS) of work.
Knit a further 3 rows.

Change to 3mm (US 2/3) needles and work in lace patt as given for back, inc 1 st at each end of 5th and every foll 8th (8th: 8th: 10th: 8th) row until there are 96 (90: 88: 72: 100) sts, taking inc sts into patt.
Small, medium, large and extra large sizes only
Inc 1 st at each end of every foll − (6th: 6th: 8th: 6th) row until there are − (98: 100: 102: 104) sts.
All sizes
Cont straight until sleeve measures 41 (41: 42: 42: 42) cm, ending with a WS row.
Shape top
Keeping patt correct, cast off 5 (6: 6: 7: 7) sts at beg of next 2 rows.
86 (86: 88: 88: 90) sts.
Dec 1 st at each end of next 5 rows, then on foll 5 alt rows, then on every foll 4th row until 56 (56: 58: 58: 60) sts rem.
Work 1 row.
Dec 1 st at each end of next and foll 4 (4: 5: 5: 6) alt rows, then on foll 3 rows. 40 sts.
Cast off 4 sts at beg of next 4 rows.
Cast off rem 24 sts.

Sweater
BACK and FRONT (both alike)
Using 2¾mm (US 2/3) needles and thumb method, work beaded cast on as folls: cast on 1 st leaving beads at ball side of this st, ★bring a bead up to within 1.5 cm of needle and cast on another st making sure that the bead is on top of the st and needle, then slip bead round to back of st so that it will sit on the RS of the work, rep from ★ until 133 (139: 145: 151: 157) sts are on right needle, cast on 1 st without a bead.
134 (140: 146: 152: 158) sts.
Knit 1 row, ensuring all beads are sitting at front (RS) of work.
Knit a further 3 rows.
Change to 3mm (US 2/3) needles and lace patt as folls:
Row 1 (RS): K1, ★bring bead up to needle, yfwd, K2, K2tog, K2, rep from ★ to last st, K1.
Row 2: P1, ★P5, slide bead along to sit next to st just worked and then purl the yfwd of the previous row, rep from ★ to last st, P1.
Row 3: K1, ★K2, K2tog, K2, bring bead up to needle, yfwd, rep from ★ to last st, K1.
Row 4: P1, ★move bead away from last st and purl the yfwd of previous row (bead sits between this P st and next st), P5, rep from ★ to last st, P1.
These 4 rows form patt.
Cont in patt until work measures 27 (28: 28: 29: 29) cm, ending with a WS row.
Shape armholes
Keeping patt correct, cast off 5 (6: 6: 7: 7) sts at beg of next 2 rows. 124 (128: 134: 138: 144) sts.
Dec 1 st at each end of next 9 (9: 11: 11: 13) rows, then on foll 2 (3: 3: 4: 4) alt rows.
102 (104: 106: 108: 110) sts.
Cont straight until armhole measures 19 (19: 20: 20: 21) cm, ending with a WS row.
Shape neck
Next row (RS): Patt 27 (27: 28: 28: 29) sts and turn, leaving rem sts on a holder.
Work each side of neck separately.
Cast off 6 sts at beg of next row. 21 (21: 22: 22: 23) sts.
Dec 1 st at neck edge of next 2 rows.
19 (19: 20: 20: 21) sts.
Shape shoulder
Cast off 6 sts at beg and dec 1 st at end of next row.
12 (12: 13: 13: 14) sts.
Work 1 row.
Rep last 2 rows once more.
Cast off rem 5 (5: 6: 6: 7) sts.
With RS facing, rejoin yarn to rem sts, cast off centre 48 (50: 50: 52: 52) sts, patt to end.
Work to match first side, reversing shapings.

SLEEVES (both alike)
Work as given for sleeves of cardigan.

MAKING UP
PRESS all pieces carefully using a warm iron over a damp cloth, taking care not to damage beads.

Cardigan
Join both shoulder seams using back stitch, or mattress stitch if preferred.
Bands (both alike)
With RS facing and using 2¾mm (US 2) needles, pick up and knit 120 (120: 120: 126: 126) sts along left front opening edge.
★★Knit 3 rows.
Row 4 (RS): K1, ★slide bead up to needle and K1 making sure bead is now on top of st just worked, rep from ★ to last st, K1.
Cast off knitwise, ensuring all beads are to RS of work.★★
Neckband
With RS facing and using 2¾mm (US 2) needles, pick up and knit 39 (40: 40: 43: 43) sts up right side of neck, 38 (40: 40: 42: 42) sts from back, then 39 (40: 40: 43: 43) sts down left side of neck.
116 (120: 120: 128: 128) sts.
Work as given for bands from ★★ to ★★.
See information page for finishing instructions, setting in sleeves using the set-in method.

Sweater
Join right shoulder seam using back stitch, or mattress stitch if preferred.
Neckband
With RS facing and using 2¾mm (US 2) needles, pick up and knit 12 sts down left side of front neck, 48 (50: 50: 52: 52) sts from front, 12 sts up right side of front neck, 12 sts down right side of back neck, 48 (50: 50: 52: 52) sts from back, then 12 sts up left side of back neck. 144 (148: 148: 152: 152) sts.
Work as given for bands of cardigan from ★★ to ★★.
See information page for finishing instructions, setting in sleeves using the set-in method.

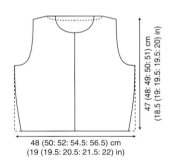

47 (48: 49: 50: 51) cm
(18.5 (19: 19.5: 19.5: 20) in)

48 (50: 52: 54.5: 56.5) cm
(19 (19.5: 20.5: 21.5: 22) in)

41 (41: 42: 42: 42) cm
(16 (16: 16.5: 16.5: 16.5) in)

Design number 21

Native

KIM HARGREAVES

YARN
Rowan Handknit DK Cotton
Childs sweater

To fit age		4-6	6-8	8-10	yrs	
A	Flame	254	2	2	2	x 50gm
B	Oasis	202	2	2	2	x 50gm
C	Raindrop	206	3	3	3	x 50gm
D	Linen	205	2	3	3	x 50gm
E	Artichoke	209	2	2	2	x 50gm
F	Tope	253	2	2	2	x 50gm
G	Popcorn	229	2	2	2	x 50gm

Ladies sweater

To fit bust		S	M	L		
		86	91	97	cm	
		34	36	38	in	
A	Gerba	223	3	3	3	x 50gm
B	Artichoke	209	3	3	3	x 50gm
C	Zing	300	4	4	4	x 50gm
D	Chime	204	4	4	4	x 50gm
E	Linen	205	3	4	4	x 50gm
F	Muddy	302	4	4	4	x 50gm
G	Carmen	201	3	3	3	x 50gm

Mens sweater

To fit chest		M	L	XL		
		102	107	112	cm	
		40	42	44	in	
A	Soft Green	228	3	3	3	x 50gm
B	Ice Water	239	3	3	3	x 50gm
C	Rainwater	206	4	4	5	x 50gm
D	Linen	205	4	4	4	x 50gm
E	Tope	253	3	4	4	x 50gm
F	Artichoke	209	4	4	4	x 50gm
G	Zing	300	3	3	3	x 50gm

NEEDLES
1 pair 3¼mm (no 10) (US 3) needles
1 pair 4mm (no 8) (US 6) needles

TENSION
20 sts and 28 rows to 10 cm measured over stocking stitch using 4mm (US 6) needles.

Pattern note: The pattern is written for the 3 childrens sizes, followed by the 3 ladies sizes in **bold**, followed by the mens sizes.

BACK
Using 3¼mm (US 3) needles, cast on as folls:
30 (33: 36: **39: 41: 43:** 45: 47: 49) sts using yarn D,
30 (33: 36: **39: 41: 43:** 45: 47: 49) sts using yarn C and 30 (33: 36: **39: 41: 43:** 45: 47: 49) sts using yarn F.
90 (99: 108: **117: 123: 129:** 135: 141: 147) sts.
Using the **intarsia** technique described on the info page, cont in striped st st from chart as folls:
Row 1 (RS): Work first 30 (33: 36: **39: 41: 43:** 45: 47: 49) sts using left panel colour, work next 30 (33: 36: **39: 41: 43:** 45: 47: 49) sts using centre panel colour, work last 30 (33: 36: **39: 41: 43:** 45: 47: 49) sts using right panel colour.
Row 2: Work first 30 (33: 36: **39: 41: 43:** 45: 47: 49) sts using right panel colour, work next 30 (33: 36: **39: 41: 43:** 45: 47: 49) sts using centre panel colour, work last 30 (33: 36: **39: 41: 43:** 45: 47: 49) sts using left panel colour.
These 2 rows set position of colours as on chart.
Keeping chart correct, cont as folls:
Work 8 rows.
Change to 4mm (US 6) needles.
Cont straight until back measures 25 (28: 31: **46: 47: 48:** 40: 41: 42) cm, ending with a WS row.
Shape armholes
Cast off 4 sts at beg of next 2 rows.
82 (91: 100: **109: 115: 121:** 127: 133: 139) sts.
Dec 1 st at each end of next 4 (**6:** 6) rows.
74 (83: 92: **97: 103: 109:** 115: 121: 127) sts.
Cont straight until armhole measures 20 (22: 23: **24: 25: 26:** 25: 26: 27) cm, ending with a WS row.
Shape shoulders and back neck
Cast off 7 (9: 10: **10: 10: 11:** 12: 12: 13) sts at beg of next 2 rows. 60 (65: 72: **77: 83: 87:** 91: 97: 101) sts.
Next row (RS): Cast off 7 (9: 10: **10: 10: 11:** 12: 12: 13) sts, K until there are 12 (12: 14: **13: 15: 15:** 15: 17: 18) sts on right needle and turn, leaving rem sts on a holder.
Work each side of neck separately.
Cast off 4 sts at beg of next row.
Cast off rem 8 (8: 10: **9: 11: 11:** 11: 13: 14) sts.
With RS facing, rejoin yarn to rem sts, cast off centre 22 (23: 24: **31: 33: 35:** 37: 39: 39) sts, K to end.
Work to match first side, reversing shapings.

FRONT
Work as given for back until 12 (**12:** 14) rows less have been worked than on back to start of shoulder shaping, ending with a WS row.
Shape neck
Next row (RS): K31 (35: 39: **38: 40: 42:** 45: 47: 50) and turn, leaving rem sts on a holder.
Work each side of neck separately.
Cast off 4 sts at beg of next row.
27 (31: 35: **34: 36: 38:** 41: 43: 46) sts.

Dec 1 st at neck edge of next 3 rows, then on foll 2 (**2:** 3) alt rows. 22 (26: 30: **29: 31: 33:** 35: 37: 40) sts.
Work 3 rows, ending with a WS row.
Shape shoulder
Cast off 7 (9: 10: **10: 10: 11:** 12: 12: 13) sts at beg of next and foll alt row.
Work 1 row.
Cast off rem 8 (8: 10: **9: 11: 11:** 11: 13: 14) sts.
With RS facing, rejoin yarn to rem sts, cast off centre 12 (13: 14: **21: 23: 25:** 25: 27: 27) sts, K to end.
Work to match first side, reversing shapings.

LEFT SLEEVE
Cast on 44 (46: 48: **56:** 62) sts using 3¼mm (US 3) needles and yarn G.
Cont in colour sequence from chart for left sleeve as folls:
Work 8 (**10:** 10) rows.
Change to 4mm (US 6) needles.
Inc 1 st at each end of next and every foll 6th row until there are 70 (64: 64: **76:** 98) sts, then on every foll 4th row until there are 80 (88: 94: **96: 100: 104:** 100: 104: 108) sts.
Cont straight until sleeve measures 39 (41: 43: **45:** 49) cm, ending with a WS row.
Shape top
Cast off 4 sts at beg of next 2 rows.
72 (80: 86: **88: 92: 96:** 92: 96: 100) sts.
Dec 1 st at each end of next and foll 4 (**4:** 5) alt rows.
Work 1 row, ending with a WS row.
Cast off rem 62 (70: 76: **78: 82: 86:** 80: 84: 88) sts.

RIGHT SLEEVE
Work as given for left sleeve, casting on with yarn E and following chart for right sleeve.

MAKING UP
PRESS all pieces as described on the information page.
Join right shoulder seam using back stitch, or mattress stitch if preferred.
Neckband
With RS facing, using 3¼mm (US 3) needles and yarn C (**F:** E), pick up and knit 19 (**19:** 21) sts down left side of neck, 12 (13: 14: **21: 23: 25:** 25: 27: 27) sts from front, 19 (**19:** 21) sts up right side of neck, and 30 (31: 32: **39: 41: 43:** 45: 47: 47) sts from back.
80 (82: 84: **98: 102: 106:** 112: 116: 116) sts.
Beg with a P row, work in st st for 6 (**8:** 8) rows.
Cast off.
See information page for finishing instructions, setting in sleeves using the shallow set-in method.

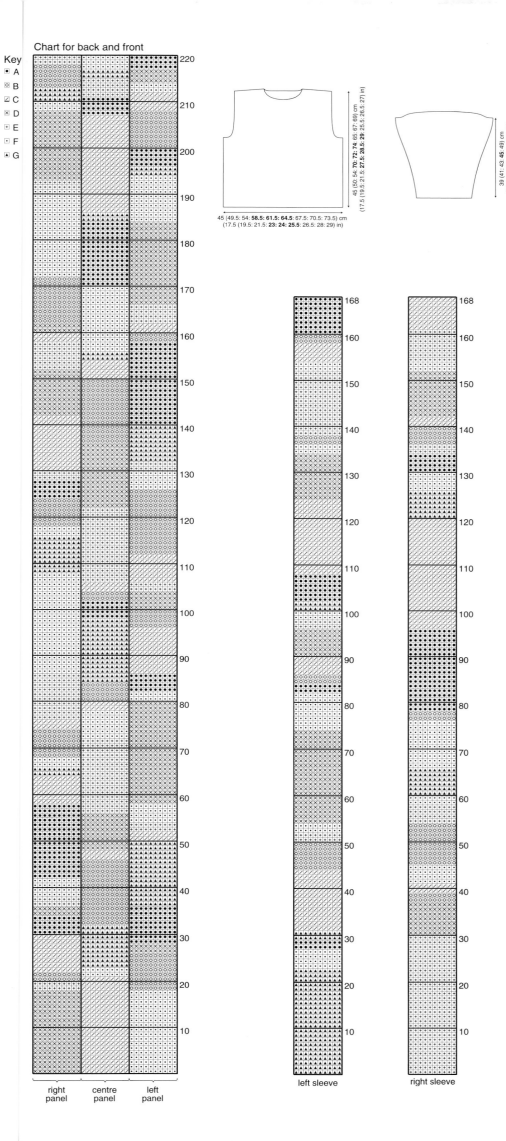

Chart for back and front

Key
• A
⊠ B
▨ C
✕ D
⊡ E
⊡ F
▲ G

right panel   centre panel   left panel

left sleeve

right sleeve

45 (50: 54: **70: 72: 74**: 65: 67: 69) cm
(17.5 (19.5: 21.5: **27.5: 28.5: 29**: 25.5: 26.5: 27) in)

45 (49.5: 54: **58.5: 61.5: 64.5**: 67.5: 70.5: 73.5) cm
(17.5 (19.5: 21.5: **23: 24: 25.5**: 26.5: 28: 29) in)

39 (41: 43: **45: 45: 49**) cm
(15.5 (16: 17: **17.5** 19.5) in)

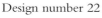

Design number 22

Splash

K I M   H A R G R E A V E S

YARN
Rowan Handknit DK Cotton

A Raindrop	206	2	x	50gm
B Zing	300	8	x	50gm

NEEDLES
1 pair 6mm (no 4) (US 10) needles

TENSION
14 sts and 24 rows to 10 cm measured over moss stitch using 6mm (US 10) needles and yarn double.

FINISHED SIZE
Completed bath mat is 55 cm (21½ in) wide and 72 cm (28½ in) long.

Pattern note: Use yarn **DOUBLE** throughout.

MAT
Cast on 77 sts using 6mm (US 10) needles and yarn A DOUBLE.
Row 1 (RS): K1, *P1, K1, rep from * to end.
Row 2: As row 1.
These 2 rows form moss st.
Keeping moss st correct throughout, cont as folls:
Work a further 8 rows using yarn A.
Join in yarn B.
Using yarn B, work 6 rows.
Using yarn A, work 6 rows.
Break off yarn A.
Cont using yarn B only until mat measures 62 cm from cast-on edge, ending with a WS row.
Join in yarn A.
Work 6 rows using yarn A.
Work 6 rows using yarn B.
Break off yarn B.
Work 10 rows using yarn A.
Cast off in moss st.

MAKING UP
PRESS as described on the information page.

103

Design number 23

Curls

SUSAN DUCKWORTH

YARN

Rowan 4 ply Cotton

		XS-S	M	L-XL		
To fit bust		81-86	91	97-102	cm	
		32-34	36	38-40	in	
A	Ripple	121	9	9	9	x	50gm
B	Pool	124	1	1	1	x	50gm
C	Bonny	104	1	1	1	x	50gm
D	Blaze	105	1	1	1	x	50gm
E	Sage	123	1	1	1	x	50gm
F	Vine	103	1	1	1	x	50gm
G	Orchid	120	1	1	1	x	50gm
H	Night Sky	115	1	1	1	x	50gm
J	Magenta	106	1	1	1	x	50gm
K	Olive	118	1	1	1	x	50gm
L	Vamp	117	1	1	1	x	50gm

NEEDLES

1 pair 2¼mm (no 13) (US 1) needles
1 pair 3mm (no 11) (US 2/3) needles

BUTTONS - 7

TENSION

28 sts and 38 rows to 10 cm measured over patterned stocking stitch using 3mm (US 2/3) needles.

BACK

Cast on 139 (147: 157) sts using 2¼mm (US 1) needles and yarn A.
Row 1 (RS): K1, *P1, K1, rep from * to end.
Row 2: As row 1.
These 2 rows form moss st.
Work a further 8 rows in moss st.
Change to 3mm (US 2/3) needles.
Using the **intarsia** technique described on the information page, place chart for back, which is worked entirely in st st, as folls:
Row 1 (RS): K34 (38: 43), work next 71 sts as given for row 1 of back chart, K34 (38: 43).
Row 2: P34 (38: 43), work next 71 sts as given for row 2 of back chart, P34 (38: 43).
These 2 rows set position of chart with side sts worked in st st.
Keeping chart correct and repeating the 52 row repeat as required, cont as folls:
Cont straight until back measures 32 cm, ending with a WS row.
Shape armholes
Keeping patt correct, cast off 4 sts at beg of next 2 rows. 131 (139: 149) sts.
Dec 1 st at each end of next 5 rows, then on foll 5 (5: 6) alt rows. 111 (119: 127) sts.
Cont straight until armhole measures 24 cm, ending with a WS row.
Shape shoulders and back neck
Cast off 11 (13: 14) sts at beg of next 2 rows.
89 (93: 99) sts.
Next row (RS): Cast off 11 (13: 14) sts, patt until there are 16 (16: 18) sts on right needle and turn, leaving rem sts on a holder.
Work each side of neck separately. Cast off 4 sts at beg of next row.
Cast off rem 12 (12: 14) sts.
With RS facing, rejoin yarn to rem sts, cast off centre 35 sts, patt to end.
Work to match first side, reversing shapings.

POCKET LININGS (make 2)

Cast on 34 sts using 3mm (US 2/3) needles and yarn A.
Beg with a K row, work in st st for 40 rows.
Break yarn and leave sts on a holder.

LEFT FRONT

Cast on 69 (73: 79) sts using 2¼mm (US 1) needles and yarn A.
Work 10 rows in moss st as given for back, inc 1 (1: 0) st at centre of last row. 70 (74: 79) sts.
Change to 3mm (US 2/3) needles.
Place chart for left front as folls:
Row 1 (RS): K17 (21: 26), work last 53 sts as given for row 1 of chart for left front.
Row 2: Work first 53 sts as given for row 2 of chart for left front, P17 (21: 26).
These 2 rows set position of chart with side sts worked in st st.
Keeping chart correct and repeating the 52 row repeat as required, cont as folls:
Cont foll chart until chart row 40 has been completed.
Place pocket
Next row (RS): Patt 11 (15: 20) sts, slip next 34 sts onto a holder and, in their place, patt across 34 sts of first pocket lining, patt 25 sts.
Cont straight until left front matches back to beg of armhole shaping, ending with a WS row.
Shape armhole
Keeping chart correct, cast off 4 sts at beg of next row. 66 (70: 75) sts.
Work 1 row. Dec 1 st at armhole edge of next 5 rows, then on foll 5 (5: 6) alt rows. 56 (60: 64) sts.
Cont straight until 19 rows less have been worked than on back to start of shoulder shaping, ending with a RS row.
Shape neck
Cast off 9 sts at beg of next row, then 4 sts at beg of foll alt row. 43 (47: 51) sts.
Dec 1 st at neck edge of next 9 rows. 34 (38: 42) sts.
Work 7 rows, ending with a WS row.
Shape shoulder
Cast off 11 (13: 14) sts at beg of next and foll alt row.
Work 1 row. Cast off rem 12 (12: 14) sts.

RIGHT FRONT

Cast on 69 (73: 79) sts using 2¼mm (US 1) needles and yarn A.
Work 10 rows in moss st as given for back, inc 1 (1: 0) st at centre of last row. 70 (74: 79) sts.
Change to 3mm (US 2/3) needles.
Place chart for right front as folls:
Row 1 (RS): Work first 53 sts as given for row 1 of chart for right front, K17 (21: 26).
Row 2: P17 (21: 26), work last 53 sts as given for row 2 of chart for right front.
These 2 rows set position of chart with side sts worked in st st.

BACK CHART

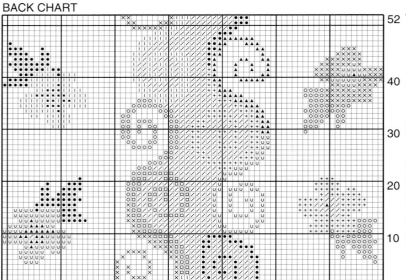

Key
☐ A
⊡ B
⊠ C
⊡ D
⊙ E
▪ F
☑ G
⊞ H
☐ J
▪ K
⊡ L

52
40
30
20
10

52 row patt rep

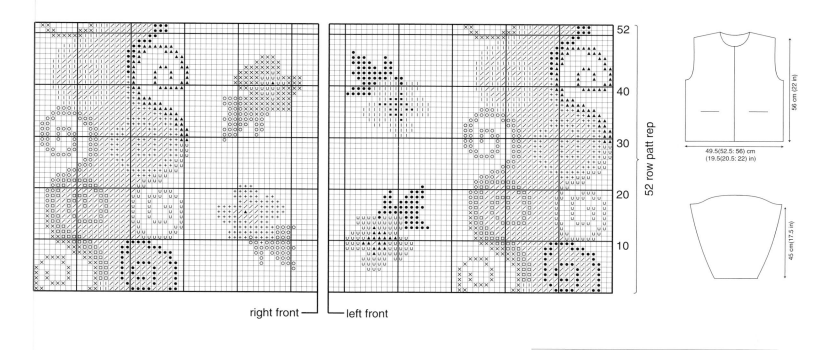

right front ⌐ └ left front

52 row patt rep

49.5(52.5: 56) cm
(19.5(20.5: 22) in)

56 cm (22 in)

45 cm (17.5 in)

Keeping chart correct and repeating the 52 row repeat as required, cont as folls:
Cont foll chart until chart row 40 has been completed.

Place pocket
Next row (RS): Patt 25 sts, slip next 34 sts onto a holder and, in their place, patt across 34 sts of second pocket lining, patt 11 (15: 20) sts.
Complete to match left front, reversing shapings.

SLEEVES (both alike)
Cast on 65 sts using 2¼mm (US 1) needles and yarn A.
Work 10 rows in moss st as given for back.
Change to 3mm (US 2/3) needles.
Place chart for sleeves as folls:
Row 1 (RS): K14, work next 36 sts as given for row 1 of chart for sleeves, K15.
Row 2: P15, work next 36 sts as given for row 2 of chart for sleeves, P14.
These 2 rows set position of chart with side sts worked in st st.
Keeping chart correct and repeating the 59 row repeat as required and **noting that on 2nd repeat of chart even numbered rows become RS (K) rows and vice versa**, cont as folls:
Inc 1 st at each end of 7th and every foll 6th row to 85 sts, then on every foll 4th row until there are 127 sts, taking inc sts into st st.
Cont straight until sleeve measures 45 cm, ending with a WS row.

Shape top
Keeping patt correct, cast off 4 sts at beg of next 2 rows. 119 sts.
Dec 1 st at each end of next 5 rows, then on foll 3 alt rows. Work 1 row.
Cast off rem 103 sts.

MAKING UP
PRESS all pieces as described on the info page.
Join shoulder seams using back stitch, or mattress stitch if preferred.
Button band
Cast on 9 sts using 2¼mm (US 1) needles and yarn A.
Work in moss st as given for back until band, when slightly stretched, fits up left front opening edge to start of neck shaping, ending with a WS row.
Cast off.
Slip stitch band in place.
Mark positions for 7 buttons on this band – lowest button 2 cm up from cast-on edge, top button 1.5 cm below neck shaping and rem 5 buttons evenly spaced between.

SLEEVE CHART

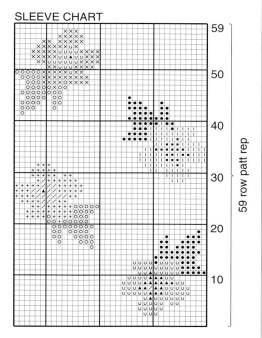

59 row patt rep

Buttonhole band
Work as given for button band, with the addition of 7 buttonholes to correspond with positions marked for buttons worked as folls:
Buttonhole row (RS): Moss st 4 sts, yrn (to make a buttonhole), work 2 tog, moss st 3 sts.
Slip stitch band in place.
Pocket tops
Slip 34 sts from pocket holder onto 2¼mm (US 1) needles and rejoin yarn A with RS facing.
Row 1 (RS): *K1, P1, rep from * to end.
Rep this row 4 times more.
Cast off in rib.
Collar
Cast on 129 sts using 2¼mm (US 1) needles and yarn A.
Work in moss st as given for back for 8 cm.
Cast off in moss st.
Sew cast-on edge of collar to neck edge, positioning ends of collar halfway across top of bands.
See information page for finishing instructions, setting in sleeves using the shallow set-in method.

Design number 24

Puppy Love

JULIA RYAN DINNER

YARN
Rowan All Seasons Cotton

		XS	S	M	L	XL	
To fit bust		81	86	91	97	102	cm
		32	34	36	38	40	in
A Jazz	185	4	4	4	4	5	x 50gm
B Gay	184	4	4	4	5	5	x 50gm
C Limedrop	197	3	3	3	4	4	x 50gm
D Orkney	196	2	2	2	2	2	x 50gm
E Jaunty	183	4	4	4	4	5	x 50gm
F Melba	198	2	2	2	2	2	x 50gm

NEEDLES
1 pair 4½mm (no 7) (US 7) needles
1 pair 5mm (no 6) (US 8) needles

BUTTONS - 5

TENSION

17 sts and 24 rows to 10 cm measured over patterned stocking stitch using 5mm (US 8) needles.

BACK

Cast on 81 (85: 89: 93: 97) sts using 4½mm (US 7) needles and yarn B.

Work in garter st for 10 rows, ending with a WS row.

Change to 5mm (US 8) needles.

Using the **intarsia** technique described on the information page, starting and ending panel as indicated and repeating the 36 row repeat throughout, cont in patt from chart, which is worked entirely in st st, as folls:

Row 1 (RS): Using yarn B K4, *work next 16 (17: 18: 19: 20) sts as given for row 1 of panel, using yarn B K3, rep from * 3 times more, using yarn B K1.

Row 2: Using yarn B P4, *work next 16 (17: 18: 19: 20) sts as given for row 2 of panel, using yarn B P3, rep from * 3 times more, using yarn B P1.

These 2 rows set the sts.

Cont straight until back measures 27 (28: 28: 29: 29) cm, ending with a WS row.

Shape armholes

Keeping patt correct, cast off 4 (4: 5: 5: 5) sts at beg of next 2 rows.

73 (77: 79: 83: 87) sts.

Dec 1 st at each end of next 3 rows, then on every foll alt row until 63 (65: 67: 69: 71) sts rem.

Cont straight until armhole measures 22 (22: 23: 23: 24) cm, ending with a WS row.

Shape shoulders and back neck

Keeping patt correct, cast off 6 (6: 7: 7: 7) sts at beg of next 2 rows.

51 (53: 53: 55: 57) sts.

Next row (RS): Cast off 6 (6: 7: 7: 7) sts, patt until there are 11 (11: 10: 10: 11) sts on right needle and turn, leaving rem sts on a holder.

Work each side of neck separately.

Cast off 4 sts at beg of next row.

Cast off rem 7 (7: 6: 6: 7) sts.

With RS facing, rejoin yarn to rem sts, cast off centre 17 (19: 19: 21: 21) sts, patt to end.

Work to match first side, reversing shapings.

LEFT FRONT

Cast on 43 (45: 47: 49: 51) sts using 4½mm (US 7) needles and yarn B.

Work in garter st for 9 rows, ending with a RS row.

Row 10 (WS): K5 and slip these sts onto a holder for button band, M1, K to end.

39 (41: 43: 45: 47) sts.

Change to 5mm (US 8) needles and cont in patt foll chart as folls:

Row 1 (RS): Using yarn B K4, work next 16 (17: 18: 19: 20) sts as given for row 1 of panel, using yarn B K3, work last 16 (17: 18: 19: 20) sts as given for row 1 of panel.

Row 2: Work first 16 (17: 18: 19: 20) sts as given for row 2 of panel, using yarn B P3, work next 16 (17: 18: 19: 20) sts as given for row 2 of panel, using yarn B P4.

These 2 rows set the sts.

Cont straight until left front matches back to beg of armhole shaping, ending with a WS row.

Shape armhole

Keeping patt correct, cast off 4 (4: 5: 5: 5) sts at beg of next row.

35 (37: 38: 40: 42) sts.

Work 1 row.

Dec 1 st at armhole edge of next 3 rows, then on every foll alt row until 30 (31: 32: 33: 34) sts rem.

Work 7 (5: 5: 3: 1) rows, ending with a WS row.

Shape neck

Dec 1 st at neck edge of next and foll 4 (6: 4: 6: 5) alt rows, then on every foll 4th row until 19 (19: 20: 20: 21) sts rem.

Cont straight until left front matches back to start of shoulder shaping, ending with a WS row.

Shape shoulder

Keeping patt correct, cast off 6 (6: 7: 7: 7) sts at beg of next and foll alt row.

Work 1 row.

Cast off rem 7 (7: 6: 6: 7) sts.

RIGHT FRONT

Cast on 43 (45: 47: 49: 51) sts using 4½mm (US 7) needles and yarn B.

Work in garter st for 4 rows, ending with a WS row.

Row 5 (buttonhole row) (RS): K2, yfwd, K2tog, K to end.

Cont in garter st for a further 4 rows, ending with a RS row.

Row 10 (WS): K to last 5 sts, M1 and turn, leaving rem 5 sts on a holder for buttonhole band.

39 (41: 43: 45: 47) sts.

Change to 5mm (US 8) needles and cont in patt foll chart as folls:

Row 1 (RS): Work first 16 (17: 18: 19: 20) sts as given for row 1 of panel, using yarn B K3, work next 16 (17: 18: 19: 20) sts as given for row 1 of panel, using yarn B K4.

Row 2: Using yarn B P4, work next 16 (17: 18: 19: 20) sts as given for row 2 of panel, using yarn B P3, work last 16 (17: 18: 19: 20) sts as given for row 2 of panel.

These 2 rows set the sts.

Complete to match left front, reversing shapings.

SLEEVES

Cast on 37 (37: 39: 41: 41) sts using 4½mm (US 7) needles and yarn B.

Work in garter st for 6 rows, ending with a WS row.

Change to 5mm (US 8) needles and cont in patt foll chart as folls:

Row 1 (RS): Using yarn B K2, work next 15 (15: 16: 17: 17) sts as given for row 1 of panel, using yarn B K3, work next 15 (15: 16: 17: 17) sts as given for row 1 of panel, using yarn B K2.

Row 2: Using yarn B P2, work next 15 (15: 16: 17: 17) sts as given for row 2 of panel, using yarn B P3, work next 15 (15: 16: 17: 17) sts as given for row 2 of panel, using yarn B P2.

These 2 rows set the sts.

Cont in patt, inc 1 st at each end of next and every foll 8th row until there are 57 (51: 55: 57: 51) sts, then on every foll 6th row until there are 59 (61: 63: 65: 67) sts, taking inc sts into patt.

Cont straight until sleeve measures 41 (41: 42: 42: 42) cm, ending with a WS row.

Shape top

Keeping patt correct, cast off 4 (4: 5: 5: 5) sts at beg of next 2 rows. 51 (53: 53: 55: 57) sts.

Dec 1 st at each end of next 3 rows, then on foll 2 alt rows, then on every foll 4th row until 31 (35: 33: 37: 39) sts rem.

Work 1 row, ending with a WS row.

Dec 1 st at each end of next and foll 0 (2: 1: 3: 4) alt rows, then on foll row, ending with a WS row. 27 sts.

Cast off 4 sts at beg of next 2 rows.

Cast off rem 19 sts.

MAKING UP

PRESS all pieces as described on the information page.

Join both shoulder seams using back stitch, or mattress stitch if preferred.

Button band

Slip 5 sts left on holder for button band onto 4½mm (US 7) needles and rejoin yarn B with RS facing.

Cont in garter st until band, when slightly stretched, fits up left front opening edge to shoulder and then across to centre back neck, ending with a WS row.

Cast off.

Slip stitch band in place.

Mark positions for 5 buttons on this band – lowest button level with buttonhole already worked in right front, top button level with start of front slope shaping and rem 3 buttons evenly spaced between.

Buttonhole band

Work as given for button band, rejoining yarn with WS facing and with the addition of a further 4 buttonholes to correspond with positions marked for buttons worked as folls:

Buttonhole row (RS): K2, yfwd, K2tog, K1.

Slip stitch band in place, joining ends at centre back neck.

See information page for finishing instructions, setting in sleeves using the set-in method.

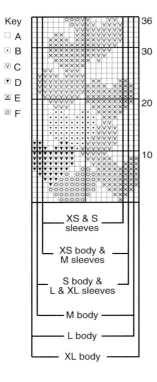

Key
- ☐ A
- ⊡ B
- ☑ C
- ▣ D
- ☒ E
- ⊚ F

XS & S sleeves

XS body & M sleeves

S body & L & XL sleeves

M body

L body

XL body

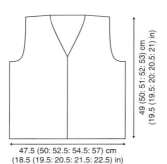

49 (50: 51: 52: 53) cm
(19.5: 19.5: 20.5: 21) in

47.5 (50: 52.5: 54.5: 57) cm
(18.5: 19.5: 20.5: 21.5: 22.5) in

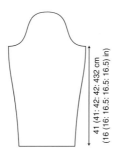

41 (41: 42: 42: 42) cm
(16: 16: 16.5: 16.5: 16.5) in

Design number 25

Prance

KIM HARGREAVES

YARN
Rowan Linen Drape

	XS	S	M	L	XL
To fit bust	81	86	91	97	102 cm
	32	34	36	38	40 in
	11	12	13	13	14 x 50gm

(photographed in Cornflower 846)

NEEDLES
1 pair 3mm (no 11) (US 2/3) needles
1 pair 3¾mm (no 9) (US 5) needles

BUTTONS - 5

TENSION
24 sts and 38 rows to 10 cm measured over moss stitch using 3¾mm (US 5) needles.

Pattern note: As row end edges of fronts form actual finished edges of garment, it is important these edges are kept neat. Therefore all new balls of yarn should be joined in at side seam or armhole edges of rows.

BACK
Cast on 101 (107: 113: 119: 125) sts using 3mm (US 2/3) needles.
Knit 3 rows.
Cont in moss st as folls:
Row 1 (WS): K0 (1: 0: 1: 0), *P1, K1, rep from * to last 1 (0: 1: 0: 1) st, P1 (0: 1: 0: 1).
Row 2: As row 1.
These 2 rows form moss st.
Work 1 row, ending with a WS row.
Change to 3¾mm (US 5) needles.
Cont in moss st, shaping side seams by dec 1 st at each end of next and every foll 4th row until 85 (91: 97: 103: 109) sts rem.
Work 7 (9: 9: 9: 9) rows, ending with a WS row.
Inc 1 st at each end of next and every foll 6th row to 101 (107: 113: 119: 125) sts, then on every foll 4th row until there are 109 (115: 121: 127: 133) sts, taking inc sts into moss st.
Cont straight until back measures 29 (30: 30: 31: 31) cm, ending with a WS row.

Shape armholes
Keeping moss st correct, cast off 3 (4: 4: 5: 5) sts at beg of next 2 rows. 103 (107: 113: 117: 123) sts.
Dec 1 st at each end of next 5 (5: 7: 7: 9) rows, then on foll 4 (5: 5: 6: 6) alt rows. 85 (87: 89: 91: 93) sts.
Cont straight until armhole measures 20 (20: 21: 21: 22) cm, ending with a WS row.

Shape shoulders and back neck
Keeping moss st correct, cast off 9 sts at beg of next 2 rows. 67 (69: 71: 73: 75) sts.
Next row (RS): Cast off 9 sts, patt until there are 12 (12: 13: 13: 14) sts on right needle and turn, leaving rem sts on a holder.
Work each side of neck separately.
Cast off 4 sts at beg of next row.
Cast off rem 8 (8: 9: 9: 10) sts.
With RS facing, rejoin yarn to rem sts, cast off centre 25 (27: 27: 29: 29) sts, patt to end.
Work to match first side, reversing shapings.

LEFT FRONT
Cast on 50 (53: 56: 59: 62) sts using 3mm (US 2/3) needles. Knit 3 rows.
Cont in moss st as folls:
Row 1 (WS): K1, *P1, K1, rep from * to last 1 (0: 1: 0: 1) st, P1 (0: 1: 0: 1).
Row 2: P1 (0: 1: 0: 1), *K1, P1, rep from * to last st, K1.
These 2 rows form moss st.
Work 1 row, ending with a WS row.
Change to 3¾mm (US 5) needles.
Cont in moss st, shaping side seams by dec 1 st at beg of next and every foll 4th row until 42 (45: 48: 51: 54) sts rem.
Work 7 (9: 9: 9: 9) rows, ending with a WS row.
Inc 1 st at beg of next and every foll 6th row to 50 (53: 56: 59: 62) sts, then on every foll 4th row until there are 54 (57: 60: 63: 66) sts, taking inc sts into moss st.
Cont straight until left front matches back to beg of armhole shaping, ending with a WS row.

Shape armhole
Keeping moss st correct, cast off 3 (4: 4: 5: 5) sts at beg of next row. 51 (53: 56: 58: 61) sts.
Work 1 row.
Dec 1 st at armhole edge of next 5 (5: 7: 7: 9) rows, then on foll 4 (5: 5: 6: 6) alt rows. 42 (43: 44: 45: 46) sts.
Work 1 row, ending with a WS row.

Shape front slope
Next row (RS): Moss st to last 6 sts, P3tog, K1, P1, K1. 40 (41: 42: 43: 44) sts.
Work 17 rows, ending with a WS row.
Next row (RS): Moss st to last 6 sts, P3tog, K1, P1, K1. 38 (39: 40: 41: 42) sts.
Cont straight until 23 (23: 23: 25: 25) rows less have been worked than on back to start of shoulder shaping, ending with a RS row.

Shape neck
Keeping moss st correct, cast off 5 (6: 6: 6: 6) sts at beg of next row. 33 (33: 34: 35: 36) sts.
Dec 1 st at neck edge of next 3 rows, then on foll 2 (2: 2: 3: 3) alt rows, then on every foll 4th row until 26 (26: 27: 27: 28) sts rem.
Work 7 rows, ending with a WS row.

Shape shoulder
Keeping moss st correct, cast off 9 sts at beg of next and foll alt row.
Work 1 row. Cast off rem 8 (8: 9: 9: 10) sts.

RIGHT FRONT
Cast on 50 (53: 56: 59: 62) sts using 3mm (US 2/3) needles. Knit 3 rows.
Cont in moss st as folls:
Row 1 (WS): P1 (0: 1: 0: 1), *K1, P1, rep from * to last st, K1.
Row 2: K1, *P1, K1, rep from * to last 1 (0: 1: 0: 1) st, P1 (0: 1: 0: 1).
These 2 rows form moss st.

Work 1 row, ending with a WS row.
Change to 3¾mm (US 5) needles.
Cont in moss st, shaping side seams by dec 1 st at end of next and every foll 4th row until 42 (45: 48: 51: 54) sts rem.
Complete to match left front, reversing shapings.

SLEEVES (both alike)
Cast on 57 (57: 59: 61: 61) sts using 3mm (US 2/3) needles.
Knit 3 rows.
Now work in moss st as folls:
Row 1 (WS): *K1, P1, rep from * to last st, K1.
Row 2: As row 1.
These 2 rows form moss st.
Work a further 5 rows in moss st, ending with a WS row.
Change to 3¾mm (US 5) needles.
Inc 1 st at each end of next and every foll 10th (10th: 10th: 10th: 8th) row to 69 (63: 65: 67: 89) sts, then on every foll 8th (8th: 8th: 8th: -) row until there are 81 (83: 85: 87: -) sts, taking inc sts into moss st.
Cont straight until sleeve measures 33 (33: 34: 34: 34) cm, ending with a WS row.

Shape top
Keeping moss st correct, cast off 3 (4: 4: 5: 5) sts at beg of next 2 rows. 75 (75: 77: 77: 79) sts.
Dec 1 st at each end of next 3 rows, then on foll 3 alt rows, then on every foll 4th row until 49 (49: 51: 51: 53) sts rem.
Work 1 row, ending with a WS row.
Dec 1 st at each end of next and foll 3 (3: 4: 4: 5) alt rows, then on foll 5 rows, ending with a WS row. 31 sts.
Cast off 6 sts at beg of next 2 rows.
Cast off rem 19 sts.

MAKING UP
PRESS all pieces as described on the information page.
Join both shoulder seams using back stitch, or mattress stitch if preferred.
Neckband
With RS facing and using 3mm (US 2/3) needles, pick up and knit 32 (33: 33: 35: 35) sts up right side of neck, 33 (35: 35: 37: 37) sts from back, and 32 (33: 33: 35: 35) sts down left side of neck.
97 (101: 101: 107: 107) sts.
Cast off knitwise (on WS).
Mark positions for 5 buttons along left front opening edge – top button 5 cm down from start of front slope shaping, lowest button 16 cm up from cast-on edge and rem 3 buttons evenly spaced between.
Button loops (make 5)
Cast on 16 sts using 3mm (US 2/3) needles.
Cast off knitwise.
Fold each strip in half to make a loop. Pin loops to inside of right front opening edge to correspond with positions marked for buttons, adjust size to match buttons and sew in place.
See information page for finishing instructions, setting in sleeves using the set-in method.

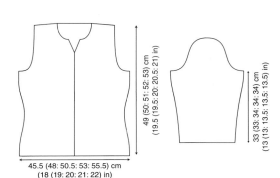

45.5 (48: 50.5: 53: 55.5) cm
(18 (19: 20: 21: 22) in)

49 (50: 51: 52: 53) cm
(19.5 (19.5: 20: 20.5: 21) in)

33 (33: 34: 34: 34) cm
(13 (13: 13.5: 13.5: 13.5) in)

Design number 26

Essence

KIM HARGREAVES

YARN
Rowan Linen Drape

	XS	S	M	L	XL	
To fit bust	81	86	91	97	102	cm
	32	34	36	38	40	in
Split neck vest	5	6	6	7	7	x 50gm

(photographed in Watermelon 848)

| **V neck vest** | 5 | 6 | 6 | 6 | 7 | x 50gm |

(photographed in Hawaii 849)

Striped vest

A	Petal	842	2	2	2	2	3	x 50gm
B	Hawaii	849	2	2	2	2	2	x 50gm
C	Cornflower	846	2	2	2	2	2	x 50gm
D	Natural	843	2	2	2	2	2	x 50gm
E	Pewter	841	2	2	2	2	2	x 50gm

NEEDLES
1 pair 3mm (no 11) (US 2/3) needles
1 pair 3¾mm (no 9) (US 5) needles
2 double pointed 3mm (no 11) (US 2/3) needles

BEADS – v neck vest only: approx 50 large glass beads (See page 117 for details).

TENSION
23 sts and 30 rows to 10 cm measured over stocking stitch using 3¾mm (US 5) needles.

Split neck vest
BACK
Cast on 93 (99: 105: 111: 117) sts using 3mm (US 2/3) needles.
Beg with a K row, work in st st throughout as folls:
Work 6 (8: 8: 8: 8) rows.
Change to 3¾mm (US 5) needles.
Dec 1 st at each end of next and every foll 4th row until 77 (83: 89: 95: 101) sts rem. Work 9 rows.
Inc 1 st at each end of next and every foll 8th row to 83 (89: 95: 101: 107) sts, then on every foll 6th row until there are 93 (99: 105: 111: 117) sts.
Cont straight until back measures 33 (34: 34: 35: 35) cm, ending with a WS row.
Shape armholes
Cast off 4 (4: 5: 5: 6) sts at beg of next 2 rows.
85 (91: 95: 101: 105) sts.
Dec 1 st at each end of next 5 (7: 7: 9: 9) rows, then on foll 5 (5: 6: 6: 7) alt rows. 65 (67: 69: 71: 73) sts.★★
Cont straight until armhole measures 20 (20: 21: 21: 22) cm, ending with a WS row.
Shape shoulders and back neck
Cast off 5 sts at beg of next 2 rows.
55 (57: 59: 61: 63) sts.
Next row (RS): Cast off 5 sts, K until there are 8 (8: 9: 9: 10) sts on right needle and turn, leaving rem sts on a holder. Work each side of neck separately.
Cast off 4 sts at beg of next row.
Cast off rem 4 (4: 5: 5: 6) sts.
With RS facing, rejoin yarn to rem sts, cast off centre 29 (31: 31: 33: 33) sts, K to end.
Work to match first side, reversing shapings.

FRONT
Work as given for back to ★★.
Work 1 row, ending with a WS row.
Divide for front opening
Next row (RS): K32 (33: 34: 35: 36) and turn, leaving rem sts on a holder.
Work each side of neck separately.
Cont straight until 17 (17: 17: 19: 19) rows less have been worked than on back to start of shoulder shaping, ending with a RS row.
Shape neck
Cast off 8 (9: 9: 9: 9) sts at beg of next row and 4 sts at beg of foll alt row. 20 (20: 21: 22: 23) sts.
Dec 1 st at neck edge of next 3 rows, then on foll 3 (3: 3: 4: 4) alt rows. 14 (14: 15: 15: 16) sts.
Work 5 rows, ending with a WS row.
Shape shoulder
Cast off 5 sts at beg of next and foll alt row.
Work 1 row. Cast off rem 4 (4: 5: 5: 6) sts.
With RS facing, rejoin yarn to rem sts, K2tog, K to end.
Work to match first side, reversing shapings.

V neck vest
BACK
Work as given for back of split neck vest to start of shoulder and back neck shaping, ending with a WS row.
Shape shoulders and back neck
Cast off 6 (6: 6: 6: 7) sts at beg of next 2 rows.
53 (55: 57: 59: 59) sts.
Next row (RS): Cast off 6 (6: 6: 6: 7) sts, K until there are 10 (10: 11: 11: 10) sts on right needle and turn, leaving rem sts on a holder.
Work each side of neck separately.
Cast off 4 sts at beg of next row.
Cast off rem 6 (6: 7: 7: 6) sts.
With RS facing, rejoin yarn to rem sts, cast off centre 21 (23: 23: 25: 25) sts, K to end.
Work to match first side, reversing shapings.

FRONT
Work as given for back of split neck vest to beg of armhole shaping, ending with a WS row.
Shape armholes and divide for front neck
Next row (RS): Cast off 4 (4: 5: 5: 6) sts, K until there are 42 (45: 47: 50: 52) sts on right needle and turn, leaving rem sts on a holder.
Work each side of neck separately.
Work 1 row.
Dec 1 st at armhole edge of next 5 (7: 7: 9: 9) rows **and at same time** dec 1 st at neck edge of 3rd and every foll 0 (4th: 4th: 4th: 4th) row.
36 (36: 38: 39: 41) sts.
Work 1 row.
Dec 1 st at armhole edge of next and foll 4 (4: 5: 5: 6) alt rows **and at same time** dec 1 st at neck edge of every foll 4th row from previous dec.
28 (29: 29: 30: 30) sts.
Dec 1 st at neck edge only on every foll 4th row from previous dec until 20 (24: 23: 27: 24) sts rem, then on every foll 3rd row until 18 (18: 19: 19: 20) sts rem.
Cont straight until front matches back to start of shoulder shaping, ending with a WS row.
Shape shoulder
Cast off 6 (6: 6: 6: 7) sts at beg of next and foll alt row.
Work 1 row.
Cast off rem 6 (6: 7: 7: 6) sts.
With RS facing, rejoin yarn to rem sts, K2tog, K to end.
Work to match first side, reversing shapings.

Striped vest
BACK and FRONT (both alike)
Working in stripe sequence throughout as given below, work as given for back of split neck vest to ★★.
Keeping stripe sequence correct, cont straight until armhole measures 19 (19: 20: 20: 21) cm, ending with a WS row.
Shape neck
Next row (RS): K12 (12: 13: 13: 14) and turn, leaving rem sts on a holder.
Work each side of neck separately.
Cast off 4 sts at beg of next row.
Dec 1 st at neck edge of next row.
7 (7: 8: 8: 9) sts.
Work 1 row, ending with a WS row.
Shape shoulder
Cast off 3 (3: 3: 3: 4) sts at beg and dec 1 st at end of next row.
Work 1 row.
Cast off rem 3 (3: 4: 4: 4) sts.
With RS facing, rejoin yarn to rem sts, cast off centre 41 (43: 43: 45: 45) sts, K to end.
Work to match first side, reversing shapings.

STRIPE SEQUENCE

Cast on using yarn A.
Rows 1 to 6: Using yarn A.
Row 7: Using yarn D.
Rows 8 and 9: Using yarn E.
Row 10: Using yarn B.
Rows 11 to 14: Using yarn C.
Rows 15 and 16: Using yarn A.
Rows 17 to 20: Using yarn E.
Row 21: Using yarn D.
Row 22: Using yarn B.
Rows 23 to 26: Using yarn C.
Rows 27 and 28: Using yarn B.
Row 29: Using yarn E.
Rows 30 to 32: Using yarn D.
Rows 33 to 36: Using yarn A.
Rows 37 and 38: Using yarn E.
Row 39: Using yarn D.
Row 40: Using yarn A.
Row 41: Using yarn C.
Rows 42 to 50: Using yarn B.
Rows 51 to 54: Using yarn A.
Row 55: Using yarn E.
Rows 56 to 58: Using yarn C.
Row 59: Using yarn B.
Row 60: Using yarn E.
Rows 61 to 65: Using yarn D.
Rows 66 and 67: Using yarn E.
Row 68: Using yarn A.
Row 69: Using yarn B.
Rows 70 to 76: Using yarn C.
Rows 77 and 78: Using yarn E.
Rows 79 and 80: Using yarn A.
Row 81: Using yarn E.
Rows 82 to 84: Using yarn B.
Rows 85 and 86: Using yarn A.
Row 87: Using yarn C.
Rows 88 to 94: Using yarn D.
Row 95: Using yarn E.
Rows 96 and 97: Using yarn A.
Rows 98 to 102: Using yarn C.
Row 103: Using yarn B.
Rows 104 and 105: Using yarn E.
Row 106: Using yarn D.
Row 107: Using yarn A.
Row 108: Using yarn C.
Rows 109 to 114: Using yarn B.
Row 115: Using yarn D.
Row 116: Using yarn A.
Rows 117 to 122: Using yarn E.
Rows 123 to 125: Using yarn D.
Row 126: Using yarn A.
Rows 127 and 128: Using yarn B.
Rows 129 to 131: Using yarn C.
Rows 132 and 133: Using yarn D.
Rows 134 and 135: Using yarn E.
Rows 136 to 140: Using yarn C.

Rows 141 to 144: Using yarn D.
Rows 145 and 146: Using yarn A.
Row 147: Using yarn E.
Row 148: Using yarn B.
Rows 149 to 153: Using yarn A.
Row 154: Using yarn E.
Row 155: Using yarn D.
Row 156: Using yarn B.
Rows 157 to 165: Using yarn E.
Rows 166 to 168: Using yarn B.
Row 169: Using yarn C.
Rows 170 and 171: Using yarn A.
Rows 172 and 173: Using yarn E.
Rows 174 to 176: Using yarn D.
Rows 177 to 180: Using yarn C.
Row 181: Using yarn E.
Row 182: Using yarn A.
Rows 183 to 185: Using yarn B.

MAKING UP

PRESS all pieces as described on the information page.
Join shoulder seams using back stitch, or mattress stitch if preferred.

Split neck vest
Front opening edging
With RS facing and using 3mm (US 2/3) needles, pick up and knit 14 (15: 16: 17: 18) sts down left side of split, then 14 (15: 16: 17: 18) sts up right side of split. 28 (30: 32: 34: 36) sts.
Cast off knitwise (on WS).
Neckband
With RS facing and using 3mm (US 2/3) needles, starting and ending at cast-off edge of front opening edging, pick up and knit 32 (33: 33: 36: 36) sts up right side of neck, 37 (39: 39: 41: 41) sts from back, and 32 (33: 33: 36: 36) sts down left side of neck. 101 (105: 105: 113: 113) sts.
Cast off knitwise (on WS).
Tie belt (optional)
Using double pointed 3mm (US 2/3) needles, cast on 3 sts.
Next row (RS): K3 – all 3 sts now on right needle, ★slip sts to opposite end of needle and transfer this needle to left hand, without turning work and taking yarn quite tightly across back of work, K same 3 sts again – all 3 sts now on right needle again, rep from ★ until tie is 135 cm long.
Next row: K3tog and fasten off.

V neck vest
Neckband
With RS facing and using 3mm (US 2/3) needles, pick up and knit 51 (52: 53: 54: 55) sts down left side of neck, 51 (52: 53: 54: 55) sts up right side of neck, and 29 (31: 31: 33: 33) sts from back. 131 (135: 137: 141: 143) sts.
Cast off knitwise (on WS).

Striped vest
Neckband
With RS facing, using 3mm (US 2/3) needles and yarn E, pick up and knit 8 sts down left side of front neck, 45 (47: 47: 49: 49) sts from front, 8 sts up right side of front neck, 8 sts down right side of back neck, 45 (47: 47: 49: 49) sts from back, 8 sts up left side of back neck. 122 (126: 126: 130: 130) sts.
Cast off knitwise (on WS).

All vests
Join left shoulder and neckband seam.
For v neck vest, sew beads around neck edge, positioning beads just in from neckband and approx 12 mm (½ in) apart.

Armhole borders
With RS facing and using 3mm (US 2/3) needles (and using yarn E for striped vest), pick up and knit 108 (108: 114: 114: 120) sts evenly all round armhole edge.
Cast off knitwise (on WS).
See information page for finishing instructions.

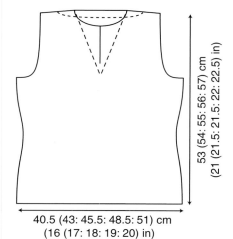

40.5 (43: 45.5: 48.5: 51) cm
(16 (17: 18: 19: 20) in)

53 (54: 55: 56: 57) cm
(21 (21.5: 21.5: 22: 22.5) in)

Aura

KIM HARGREAVES

YARN
Rowan Linen Drape 6 x 50gm
(photographed in Cornflower 846)

NEEDLES
1 pair 3¼mm (no 10) (US 3) needles

BEADS
– approx 60 rectangular glass beads (See page 117 for details).

TENSION
25 sts and 34 rows to 10 cm measured over stocking stitch using 3¼mm (US 3) needles.

FINISHED SIZE
Completed cushion is approx 46 cm (18 in) x 28 cm (11 in) excluding fringe.

MAIN SECTION
Cast on 115 sts using 3¼mm (US 3) needles.
Beg with a K row, work in st st for 56 cm from cast-on edge, ending with a WS row. Cast off.

END PANELS (both alike)
Place markers half way along row end edges.
With RS facing and using 3¼mm (US 3) needles, pick up and knit 67 sts along side of main section between cast-on edge and marker.
Row 1 (WS): K1, ★P1, K1, rep from ★ to end.
Rep this row 5 times more. Cast off.

MAKING UP
PRESS as described on the information page.
Work embroidery next to moss st end panels as folls: placing beads on every 4th row, sew a row of beads across cushion, positioning them over 3rd st in from moss st panels (see sketch on page 117 for details). Leaving one st between beads and cross stitches, now work a line of cross stitches next to line of beads, working each cross stitch over 2½ sts. With RS facing, fold main section in half to form rectangle 46 cm x 28 cm. Sew short ends closed and turn RS out. Insert cushion pad and close last side. Cut 7 cm lengths of yarn and knot to cast-off edges of end panels to form fringe.

Design number 28

Nancy

DEBBIE BLISS

YARN
Rowan Wool Cotton

		XS	S	M	L	XL	
To fit bust		81	86	91	97	102	cm
		32	34	36	38	40	in

Multi colour version

		XS	S	M	L	XL	
A Riviera	930	12	12	13	14	14 x 50gm
B Gypsy	910	1	1	1	1	1 x 50gm
C Tulip	944	1	1	1	1	1 x 50gm
D Deepest Olive	907	1	1	1	1	1 x 50gm

One colour version 12 12 13 14 14 x 50gm
(photographed in Clear 941)

NEEDLES
1 pair 3¼mm (no 10) (US 3) needles
1 pair 4mm (no 8) (US 6) needles

BUTTONS
7

TENSION
21 sts and 33 rows to 10 cm measured over pattern using 4mm (US 6) needles.

Special note: For one colour version, work as given for floral version using same colour throughout.

BACK
Cast on 93 (99: 105: 111: 117) sts using 3¼mm (US 3) needles and yarn A.
Row 1 (RS): P1 (0: 1: 0: 1), ★K1, P1, rep from ★ to last 0 (1: 0: 1: 0) st, K0 (1: 0: 1: 0).
Row 2: As row 1.
These 2 rows form moss st. Work in moss st for a further 4 rows, ending with a WS row.
Change to 4mm (US 6) needles.
Using the intarsia technique described on the info page, starting and ending rows as indicated and rep the 28 row repeat throughout, cont in patt foll chart as folls:
Work 4 (6: 6: 8: 8) rows.
Dec 1 st at each end of next and every foll 6th row until 79 (85: 91: 97: 103) sts rem.
Work 11 rows.
Inc 1 st at each end of next and every foll 6th row until there are 93 (99: 105: 111: 117) sts.
Cont straight until back measures 32 (33: 33: 34: 34) cm, ending with a WS row.
Shape armholes
Keeping chart correct, cast off 3 (4: 5: 6: 7) sts at beg of next 2 rows. 87 (91: 95: 99: 103) sts.
Dec 1 st at each end of next 7 rows, then on every foll alt row until 71 (73: 75: 77: 79) sts rem.
Cont straight until armhole measures 22 (22: 23: 23: 24) cm, ending with a WS row.
Shape shoulders and back neck
Cast off 6 (6: 7: 7: 7) sts at beg of next 2 rows. 59 (61: 61: 63: 65) sts.
Next row (RS): Cast off 6 (6: 7: 7: 7) sts, patt until there are 11 (11: 10: 10: 11) sts on right needle and turn, leaving rem sts on a holder.
Work each side of neck separately.
Cast off 4 sts at beg of next row.
Cast off rem 7 (7: 6: 6: 7) sts.
With RS facing, rejoin yarn to rem sts, cast off centre 25 (27: 27: 29: 29) sts, patt to end.
Work to match first side, reversing shapings.

LEFT FRONT
Cast on 52 (55: 58: 61: 64) sts using 3¼mm (US 3) needles and yarn A.
Row 1 (RS): K0 (1: 0: 1: 0), ★P1, K1, rep from ★ to end.
Row 2: ★K1, P1, rep from ★ to last 0 (1: 0: 1: 0) st, K0 (1: 0: 1: 0).
These 2 rows form moss st. Work in moss st for a further 3 rows, ending with a RS row.
Row 6 (WS): Moss st 6 and slip these 6 sts onto a holder for button band, M1, moss st to end.
47 (50: 53: 56: 59) sts.
Change to 4mm (US 6) needles.
Cont in patt foll chart as folls:
Work 4 (6: 6: 8: 8) rows.
Dec 1 st at beg of next and every foll 6th row until 40 (43: 46: 49: 52) sts rem.
Work 11 rows. Inc 1 st at beg of next and every foll 6th row until there are 47 (50: 53: 56: 59) sts.
Cont straight until left front matches back to beg of armhole shaping, ending with a WS row.
Shape armhole
Keeping chart correct, cast off 3 (4: 5: 6: 7) sts at beg of next row. 44 (46: 48: 50: 52) sts.
Work 1 row.
Dec 1 st at armhole edge of next 7 rows, then on every foll alt row until 36 (37: 38: 39: 40) sts rem.
Cont straight until 25 (25: 25: 27: 27) rows less have been worked than on back to start of shoulder shaping, ending with a RS row.

Shape neck
Keeping chart correct, cast off 4 (5: 5: 5: 5) sts at beg of next row, then 4 sts at beg of foll alt row.
28 (28: 29: 30: 31) sts.
Dec 1 st at neck edge of next 3 rows, then on foll 4 (4: 4: 5: 5) alt rows, then on every foll 4th row until 19 (19: 20: 20: 21) sts rem.
Work 3 rows, ending with a WS row.
Shape shoulder
Cast off 6 (6: 7: 7: 7) sts at beg of next and foll alt row.
Work 1 row. Cast off rem 7 (7: 6: 6: 7) sts.

RIGHT FRONT
Cast on 52 (55: 58: 61: 64) sts using 3¼mm (US 3) needles and yarn A.
Row 1 (RS): ★K1, P1, rep from ★ to last 0 (1: 0: 1: 0) st, K0 (1: 0: 1: 0).
Row 2: K0 (1: 0: 1: 0), ★P1, K1, rep from ★ to end.
These 2 rows form moss st.
Work in moss st for a further 3 rows, ending with a RS row.
Row 6 (WS): Moss st to last 6 sts, M1 and turn, leaving last 6 sts on a holder for buttonhole band.
47 (50: 53: 56: 59) sts.
Change to 4mm (US 6) needles.
Cont in patt foll chart as folls:
Work 4 (6: 6: 8: 8) rows.
Dec 1 st at end of next and every foll 6th row until 40 (43: 46: 49: 52) sts rem.
Complete to match left front, reversing shapings.

SLEEVES (both alike)
Cast on 41 (41: 43: 45: 45) sts using 3¼mm (US 3) needles and yarn A.
Row 1 (RS): P1 (1: 0: 1: 1), ★K1, P1, rep from ★ to last 0 (0: 1: 0: 0) st, K0 (0: 1: 0: 0).
Row 2: As row 1.
These 2 rows form moss st. Work in moss st for a further 4 rows, ending with a WS row.
Change to 4mm (US 6) needles.
Cont in patt foll chart as folls:
Work 4 rows. Inc 1 st at each end of next and every foll 8th row until there are 49 (59: 57: 59: 69) sts, then on every foll 10th row until there are 67 (69: 71: 73: 75) sts, taking inc sts into patt.
Cont straight until sleeve measures 42 (42: 43: 43: 43) cm, ending with a WS row.
Shape top
Keeping chart correct, cast off 3 (4: 5: 6: 7) sts at beg of next 2 rows. 61 sts.
Dec 1 st at each end of next 3 rows, then on foll 3 (3: 3: 3: 2) alt rows, then on every foll 4th row until 35 (35: 33: 33: 33) sts rem.
Work 1 row, ending with a WS row.
Dec 1 st at each end of next and foll 1 (1: 0: 0: 0) alt rows, then on foll 3 rows, ending with a WS row.
25 sts.
Cast off 4 sts at beg of next 2 rows.
Cast off rem 17 sts.

MAKING UP
PRESS all pieces as described on the information page.
Join both shoulder seams using back stitch, or mattress stitch if preferred.
Button band
Slip 6 sts left on holder for button band onto 3¼mm (US 3) needles and rejoin yarn A with RS facing.
Cont in moss st as set until band, when slightly stretched, fits up left front to neck shaping, ending with a WS row.
Cast off.
Slip stitch band in place.
Mark positions for 7 buttons on this band – lowest button 10cm up from cast-on edge, top button 1.2cm below neck shaping and rem 5 buttons evenly spaced between.

Buttonhole band

Work as given for button band, rejoining yarn A with WS facing and with the addition of 7 buttonholes to correspond with positions marked for buttons worked as folls:

Buttonhole row (RS): K1, P1, yrn, P2tog, K1, P1. Slip stitch band in place.

Collar

Cast on 81 (85: 85: 93: 93) sts using 3¼mm (US 3) needles and yarn A.

Row 1 (RS): K1, *P1, K1, rep from * to end.
Row 2: As row 1.
These 2 rows form moss st.
Cont in moss st until collar measures 10 cm, ending with a WS row.
Cast off in moss st.
Sew cast-on edge of collar to neck edge, positioning ends of collar halfway across top of bands.
See information page for finishing instructions, setting in sleeves using the set-in method.

54 (55: 56: 57: 58) cm
(21.5 (21.5: 22: 22.5: 23) in)

44.5 (47: 50: 53: 55.5) cm
(17.5 (18.5: 19.5: 21: 22) in)

42 (42: 42: 43: 43) cm
(16.5 (16.5: 17: 17: 17) in)

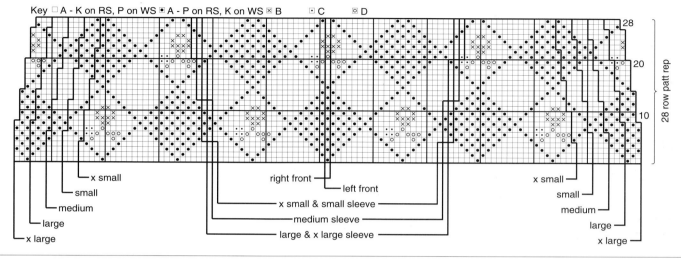

Key □ A - K on RS, P on WS ● A - P on RS, K on WS ⊠ B ⊡ C ◉ D

28
20
10

28 row patt rep

x small
small
medium
large
x large

right front — left front
x small & small sleeve
medium sleeve
large & x large sleeve

x small
small
medium
large
x large

Design number 29

Swank

KIM HARGREAVES

YARN

Rowan All Seasons Cotton

	XS	S	M	L	XL	
To fit bust	81	86	91	97	102	cm
	32	34	36	38	40	in
Hooded coat	17	18	19	19	20	x 50gm
Collared coat	16	16	17	18	19	x 50gm

(straight hooded coat photographed in Jaunty 183, fitted collared coat in Mellow 190)

NEEDLES

1 pair 4½mm (no 7) (US 7) needles
1 pair 5mm (no 6) (US 8) needles

TENSION

17 sts and 24 rows to 10 cm measured over stocking stitch using 5mm (US 8) needles.

Pattern note: As row end edges of fronts form actual finished edges of garment, it is important these edges are kept neat. Therefore all new balls of yarn should be joined in at side seam or armhole edges of rows.

BACK

Cast on 95 (99: 103: 107: 111) sts using 4½mm (US 7) needles.
Row 1 (RS): P1, *K1, P1, rep from * to end.
Row 2: As row 1.
These 2 rows form moss st.
Work a further 8 rows in moss st.
Change to 5mm (US 8) needles.
Next row (RS): (P1, K1) 3 times, P to last 6 sts, (K1, P1) 3 times.

Next row: (P1, K1) 3 times, K to last 6 sts, (K1, P1) 3 times.
These 2 rows set the sts – first and last 6 sts worked in moss st with all other sts worked in rev st st.
Keeping sts correct as set, cont as folls:
Work a further 20 rows.
Next row (RS): (P1, K1) twice, P to last 4 sts, (K1, P1) twice.
Next row: (P1, K1) twice, K to last 4 sts, (K1, P1) twice.
Next row: P1, K1, P to last 2 sts, K1, P1.
Next row: P1, K to last st, P1.
Beg with a P row, cont in rev st st as folls:
Fitted version only
Work 2 rows.
Dec 1 st at each end of next and every foll 6th row until 81 (85: 89: 93: 97) sts rem.
Work 9 rows.

Inc 1 st at each end of next and every foll 4th row until there are 95 (99: 103: 107: 111) sts.
Both versions
Cont straight until back measures 49 cm, ending with a WS row.
Shape raglan armholes
Cast off 5 sts at beg of next 2 rows.
85 (89: 93: 97: 101) sts.
Next row (RS): K1, (K1, P1) 3 times, P2tog, P to last 9 sts, P2tog tbl, (P1, K1) 3 times, K1.
Next row: K1, (P1, K1) 3 times, K2tog tbl, K to last 9 sts, K2tog, (K1, P1) 3 times, K1.
Rep last 2 rows 1 (1: 2: 2: 3) times more.
77 (81: 81: 85: 85) sts.
Next row (RS): K1, (K1, P1) 3 times, P2tog, P to last 9 sts, P2tog tbl, (P1, K1) 3 times, K1.
Next row: K1, (P1, K1) 3 times, K to last 7 sts, (K1, P1) 3 times, K1.

Rep last 2 rows 25 (26: 26: 27: 27) times more.
Cast off rem 25 (27: 27: 29: 29) sts.

LEFT FRONT

Cast on 56 (58: 60: 62: 64) sts using 4½mm (US 7) needles.
Row 1 (RS): *P1, K1, rep from * to last 8 sts, (K1, P1) 3 times, K2.
Row 2: *K1, P1, rep from * to end.
These 2 rows set the sts – front opening edge 8 sts in rib with all other sts in moss st.
Work a further 8 rows as set.
Change to 5mm (US 8) needles.
Next row (RS): (P1, K1) 3 times, P to last 8 sts, (K1, P1) 3 times, K2.
Next row: (K1, P1) 4 times, K to last 6 sts, (K1, P1) 3 times.
Keeping sts correct as set, cont as folls:
Work a further 20 rows.
Next row (RS): (P1, K1) twice, P to last 8 sts, (K1, P1) 3 times, K2.
Next row: (K1, P1) 4 times, K to last 4 sts, (K1, P1) twice.
Next row: P1, K1, P to last 8 sts, (K1, P1) 3 times, K2.
Next row: (K1, P1) 4 times, K to last st, P1.
Next row: P to last 8 sts, (K1, P1) 3 times, K2.
Next row: (K1, P1) 4 times, K to end.
Last 2 rows set the sts – front opening edge still worked in rib with all other sts now worked in rev st st.
Keeping sts correct as set, cont as folls:
Fitted version only
Dec 1 st at beg of next and every foll 6th row until 49 (51: 53: 55: 57) sts rem.
Work 9 rows.
Inc 1 st at beg of next and every foll 4th row until there are 56 (58: 60: 62: 64) sts.
Both versions
Cont straight until left front matches back to beg of raglan armhole shaping, ending with a WS row.
Shape raglan armhole
Cast off 5 sts at beg of next row.
51 (53: 55: 57: 59) sts.
Work 1 row.
Next row (RS): K1, (K1, P1) 3 times, P2tog, patt to end.
Next row: Patt to last 9 sts, K2tog, (K1, P1) 3 times, K1.
Rep last 2 rows 1 (1: 2: 2: 3) times more.
47 (49: 49: 51: 51) sts.
Next row (RS): K1, (K1, P1) 3 times, P2tog, patt to end.
Next row: Patt to last 7 sts, (K1, P1) 3 times, K1.
Rep last 2 rows 22 (23: 23: 24: 24) times more.
Leave rem 24 (25: 25: 26: 26) sts on a holder.

RIGHT FRONT

Cast on 56 (58: 60: 62: 64) sts using 4½mm (US 7) needles.
Row 1 (RS): K2, (P1, K1) 3 times, *K1, P1, rep from * to end.
Row 2: *P1, K1, rep from * to end.
These 2 rows set the sts – front opening edge 8 sts in rib with all other sts in moss st.
Work a further 8 rows as set.
Change to 5mm (US 8) needles.
Next row (RS): K2, (P1, K1) 3 times, P to last 6 sts, (K1, P1) 3 times.
Next row: (P1, K1) 3 times, K to last 8 sts, (P1, K1) 4 times.
Keeping sts correct as set, cont as folls:
Work a further 20 rows.
Next row (RS): K2, (P1, K1) 3 times, P to last 4 sts, (K1, P1) twice.
Next row: (P1, K1) twice, K to last 8 sts, (P1, K1) 4 times.
Next row: K2, (P1, K1) 3 times, P to last 2 sts, K1, P1.
Next row: P1, K to last 8 sts, (P1, K1) 4 times.

Next row: K2, (P1, K1) 3 times, P to end.
Next row: K to last 8 sts, (P1, K1) 4 times.
Last 2 rows set the sts – front opening edge still worked in rib with all other sts now worked in rev st st.
Keeping sts correct as set, complete to match left front, reversing all shaping.
Do NOT break off yarn but set aside this ball – it will be used later.

SLEEVES

Cast on 59 (59: 61: 63: 63) sts using 4½mm (US 7) needles.
Work in moss st as given for back for 10 rows.
Change to 5mm (US 8) needles.
Beg with a P row, cont in rev st st as folls:
Work 2 rows.
Inc 1 st at each end of next and every foll 8th row until there are 79 (73: 77: 79: 73) sts, then on every foll 6th row until there are 83 (85: 87: 89: 91) sts.
Cont straight until sleeve measures 43 (43: 44: 44: 44) cm, ending with a WS row.
Shape raglan
Cast off 5 sts at beg of next 2 rows.
73 (75: 77: 79: 81) sts.
Next row (RS): K1, (K1, P1) 3 times, P2tog, P to last 9 sts, P2tog tbl, (P1, K1) 3 times, K1.
Next row: K1, (P1, K1) 3 times, K2tog tbl, K to last 9 sts, K2tog, (K1, P1) 3 times, K1.
Rep last 2 rows once more. 65 (67: 69: 71: 73) sts.
Next row (RS): K1, (K1, P1) 3 times, P2tog, P to last 9 sts, P2tog tbl, (P1, K1) 3 times, K1.
Next row: K1, (P1, K1) 3 times, K to last 7 sts, (K1, P1) 3 times, K1.
Rep last 2 rows 22 (23: 24: 25: 26) times more.
19 sts.
Left sleeve only
Next row (RS): K1, (K1, P1) 3 times, P2tog, P1, P2tog tbl, (P1, K1) 3 times, K1.
Next row: Cast off 3 sts, patt to end. 14 sts.
Next row: K1, (K1, P1) 3 times, P2tog, patt to end.
Next row: Cast off 4 sts, patt to end. 9 sts.
Next row: K1, (K1, P1) 3 times, P2tog.
Next row: Cast off 4 sts, patt to end. 4 sts.
Right sleeve only
Next row (RS): Cast off 4 sts, patt to last 9 sts, P2tog tbl, (P1, K1) 3 times, K1.
Next row: Patt to end. 14 sts.
Next row: Cast off 4 sts (one st on right needle), P2tog tbl, (P1, K1) 3 times, K1.
Next row: Patt to end. 9 sts.
Next row: Cast off 5 sts, patt to end.
Next row: Patt to end. 4 sts.
Both sleeves
Cast off rem 4 sts.

MAKING UP

PRESS all pieces as described on the information page.
Join raglan seams using back stitch, or mattress stitch if preferred.

Hooded coat
Hood
With RS facing, 5mm (US 8) needles and ball of yarn left at top of right front, patt across 24 (25: 25: 26: 26) sts of right front, pick up and knit 16 sts from right sleeve, 25 (27: 27: 29: 29) sts from back (place marker on centre st), and 16 sts from left sleeve, then patt across 24 (25: 25: 26: 26) sts of left front. 105 (109: 109: 113: 113) sts.
Keeping front opening edge 8 sts in rib as set and working all other sts in rev st st, cont as folls:
Work 1 row.
Next row (RS): Patt to marked centre st, M1 purlwise, P marked st, M1 purlwise, patt to end.
Work 3 rows.
Rep last 4 rows 4 times more and then first of these rows (the inc row) again. 117 (121: 121: 125: 125) sts.

Cont straight until hood measures 30 cm from pick-up row, ending with a WS row.
Shape top
Row 1 (RS): Patt to within 2 sts of marked st, P2tog, P marked st, P2tog tbl, patt to end.
Work 3 rows.
Row 5: As row 1.
Work 1 row.
Row 7: Patt to within 2 sts of marked st, P2tog, P marked st, P2tog tbl, patt to end.
Row 8: Patt to within 2 sts of marked st, K2tog tbl, K marked st, K2tog, patt to end.
Rows 9 to 12: As rows 7 and 8, twice.
Row 13: As row 7.
Work 1 row, dec 1 st at centre.
98 (102: 102: 106: 106) sts.
Row 15: Patt 49 (51: 51: 53: 53) sts and turn.
Fold work in half with WS tog and, using a spare needle, cast off sts from both needles tog to form hood seam.

Collared coat
Collar
With RS facing, 4½mm (US 7) needles and ball of yarn left at top of right front, patt across 24 (25: 25: 26: 26) sts of right front dec 1 (0: 0: 1: 1) st at centre, pick up and knit 16 sts from right sleeve, 25 (27: 27: 29: 29) sts from back, and 16 sts from left sleeve, then patt across 24 (25: 25: 26: 26) sts of left front dec 1 (0: 0: 1: 1) st at centre. 103 (109: 109: 111: 111) sts.
Working all sts in rib as set by front opening edge sts, cont in rib for 11 cm.
Cast off in rib.

Both coats
Tie belt (optional)
Cast on 9 sts using 4½mm (US 7) needles.
Row 1 (RS): K2, (P1, K1) 3 times, K1.
Row 2: (K1, P1) 4 times, K1.
Rep these 2 rows until belt measures 140 cm.
Cast off.
See information page for finishing instructions, leaving side seams open for first 30 rows.

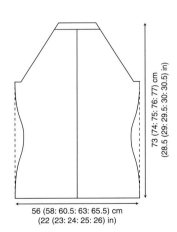

56 (58: 60.5: 63: 65.5) cm
(22 (23: 24: 25: 26) in)

73 (74: 75: 76: 77) cm
(28.5 (29: 29.5: 30: 30.5) in)

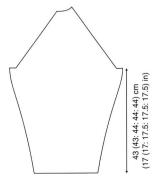

43 (43: 44: 44: 44) cm
(17 (17: 17.5: 17.5: 17.5) in)

Design number 30

Navigator

KIM HARGREAVES

YARN
Rowan All Seasons Cotton

childrens	4-6	6-8	8-10		years
Striped sweater					
A Midnight 188	7	8	9	x	50gm
B Bleached 182	2	2	2	x	50gm
Plain sweater	8	8	9	x	50gm

(photographed in Iceberg 192)

	ladies			mens		
	S	M	L	S	M	L
To fit bust/chest	86	91	97	102	107	112cm
	34	36	38	40	42	44 in
Striped sweater						
A Midnight188	10	11	11	13	13	14 x 50gm
B Bleached 182	3	3	3	3	4	4 x 50gm
Plain sweater	11	12	13	14	15	16 x 50gm

(photographed in Jazz 185)

NEEDLES
1 pair 4½mm (no 7) (US 7) needles
1 pair 5mm (no 6) (US 8) needles

TENSION
17 sts and 24 rows to 10 cm measured over stocking stitch using 5mm (US 8) needles.

Pattern note: The pattern is written for the 3 childrens sizes, followed by the 3 ladies sizes in **bold**, followed by the mens sizes.

SPECIAL ABBREVIATIONS
Right dec = sl 1, K1, psso, slip st now on right needle back onto left needle, lift 2nd st on left needle over this st and then slip this st back onto right needle
Left dec = sl 1, K2tog, psso

Striped sweater
BACK
Cast on 78 (82: 88: **96: 100: 104:** 108: 112: 116) sts using 4½mm (US 7) needles and yarn A.
Beg with a K row, work in st st as folls:
Work 10 rows.
Change to 5mm (US 8) needles and cont in striped st st patt as folls:
Work 2 rows using yarn B.
Work 8 rows using yarn A.
These 10 rows form striped st st patt.
Cont straight until back measures 23 (24: 25: **30:** 36: 37: 38) cm, ending with a WS row.
Shape armholes
Cast off 3 (4: **4:** 4) sts at beg of next 2 rows.
72 (76: 82: **88: 92: 96:** 100: 104: 108) sts.
Next row (RS): K2, right dec, K to last 5 sts, left dec, K2. 68 (72: 78: **84: 88: 92:** 96: 100: 104) sts.
Working all decreases as set by last row, cont as folls:
Work 1 row.
Dec 2 sts at each end of next and foll 0 (**1:** 1) alt row. 64 (68: 74: **76: 80: 84:** 88: 92: 96) sts.
Cont straight until armhole measures approx 11 (**13:** 13) cm, ending after 2 rows using yarn B.
Break off yarn B and cont using yarn A only.
Cont straight until armhole measures 20 (21: 22: **23: 24: 25:** 24: 25: 26) cm, ending with a WS row.
Shape shoulders and back neck
Cast off 6 (7: 7: **5: 5: 6:** 8: 9: 9) sts at beg of next 2 rows. 52 (54: 60: **66: 70: 72:** 72: 74: 78) sts.
Next row (RS): Cast off 6 (7: 7: **5: 5: 6:** 8: 9: 9) sts, K until there are 11 (10: 12: **8: 10: 9:** 13: 13: 14) sts on right needle and turn, leaving rem sts on a holder.
Work each side of neck separately.
Cast off 4 sts at beg of next row.
Cast off rem 7 (6: 8: **4: 6: 5:** 9: 9: 10) sts.
With RS facing, slip centre 18 (20: 22: **40: 40: 42:** 30: 30: 32) sts onto a holder, rejoin yarn to rem sts, K to end.
Work to match first side, reversing shapings.

FRONT
Work as given for back until 12 (**4:** 14) rows less have been worked than on back to start of shoulder shaping, ending with a WS row.
Shape neck
Next row (RS): K25 (26: 28: **18: 20: 21:** 33: 35: 36) and turn, leaving rem sts on a holder.
Work each side of neck separately.
Work 1 row.
Working all neck decreases in same way as armhole decreases (by working "left dec" or "right dec" 2 sts in from beg or end of row), dec 2 sts at neck edge of next and foll 2 (**0:** 2) alt rows.
19 (20: 22: **16: 18: 19:** 27: 29: 30) sts.
Mens sizes only
Dec 2 sts at neck edge of foll 4th row.
- (-: 25: 27: 28) sts.
All sizes
Work 5 (**1:** 3) rows.
Shape shoulder
Cast off 6 (7: 7: **5: 5: 6:** 8: 9: 9) sts at beg and dec 0 (**2:** 0) sts at end of next row.
Work 1 row.

Cast off 6 (7: 7: **5: 5: 6:** 8: 9: 9) sts at beg of next row.
Work 1 row.
Cast off rem 7 (6: 8: **4: 6: 5:** 9: 9: 10) sts.
With RS facing, slip centre 14 (16: 18: **40: 40: 42:** 22: 22: 24) sts onto a holder, rejoin yarn to rem sts, K to end.
Work to match first side, reversing shapings.

SLEEVES (both alike)
Cast on 38 (39: 40: **43: 45: 47:** 51: 53: 55) sts using 4½mm (US 7) needles and yarn A.
Beg with a K row, work in st st as folls:
Work 8 (**10:** 10) rows.
Change to 5mm (US 8) needles and, beg with 2 rows using yarn B, cont in striped st st patt as given for back as folls:
Work 0 (**0:** 2) rows.
Next row (RS): K3, M1, K to last 3 sts, M1, K3.
Working all increases as set by last row, cont as folls:
Inc 1 st at each end of every foll 6th (**6th:** 8th) row until there are 60 (59: 58: **67: 71: 77:** 61: 61: 59) sts, then on every foll 4th (**4th:** 6th) row until there are 68 (71: 74: **79: 81: 81:** 81: 85: 89) sts.
Cont straight until sleeve measures 40 (41: 42: **43: 44: 44:** 47: 48: 49) cm, ending with a WS row.
Shape top
Cast off 3 (**4:** 4) sts at beg of next 2 rows.
62 (65: 68: **71: 73: 73:** 73: 77: 81) sts.
Childrens sizes only
Working all decreases in same way as armhole decreases, dec 2 sts at each end of next and foll 2 alt rows. 50 (53: 56: **-:** -) sts.
Ladies and mens sizes only
Work 2 rows.
Working all decreases in same way as armhole decreases, dec 2 sts at each end of next and foll 4th row. – (**63: 65: 65:** 65: 69: 73) sts.
All sizes
Work 1 (**3:** 3) rows.
Cast off rem 50 (53: 56: **63: 65: 65:** 65: 69: 73) sts.

Plain sweater
Work as given for striped sweater but using same colour throughout.

MAKING UP
PRESS all pieces as described on the info page.
Join right shoulder seam using back stitch, or mattress stitch if preferred.
Neckband
With RS facing, using 4½mm (US 7) needles and yarn A, pick up and knit 12 (**8:** 18) sts down left side of neck, 14 (16: 18: **40: 40: 42:** 22: 22: 24) sts from front, 12 (**8:** 18) sts up right side of neck, and 26 (28: 30: **48: 48: 50:** 38: 38: 40) sts from back.
64 (68: 72: **104: 104: 108:** 96: 96: 100) sts.
Beg with a P row, work in st st for 8 (**6:** 24) rows.
Cast off.
See information page for finishing instructions, setting in sleeves using the shallow set-in method.

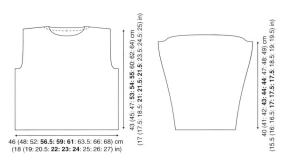

46 (48: 52: **56.5: 59: 61:** 63.5: 66: 68) cm
(18 (19: 20.5: **22: 23: 24:** 25: 26: 27) in)

43 (45: 47: **53: 54: 55:** 60: 62: 64) cm
(17 (17.5: 18.5: **21: 21.5: 21.5:** 23.5: 24.5: 25) in)

40 (41: 42: **43: 44: 44:** 47: 48: 49) cm
(15.5 (16: 16.5: **17: 17.5: 17.5:** 18.5: 19: 19.5) in)

113

Design number 31

Aerial

KIM HARGREAVES

YARN

Rowan 4 ply Cotton

	XS	S	M	L	XL
To fit bust	81	86	91	97	102 cm
	32	34	36	38	40 in
	3	3	3	4	4 x 50gm

(photographed in Allure 119 and Pool 124)

NEEDLES

1 pair 3mm (no 11) (US 2/3) needles
Cable needle
2 double-pointed 2¼mm (UK 13) (US 1) needles

ELASTIC – length of 6 mm ¼ in) elastic to fit snugly above bust

RIBBON – 2 m (for optional shoulder ties)

TENSION

28 sts and 38 rows to 10 cm measured over stocking stitch using 3mm (US 2/3) needles.

SPECIAL ABBREVIATIONS

C2F = Cable 2 front Slip next st onto cn and leave at front of work, K1, then K1 from cn.
C4F = Cable 4 front Slip next 2 sts onto cn and leave at front of work, K2, then K2 from cn.
C4B = Cable 4 back Slip next 2 sts onto cn and leave at back of work, K2, then K2 from cn.
C6F = Cable 6 front Slip next 3 sts onto cn and leave at front of work, K3, then K3 from cn.
C6B = Cable 6 back Slip next 3 sts onto cn and leave at back of work, K3, then K3 from cn.
Cr3R = Cross 3 right Slip next st onto cn and leave at back of work, K2, then P1 from cn.
Cr3L = Cross 3 left Slip next 2 sts onto cn and leave at front of work, P1, then K2 from cn.
Cr2R = Cross 2 right Slip next st onto cn and leave at back of work, K1, then P1 from cn.
Cr2L = Cross 2 left Slip next st onto cn and leave at front of work, P1, then K1 from cn.

FRONT

Cast on 90 (98: 104: 112: 118) sts using 3mm (US 2/3) needles.
Row 1 (WS): K8 (12: 15: 19: 22), inc once in each of next 2 sts, K8, inc once in each of next 3 sts, K8, inc once in each of next 2 sts, K7, inc once in each of next 2 sts, K10, inc once in each of next 2 sts, K7, inc once in each of next 2 sts, K8, inc once in each of next 3 sts, K8, inc once in each of next 2 sts, K8 (12: 15: 19: 22).
108 (116: 122: 130: 136) sts.
Place chart as folls:
Next row (RS): K0 (0: 1: 1: 0), (P1, K1) 3 (5: 6: 8: 10) times, work next 96 sts as row 1 of chart, (K1, P1) 3 (5: 6: 8: 10) times, K0 (0: 1: 1: 0).
Next row: K0 (0: 1: 1: 0), (P1, K1) 3 (5: 6: 8: 10) times, work next 96 sts as row 2 of chart, (K1, P1) 3 (5: 6: 8: 10) times, K0 (0: 1: 1: 0).
These 2 rows set the sts – edge 6 (10: 13: 17: 20) sts in moss st with centre sts worked foll chart.
Keeping sts correct as set and repeating the 24 row patt rep throughout, cont as folls:
Work a further 10 (12: 14: 16: 18) rows.
Inc 1 st at each end of next and every foll 14th row until there are 116 (124: 130: 138: 144) sts, taking inc sts into moss st. Work 3 rows.
Shape bust darts
Place markers either side of centre 96 sts of chart.
Next row (RS): Moss st to marker, M1, slip marker to right needle, patt 96 sts, slip marker to right needle, M1, moss st to end. Work 3 rows.
Rep from ** to ** once more and then first of these rows (the inc row) again.
122 (130: 136: 144: 150) sts.
Work 1 row.
Inc 1 st at each end of next row.
124 (132: 138: 146: 152) sts.
Work 1 row.
Rep from ** to ** once more and then first of these rows (the inc row) again. 128 (136: 142: 150: 156) sts.
Work 13 (13: 15: 17: 19) rows.
Next row (RS): Moss st to within 2 sts of marker, work 2 tog, slip marker to right needle, patt 96 sts, slip marker to right needle, work 2 tog, moss st to end. Work 3 rows.
Next row (RS): Moss st to within 2 sts of marker, work 2 tog, slip marker to right needle, patt 96 sts, slip marker to right needle, work 2 tog, moss st to end. 124 (132: 138: 146: 152) sts.
Work 2 rows.
Next row (WS): Moss st to marker, K2, (P2tog) twice, patt 8 sts, (P2tog) 3 times, patt 8 sts, (P2tog) twice, patt 7 (7: 5: 3: 2) sts, P2tog, patt 0 (0: 4: 8: 10) sts,

P2tog, patt 10 (10: 6: 2: 0) sts, P2tog, patt 0 (0: 4: 8: 10) sts, P2tog, patt 7 (7: 5: 3: 2) sts, (P2tog) twice, patt 8 sts, (P2tog) 3 times, patt 8 sts, (P2tog) twice, K2, moss st to end.
Cast off rem 106 (114: 120: 128: 134) sts knitwise.

Pattern note: As row end edges of backs form actual finished edges of garment, it is important these edges are kept neat. Therefore all new balls of yarn should be joined in at side seam edges of rows.

RIGHT BACK

Cast on 45 (49: 52: 56: 59) sts using 3mm (US 2/3) needles.
Row 1 (WS): K16, inc once in each of next 2 sts, K8, inc once in each of next 3 sts, K8, inc once in each of next 2 sts, K6 (10: 13: 17: 20).
52 (56: 59: 63: 66) sts.
Starting and ending at positions indicated on chart, place side section of chart as folls:
Next row (RS): K0 (0: 1: 1: 0), (P1, K1) 2 (4: 5: 7: 9) times, work next 34 sts as row 1 of chart, (K1, P1) 7 times.
Next row: (P1, K1) 7 times, work next 34 sts as row 2 of chart for back, (K1, P1) 2 (4: 5: 7: 9) times, K0 (0: 1: 1: 0).
These 2 rows set the sts – side edge 4 (8: 11: 15: 18) sts and centre back 14 sts in moss st with sts between worked foll chart.
Keeping sts correct as set and repeating the 24 row patt rep throughout, cont as folls:
Work a further 0 (2: 0: 4: 4) rows.
Next row (eyelet row) (RS): Patt to last 5 sts, yfwd, K2tog, moss st 3.
Repeating this eyelet row every foll 10th (10th: 12th: 12th: 10th) row, cont as folls:
Work 9 (9: 13: 11: 13) rows.
Inc 1 st at beg (side seam edge) of next and every foll 14th row until there are 57 (61: 64: 68: 71) sts, taking inc sts into moss st.
Work 26 (26: 28: 30: 32) rows, ending with a RS row.
Next row (WS): Patt 16 sts, (P2tog) twice, patt 8 sts, (P2tog) 3 times, patt 8 sts, (P2tog) twice, patt to end.
Cast off rem 50 (54: 57: 61: 64) sts knitwise.

LEFT BACK

Cast on 45 (49: 52: 56: 59) sts using 3mm (US 2/3) needles.
Row 1 (WS): K6 (10: 13: 17: 20), inc once in each of next 2 sts, K8, inc once in each of next 3 sts, K8, inc once in each of next 2 sts, K16.
52 (56: 59: 63: 66) sts.

Key

☐ K on RS, P on WS	◺ C2F
	◹ C4B
▣ P on RS, K on WS	◸ C4F
	C6B
⊠ Cr2R	C6F
⊠ Cr2L	⊠ Cr3R
⊡ P1tbl	⊠ Cr3L

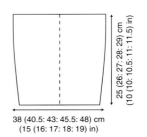

25 (26: 27: 28: 29) cm
(10: 10: 10.5: 11: 11.5) in)

38 (40.5: 43: 45.5: 48) cm
(15 (16: 17: 18: 19) in)

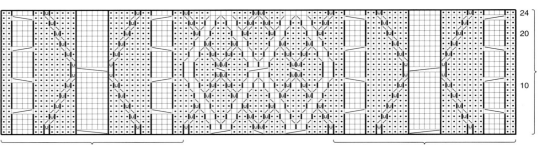

Left Back   Right Back

Starting and ending at positions indicated on chart, place side section of chart as folls:

Next row (RS): (P1, K1) 7 times, work next 34 sts as row 1 of chart, (K1, P1) 2 (4: 5: 7: 9) times, K0 (0: 1: 1: 0).

Next row: K0 (0: 1: 1: 0), (P1, K1) 2 (4: 5: 7: 9) times, work next 34 sts as row 2 of chart, (K1, P1) 7 times.

These 2 rows set the sts – side edge 4 (8: 11: 15: 18) sts and centre back 14 sts in moss st with sts between worked foll chart.

Keeping sts correct as set and repeating the 24 row patt rep throughout, cont as folls:

Work a further 0 (2: 0: 4: 4) rows.

Next row (eyelet row) (RS): Moss st 3, K2tog, yfwd, patt to end.

Repeating this eyelet row every foll 10th (10th: 12th: 12th: 10th) row, cont as folls:

Work 9 (9: 13: 11: 13) rows.

Inc 1 st at end (side seam edge) of next and every foll 14th row until there are 57 (61: 64: 68: 71) sts, taking inc sts into moss st.

Work 26 (26: 28: 30: 32) rows, ending with a RS row.

Next row (WS): Patt 11 (15: 18: 22: 25) sts, (P2tog) twice, patt 8 sts, (P2tog) 3 times, patt 8 sts, (P2tog) twice, patt to end.

Cast off rem 50 (54: 57: 61: 64) sts knitwise.

MAKING UP

PRESS all pieces as described on the information page.

Join side seams using back stitch, or mattress stitch if preferred.

Work a herringbone stitch casing along inside of upper (cast-off) edge and thread elastic through this casing. Adjust elastic so it is a snug fit and sew ends securely in place.

Back tie

Using double pointed 2¼mm (US 1) needles, cast on 3 sts.

Next row (RS): K3 – all 3 sts now on right needle, *slip sts to opposite end of needle and transfer this needle to left hand, without turning work and taking yarn quite tightly across back of work, K same 3 sts again – all 3 sts now on right needle again, rep from * until tie is 100 cm long.

Next row: K3tog and fasten off.

With centre of each tie at upper edge, thread tie in and out of eyelet holes along centre back, knotting ends at lower edge.

Shoulder ties (optional)

Cut ribbon into 4 equal lengths and neatly sew to upper edge to form shoulder ties. Tie ribbons on shoulders.

Spruce

KIM HARGREAVES

YARN

	XS-S	M	L-XL	
To fit bust	81-86	91	97-102	cm
	32-34	36	38-40	in

Rowan Linen Drape

	13	15	16	x	50gm

(photographed in Petal 842 and Watery 844)

NEEDLES

1 pair 3mm (no 11) (US 2/3) needles
1 pair 3¼mm (no 10) (US 3) needles
1 pair 3¾mm (no 9) (US 5) needles
Cable needle

TENSION

23 sts and 30 rows to 10 cm measured over stocking stitch using 3¾mm (US 5) needles.

SPECIAL ABBREVIATIONS

C4F = Cable 4 front Slip next 2 sts onto cn and leave at front of work, K2, then K2 from cn.
C4B = Cable 4 back Slip next 2 sts onto cn and leave at back of work, K2, then K2 from cn.

BACK

Using 3mm (US 2/3) needles, cast on 137 (147: 157) sts.

Row 1 (RS): (P1, K1) 12 (13: 14) times, *P2, K4, P2, (K1, P1) 9 (10: 11) times, K1, rep from * twice more, P2, K4, P2, (K1, P1) 12 (13: 14) times.

Row 2: (P1, K1) 12 (13: 14) times, *K2, P4, K2, (K1, P1) 9 (10: 11) times, K1, rep from * twice more, K2, P4, K2, (K1, P1) 12 (13: 14) times.

Rep last 2 rows 3 times more.

Change to 3¼mm (US 3) needles.

Now place star chart as folls:

Row 9 (RS): (P1, K1) twice, P1, *work next 19 (21: 23) sts as row 1 of star chart, P2, K4, P2, rep from * 3 times more, work next 19 (21: 23) sts as row 1 of star chart, P1, (K1, P1) twice.

Row 10: (P1, K1) twice, P1, *work next 19 (21: 23) sts as row 2 of star chart, K2, P4, K2, rep from * 3 times more, work next 19 (21: 23) sts as row 2 of star chart, P1, (K1, P1) twice.

These 2 rows set the sts.

Cont as set until all 33 rows of star chart have been completed, ending with a RS row.

Row 42 (WS): As row 2.

Rows 43 to 48: As rows 1 and 2, 3 times.

Change to 3¾mm (US 5) needles and work in cable patt as folls:

Row 1 (RS): K24 (26: 28), *P2, C4B, P2, K19 (21: 23), rep from * once more, P2, C4F, P2, K19 (21: 23), P2, C4F, P2, K24 (26: 28).

Row 2 and every foll alt row: P24 (26: 28), *K2, P4, K2, P19 (21: 23), rep from * twice more, K2, P4, K2, P24 (26: 28).

Row 3: K24 (26: 28), *P2, K4, P2, K19 (21: 23), rep from * twice more, P2, K4, P2, K24 (26: 28).

Row 5: As row 3.

Row 7: K24 (26: 28), *P2, C4F, P2, K19 (21: 23), rep from * once more, P2, C4B, P2, K19 (21: 23), P2, C4B, P2, K24 (26: 28).

Rows 9 and 11: As row 3.

Row 12: As row 2.

These 12 rows form cable patt.

Cont in cable patt until back measures 30 (31: 32) cm, ending with a WS row.

Shape armholes

Keeping patt correct, cast off 4 sts at beg of next 2 rows. 129 (139: 149) sts.

Dec 1 st at each end of next 8 (10: 12) rows. 113 (119: 125) sts.

Cont straight until armhole measures 23 (24: 25) cm, ending with a WS row.

Shape shoulders and back neck

Keeping patt correct, cast off 9 (9: 10) sts at beg of next 2 rows. 95 (101: 105) sts.

Next row (RS): Cast off 9 (9: 10) sts, patt until there are 12 (14: 14) sts on right needle and turn, leaving rem sts on a holder.

Work each side of neck separately.

Cast off 4 sts at beg of next row.

Cast off rem 8 (10: 10) sts.

With RS facing, rejoin yarn to rem sts, cast off centre 53 (55: 57) sts, patt to end.

Work to match first side, reversing shapings.

FRONT

Work as given for back until 12 rows less have been worked than on back to start of shoulder shaping, ending with a WS row.

Shape neck

Next row (RS): Patt 36 (38: 40) sts and turn, leaving rem sts on a holder.

Work each side of neck separately.

Cast off 4 sts at beg of next row. 32 (34: 36) sts.

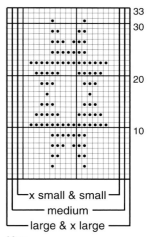

x small & small
medium
large & x large

Key
□ K on RS, P on WS
▣ P on RS, K on WS

Dec 1 st at neck edge of next 3 rows, then on foll 3 alt rows. 26 (28: 30) sts.
Work 1 row, ending with a WS row.

Shape shoulder
Keeping patt correct, cast off 9 (9: 10) sts at beg of next and foll alt row.
Work 1 row.
Cast off rem 8 (10: 10) sts.
With RS facing, rejoin yarn to rem sts, cast off centre 41 (43: 45) sts, patt to end.
Work to match first side, reversing shapings.

SLEEVES
Using 3mm (US 2/3) needles, cast on 73 (75: 77) sts.
Row 1 (RS): K1, (P1, K1) 9 times, P2, K4, P2, (K1, P1) 9 (10: 11) times, K1, P2, K4, P2, (K1, P1) 9 times, K1.
Row 2: K1, (P1, K1) 9 times, K2, P4, K2, (K1, P1) 9 (10: 11) times, K1, K2, P4, K2, (K1, P1) 9 times, K1.
Rep last 2 rows 7 times more, inc 1 st at each end of 11th of these rows. 75 (77: 79) sts.
Change to 3¾mm (US 5) needles and work in cable patt as folls:
Row 1 (RS): P1 (0: 0), K19 (20: 20), P2, C4B, P2, K19 (21: 23), P2, C4F, P2, K19 (20: 20), P1 (0: 0).
Row 2: K1 (0: 0), P19 (20: 20), K2, P4, K2, P19 (21: 23), K2, P4, K2, P19 (20: 20), K1 (0: 0).
These 2 rows set position of cable patt as given for back.
Cont in cable patt, inc 1 st at each end of next and every foll 6th row until there are 87 (89: 87) sts, then on every foll 4th row until there are 121 (125: 129) sts, taking inc sts into cable patt.
Cont straight until sleeve measures 45 (46: 46) cm, ending with a WS row.

Shape top
Keeping patt correct, cast off 4 sts at beg of next 2 rows. 113 (117: 121) sts.
Dec 1 st at each end of next and foll 6 (7: 8) alt rows.
Work 1 row, ending with a WS row.
Cast off rem 99 (101: 103) sts.

MAKING UP
PRESS all pieces as described on the info page.
Join right shoulder seam using back stitch, or mattress stitch if preferred.

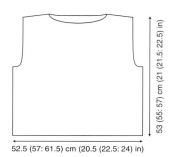

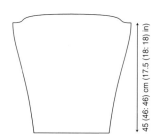

52.5 (57: 61.5) cm (20.5 (22.5: 24) in)
53 (55: 57) cm (21 (21.5: 22.5) in)
45 (46: 46) cm (17.5 (18: 18) in)

Neckband
With RS facing and using 3mm (US 2/3) needles, pick up and knit 19 sts down left side of neck, 41 (43: 45) sts from front, 19 sts up right side of neck, and 60 (62: 64) sts from back.
139 (143: 147) sts.
Row 1 (WS): K1, *P1, K1, rep from * to end.
Rep this row 5 times more. Cast off in patt.
See information page for finishing instructions, setting in sleeves using the shallow set-in method.

Design number 33

Double Seed Stitch Cushion

MARY NORDEN

YARN
Rowan Handknit DK Cotton 8 x 50gm
(photographed in Muddy 302 and Carmen 201)

NEEDLES
1 pair 4mm (no 8) (US 6) needles

TENSION
20 sts and 30 rows to 10 cm measured over double seed stitch using 4mm (US 6) needles.

FINISHED SIZE
Completed cushion is approx 45 cm (18 in) square.

CUSHION
Cast on 90 sts using 4mm (US 6) needles.
Row 1 (RS): K2, (P2, K2) to end.
Row 2: P2, (K2, P2) to end.
Row 3: As row 2.
Row 4: As row 1.
These 4 rows form double seed st.
Cont in double seed st until work measures 90 cm from cast-on edge, ending with a WS row.
Cast off.

MAKING UP
PRESS as described on the information page.
Fold knitted section in half and sew the 3 open sides closed, inserting cushion pad before closing third side.

Design number 34

Ridge & Garter Stitch Cushions

MARY NORDEN

YARN
Rowan Handknit DK Cotton
Ridge pattern cushion
8 x 50gm
Garter stitch cushion
9 x 50gm
(ridge pattern cushions photographed in Zing 300 and Gerba 223, garter stitch cushion in Foggy 301)

NEEDLES
1 pair 4mm (no 8) (US 6) needles

TENSION
20 sts and 28 rows to 10 cm measured over stocking stitch using 4mm (US 6) needles.

FINISHED SIZE
Ridge pattern cushion is approx 45 cm (18 in) square.
Garter stitch cushion is approx 50 cm (19½ in) square.

RIDGE PATTERN CUSHION
Cast on 90 sts using 4mm (US 6) needles.
Row 1 (RS): Knit.
Row 2: Purl.
Rows 3 to 6: As rows 1 and 2, twice.
Rows 7 and 8: Knit.
These 8 rows form ridge patt.
Cont in ridge patt until work measures 90 cm from cast-on edge, ending with a WS row.
Cast off.

GARTER STITCH CUSHION
Cast on 100 sts using 4mm (US 6) needles.
Work in garter st until work measures 100 cm from cast-on edge, ending with a WS row.
Cast off.

MAKING UP
PRESS as described on the information page.
Fold knitted section in half and sew the 3 open sides closed, inserting cushion pad before closing third side.

Design number 35

Sway Wrap

KIM HARGREAVES

YARN
Rowan Linen Drape
      13   x   50gm
(photographed in Petal 842)

NEEDLES
1 pair 3¾mm (no 9) (US 5) needles

BEADS
approx 112 rectangular glass beads

TENSION
23 sts and 30 rows to 10 cm measured over stocking stitch using 3¾mm (US 5) needles.

FINISHED SIZE
Completed shawl is 48 cm (19 in) x 213 cm (84 in) excluding fringe.

SHAWL
Cast on 111 sts using 3¾mm (US 5) needles.
Row 1 (RS): K1, ★P1, K1, rep from ★ to end.
Row 2: As row 1.
These 2 rows form moss st.
Work a further 4 rows in moss st.
Row 7 (RS): Moss st 5, K to last 5 sts, moss st 5.
Row 8: Moss st 5, P to last 5 sts, moss st 5.
Rep last 2 rows until work measures 211 cm, ending with a WS row.
Work 6 rows in moss st.
Cast off.

MAKING UP
PRESS as described on the information page.
Work embroidery across both ends of shawl as folls: placing beads 2 sts apart, sew a row of beads across each end, positioning beads on 3rd row of stocking stitch.
Leaving one row between beads and cross stitches, now work a line of cross stitches next to line of beads, working each cross stitch over 2 sts.
Cut 20 cm lengths of yarn and knot to cast-off and cast-on edges to form fringe.

Design number 36

Knitting Bag

JANE BUNCE

YARN
Rowan Handknit DK Cotton
      5   x   50gm
(photographed in Fruit Salad 203)

NEEDLES
1 pair 4mm (no 8) (US 6) needles

BUTTONS - 1

LINING – 0.50m of GP01-P Rowan/Kaffe Fassett "Roman Glass" fabric

TENSION
20 sts and 28 rows to 10 cm measured over stocking stitch using 4mm (US 6) needles.

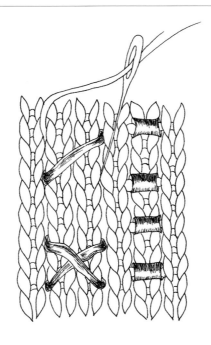

FINISHED SIZE
Completed bag is approx 35 cm (14 in) x 15 cm (6 in), with sides approx 12 cm (4½ in) deep.

BASE
Cast on 80 sts using 4mm (US 6) needles.
Row 1 (RS): (K1, P1) to end.
Row 2: (P1, K1) to end.
These 2 rows form moss st.
Work a further 52 rows in moss st.
Cast off.

SIDES (both alike)
Cast on 106 sts using 4mm (US 6) needles.
Row 1 (RS): K2, (P1, K3) to end.
Row 2: P2, (K1, P3) to end.
Rep rows 1 and 2, 10 times more.
Row 23 (RS): (P1, K1) to end.
Row 24: (K1, P1) to end.
Beg with a K row, work 12 rows in st st.
Rows 37 and 38: As rows 23 and 24.
Keeping moss st correct as set, cast off 25 sts at beg of next row. 81 sts.
Beg with a P row, cont in st st as folls:
Cast off 25 sts at beg of next row. 56 sts.
Next row (RS): K2, K2tog tbl, K to last 4 sts, K2tog, K2.
Next row: Purl.
Rep last 2 rows 22 times more. 10 sts.
Work a further 26 rows in st st.
Cast off.

MAKING UP
PRESS all pieces as described on the information page.
Lay knitted pieces onto lining fabric and cut out all shapes again from lining fabric, allowing 1 cm on all edges for seams.
Make up knitted pieces as folls: join short row end edges of sides using mattress stitch.
Positioning side seams halfway along cast-on and cast-off edges of base and with WS facing, sew cast-on edges of sides to outer edge of base using back stitch.
Join cast-off ends of sides to complete handle.
Make up lining in same way.
Fold seam allowance to inside along all outer edges, slip lining bag inside knitted bag and slip stitch edges in place.
Make button loop at top of one side seam and attach button to top of other side seam to fasten bag.

NEW GENERATION

Friendship Bracelet

1) Cut 5 lengths of coloured yarn (DK) the length of your arm to the tips of your fingers.

2) Knot them all together at one end and attach to a chair or ask a friend to hold the knot tightly.

3) Take the 1st colour on the right hand side and knot it to the 2nd colour like this:
Keep the 2nd colour tight, take the 1st colour over and under it to make a D shape, pull it up to make a knot.

4) Now take the 1st colour again and knot it to the 3rd, 4th and 5th colours in the same way.

5) You will now have a new 1st colour on the right hand side, knot it to the other 4 colours like before.

6) Repeat this until you have made a braid and there are only short lengths of wool left. Knot these ends together, trim both end neatly and tie the Friendship Bracelet round your friend's wrist.

CLEVER IDEAS

Dining chair cover

Note: add 1cm to all seams for turnings.

1) **For the front**: measure fabric to fit from the top of the front, along the seat and to the floor x the width of the chair.

2) **For the back**: cut a piece of fabric the length of the back x the width of the chair, plus enough fabric to make a large inverted pleat at the centre back (approx 80cm).

3) **For the sides**: cut 2 pieces the width and length of the sides.

4) With right sides together, machine stitch all pieces together, turn through to right side and press. Turn up hem.

5) **For the ties**: cut 2 lengths 70cm x 12cm, press 1cm all round edges to the wrong side. Fold in half length wise and machine round edges.

6) Machine stitch the ties in place at the sides of the pleat, halfway down from top edge.

Floor cushions

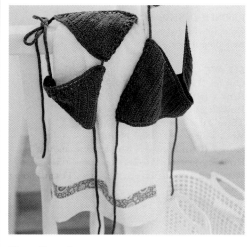

You will need:
• 80cm of fabric
• 80cm of calico
• 50cm zip
• 1 bag polystyrene craft beads

1) **For inner and outer cushions**: cut 2 squares 80cm x 80cm plus 1cm all round for turnings.

2) **For calico inner cushion**: With right sides together, machine stitch around edges, leaving a 50cm gap. Turn to right sides and press, fill with beads and hand stitch gap to close.

3) **For cotton outer cover**: with right sides together, insert the zip into one edge of the cotton squares. Machine stitch all round and turn through to right side, press and place over calico inner cushion.

Personalised towel

You will need:
• White towel
• off-cut of cotton fabric
• matching thread

Cut a length of cotton fabric to fit over the 'herringbone' band at both ends of the towel, plus 1cm all round for turnings. Press 1cm under all round and pin and machine stitch fabric in place with a zigzag stitch.

INFORMATION PAGE

TENSION

Obtaining the correct tension is perhaps the single factor which can make the difference between a successful garment and a disastrous one. It controls both the shape and size of an article, so any variation, however slight, can distort the finished look of the garment.

Different designers feature in our books and it is **their** tension, given at the **start** of each pattern, which you must match. We recommend that you knit a square in pattern and/or stocking stitch (depending on the pattern instructions) of perhaps 5 - 10 more stitches and 5 - 10 more rows than those given in the tension note. Press the finished square under a damp cloth and mark out the central 10cm square with pins. If you have too many stitches to 10cm try again using thicker needles, if you have too few stitches to 10cm try again using finer needles. Once you have achieved the correct tension your garment will be knitted to the measurements indicated in the size diagram shown at the end of the pattern.

SIZING AND SIZE DIAGRAM NOTE

The instructions are given for the smallest size. Where they vary, work the figures in brackets for the larger sizes. **One set of figures refers to all sizes**.

Included with every pattern in this magazine is a '**size diagram**', or sketch of the finished garment and its dimensions. The purpose of this is to enable you to accurately achieve a perfect fitting garment without the need for worry during knitting. The size diagram shows the finished width of the garment at the under-arm point, and it is this measurement that the knitter should choose first; a useful tip is to measure one of your own garments which is a comfortable fit. Having chosen a size based on width, look at the corresponding length for that size; if you are not happy with the total length which we recommend, adjust your own garment before beginning your armhole shaping – any adjustment after this point will mean that your sleeve will not fit into your garment easily - don't forget to take your adjustment into account if there is any side seam shaping. Finally, look at the sleeve length; the size diagram shows the finished sleeve measurement, taking into account any top-arm insertion length. Measure your body between the centre of your neck and your wrist, this measurement should correspond to half the garment width plus the sleeve length. Again, your sleeve length may be adjusted, but remember to take into consideration your sleeve increases if you do adjust the length - you must increase more frequently than the pattern states to shorten your sleeve, less frequently to lengthen it.

CHART NOTE

Many of the patterns in the book are worked from charts. Each square on a chart represents a stitch and each line of squares a row of knitting. Each colour used is given a different symbol or letter and these are shown in the **materials** section, or in the **key** alongside the chart of each pattern. When working from the charts, read odd rows (K) from right to left and even rows (P) from left to right, unless otherwise stated.

KNITTING WITH COLOUR

There are two main methods of working colour into a knitted fabric: **Intarsia** and **Fairisle** techniques. The first method produces a single thickness of fabric and is usually used where a colour is only required in a particular area of a row and does not form a repeating pattern across the row, as in the fairisle technique.

Intarsia: The simplest way to do this is to cut short lengths of yarn for each motif or block of colour used in a row. Then joining in the various colours at the appropriate point on the row, link one colour to the next by twisting them around each other where they meet on the wrong side to avoid gaps. All ends can then either be darned along the colour join lines, as each motif is completed or then can be "knitted-in" to the fabric of the knitting as each colour is worked into the pattern. This is done in much the same way as "weaving-in" yarns when working the Fairisle technique and does save time darning-in ends. It is essential that the tension is noted for **Intarsia** as this may vary from the stocking stitch if both are used in the same pattern.

Fairisle type knitting: When two or three colours are worked repeatedly across a row, strand the yarn **not** in use loosely behind the stitches being worked. If you are working with more than two colours, treat the "floating" yarns as if they were one yarn and always spread the stitches to their correct width to keep them elastic. It is advisable not to carry the stranded or "floating " yarns over more than three stitches at a time, but to weave them under and over the colour you are working. The "floating" yarns are therefore caught at the back of the work.

ALL ribs should be knitted to a firm tension, for some knitters it may be necessary to use a smaller needle. In order to prevent sagging in cuffs and welts we suggest you use a "knitting-in" elastic.

FINISHING INSTRUCTIONS

After working for hours knitting a garment, it seems a great pity that many garments are spoiled because such little care is taken in the pressing and finishing process. Follow the following tips for a truly professional-looking garment.

PRESSING

Darn in all ends neatly along the selvage edge or a colour join, as appropriate.

Block out each piece of knitting using pins and gently press each piece, omitting the ribs, using a warm iron over a damp cloth. **Tip**: Take special care to press the edges, as this will make sewing up both easier and neater.

STITCHING

When stitching the pieces together, remember to match areas of colour and texture very carefully where they meet.

Use a seam stitch such as back stitch or mattress stitch for all main knitting seams and join all ribs and neckband with a flat seam, unless otherwise stated.

CONSTRUCTION

Having completed the pattern instructions, join left shoulder and neckband seams as detailed above.

Sew the top of the sleeve to the body of the garment using the method detailed in the pattern, referring to the appropriate guide:
Straight cast-off sleeves: Place centre of cast-off edge of sleeve to shoulder seam. Sew top of sleeve to body, using markers as guidelines where applicable.
Square set-in sleeves: Set sleeve head into armhole, the straight sides at top of sleeve to form a neat right-angle to cast-off sts at armhole on back and front.
Shallow set-in sleeves: Join cast-off sts at beg of armhole shaping to cast-off sts at start of sleeve-head shaping. Sew sleeve head into armhole, easing in shapings.
Set-in sleeves: Set in sleeve, easing sleeve head into armhole.

Join side and sleeve seams.
Slip stitch pocket edgings and linings into place.
Sew on buttons to correspond with buttonholes.
After sewing up, press seams and hems.
Ribbed welts and neckbands and any areas of garter stitch should not be pressed.

= Easy, straight forward knitting

= Suitable for the average knitter

= For the more experienced knitter

ABBREVIATIONS

K	knit
P	purl
st(s)	stitch(es)
inc	increas(e)(ing)
dec	decreas(e)(ing)
st st	stocking stitch (1 row K, 1 row P)
garter st	garter stitch (K every row)
beg	begin(ning)
foll	following
rem	remain(ing)
rev	revers(e)(ing)
rep	repeat
alt	alternate
cont	continue
patt	pattern
tog	together
mm	millimetres
cm	centimetres
in(s)	inch(es)
RS	right side
WS	wrong side
sl1	slip one sticth
psso	pass slipped stitch over
p2sso	pass 2 slipped stitches over
tbl	through back of loop
M1	make one stitch by picking up horizontal loop before next stitch and knitting into back of it
yfwd	yarn forward
yrn	yarn round needle
yon	yarn over needle
cn	cable needle

Rowan Stockists - Overseas

For more information on Overseas Stockists and Mail Order details please contact the Rowan distributor/agent listed under each country
'ROWAN AT ....' stockists who carry a large range of Rowan Yarns

AUSTRALIA

DISTRIBUTOR: Sunspun, 185 Canterbury Road, Canterbury VIC 3126 Tel (03) 9830 1609 Email: sunspun@labyrinth.net.au www.melbourne.citysearch.com.au

Canberra - The Shearing Shed, Shop 7B Manuka Court, Bougainville Street, Manuka, ACT 2603 Tel (02) 62950061
CANTERBURY - ROWAN AT Sunspun, 185 Canterbury Road VIC 3126 Tel (03) 9830 1609 Mail Order
Cottesloe - Ivy and Maude, 1A Station Street, WA 6011. Tel 08 9383 3794
Darwin - Frangipani, 2/6 Parap Place, Parap NT 0820. Tel 08 8 981 278
Essendon - The Stitchery, 171 Mount Alexander Road VIC 3040. Tel 03 9379 9790
LINFIELD - ROWAN AT Greta's Handcrafts Centre, 321 Pacific Highway, Lindfield NSW 2070 Tel (02) 9416 2489
Malvern - Wondaflex Yarncraft Centre, 1353 Malvern Road, VIC 3144 Tel (03) 9822 6231
Queens Park - Atelier Kumi, 2a Ashton Street, NSW 2022. Tel 02 9369 3705

AUSTRIA

WIEN - ROWAN AT Wolle & Knopfe - Christine Withhalm, Josefstadter Str. 14, A-1080 Tel 1/40 35 735 Email: wolle@zweiglattzweiverkehrt.at www.zweiglattzweiverkehrt.at

BELGIUM

DISTRIBUTOR: Pavan, Koningin Astridlaan 78, B9000 Gent Tel (09) 221 8594

ANTWERPEN - ROWAN AT Lana, Anselmostraat 92, 2018 Tel (03) 238 70 17
Brugge - Stikkestek, Walweinstraat 3, 8000 Tel (050) 34 03 45
Bruxelles - Art et Fil, Rue du Bailli 25 Tel (02) 647 64 51
Bruxelles - ROWAN AT Boutique Laines, Galerie du Centre 53 - 55, 1000 Tel (02) 223 05 51.
GENT - ROWAN AT Pavan, Kon. Astridlaan 78, 9000 Tel (09) 221 85 94
LEUVEN - ROWAN AT Twolwinkeltje, Parijsstraat 25. Tel (016) 22 75 48
ST-NIKLAAS - ROWAN AT 't Wolleken, Ankerstraat 28, 9100 Tel (03) 777 64 15
WILSELE - ROWAN AT D. Yarns, P Van Langendoncklaan 17, Tel (016) 20 13 81

CANADA

DISTRIBUTOR: Diamond Yarn, 9697 St Laurent, Montreal, Quebec H3L 2N1 Tel (514) 388-6188 / Diamond Yarn (Toronto), 155 Martin Ross, Unit 3, Toronto, Ontario M3J 2L9 Tel (416) 736-6111

ALBERTA
Calgary - Gina Brown's, 17, 6624 Centre Sr S.E., T2C 0C6. Tel (403) 225-2200
Calgary - Fiber Hut. 2614 4th Street N W, T2M 3A1. Tel (403) 230-3822 Toll Free 1-800-816-7764 Email: fiberhut@nucleus.com
Edmonton - Knit & Purl, 10412-124 Street, T5N 1R5. Tel (403) 482-2150
Edmonton - Wool Revival, 6513-112 Avenue, T5W 0P1. Tel (403) 471-2749
St Albert - Burwood House, 205 Carnegie Drive T8N 5B2. Tel (403) 459-4828 Toll Free 1-888-600-4525

BRITISH COLUMBIA
Chilliwack - Country Craft Creations, 46291 Yale Road East, V2P 2P7 Tel (604) 792-5434 Fax (604) 858-3409
Duncan - The Loom, Whippletree Junction, Box H, 4705 Trans Canada Hwy, V9L 6E1 Tel (250) 746-5250
Port Alberni - Heartspun, 5242 Mary Street, V9Y 7H6. Tel (250) 724-2285
Prince George - House of Wool, 1282 N.Nechako Road, V2K 1A6 Tel (250) 562-2803
RICHMOND - ROWAN AT Craft Cottage, 7451 Elmbridge Way, V6X 1B8 Tel (604) 278-0313 Toll Free 1-800-329-6838
Richmond - Wool & Wicker, 120-12051 2nd Ave Tel (604) 275 1239 www.woolandwicker.com
Victoria - Beehive Wool Shop, 2207 Oak Bay Avenue, V8R 1G4. Tel (250) 598-22721 Toll Free 1-888-334-9005 www.beehivewool.com
West Vancouver - The Knit & Stitch Shoppe, 2419 Marine Drive, V7V 1L3 Tel (604) 922-1023 Toll Free 1-800-565-KNIT (5648) Email ingy@knit-n-stitch.com www.knit-n-stitch.com

MANITOBA
WINNIPEG - ROWAN AT Ram Wools, 1266 Fife Street, R2X 2N6 Tel (204) 942-2797 Toll Free 1-800-263-8002 Fax (204) 947-0024 Email ram@gaspard.ca MAIL ORDER AVAILABLE www.gaspard.ca/ramwools.htm

NOVA SCOTIA
Dartmouth - Fleece Artist, 1174 Mineville Road, B2Z 1K8 Tel (902) 462-0602

ONTARIO
ANCASTER - ROWAN AT The Needle Emporium, 420 Wilson St. East, L9G 4S4 Tel 01 800 667-9167 Mail Order Service
Carleton Place - Real Wool Shop, 142 Franktown Road, Box 130. K7C 3P3 Tel (613) 257-2714 www.needleemporium.com
Haliburton - Marty's Custom Knits, Box 857, Highland Street, KOM 1SO Tel (705) 457-3216
Kemptville - Your Creation (Jill Andrew), 3767 Mapleshore Drive. K0G 1J0 Tel (613) 826-3261
KINGSTON - ROWAN AT The Wool Room, 2-313 University Avenue, K7L 3R3 Tel (613) 544-9544 or Tel TOLL FREE 1 800 449-5868
Oakville - The Wool Bin, 236 Lakeshore Road East, L6J 1H8 Tel (905) 845-9512
Orillia - Imaginit 2000, 3493 Bayou Road, R R No 3, L3V 6H3 Tel (705) 689-8676
Orleans - Woolaine, Orleans Shopping Center Tel (613) 824-3525
Ottawa - Your Creation (Jill Andrew), 3767 Mapleshore Drive (Kemptville). K0G 1J0 Tel (613) 826 3261
TORONTO - ROWAN AT Passionknit Ltd., 3467 Yonge Street, M4N 2N3 Tel (416) 322-0688 or Fax (416) 864 0984
TORONTO - ROWAN AT Romni Wools Ltd, 658 Queen St. West M6J 1E6 Tel (416) 368-0202 Mail Order Service available
Toronto - (The) Wool Mill, 2170 Danforth Avenue, M4C 1K3 Tel (416) 696-2670
Toronto - Village Yarns, 4895 Dundas Street West, M9A 1B2 Tel (416) 232-2361 www.villageyarns.com
Toronto - (The) Yarn Boutique, 1719A Bloor Street West, M6P 1B2 Tel (416) 760-9129
Toronto - Studio Limestone, 16 Fenwick Ave, M4K 3H3 Tel (416) 469-4018 (MAIL ORDER ONLY)

QUEBEC
Montreal - A la Tricoteuse, 779 Rachel Est, H2J 2H4 Tel (514) 527-2451
St Lambert - Saute Mouton, 20 Webster, J4P 1N8 Tel (514) 671-1155
Westmount - Brickpoint Studios, 317-319 Victoria Avenue, H3Z 2L6 Tel (514) 489-0993

SASKATCHEWAN
Saskatoon - Prairie Lily Knitting & Weaving Shop, 7- 1730 Quebec Avenue, S7K 1V9 Tel (306) 665 2771 Fax (306) 343-9095

DENMARK

AARHUS C - ROWAN AT Inger's, Volden 19, 8000 Tel 86 19 40 44
KOBENHAVN K - ROWAN AT Sommerfuglen, Vandkunsten 3, 1467 Tel 33 32 82 90. Email : mail@sommerfuglen.dk
NYKOBING F - ROWAN AT Ruzicka, St Kirkestraede 5 B, 4800 Tel 54 70 78 04 Email: anne-lise@rudzicka.dk
ROSKILDE - ROWAN AT Garnhoekeren, Karen Olsdatterstraede 9, 4000 Tel 46 37 20 63

EIRE

Dublin - Hickey's Fabrics, 5 Henry Street Tel: +3531 873 0714
DUBLIN - ROWAN AT Needle Craft Ltd, 27/28 Dawson Street, 2 Tel: +3531 6772493 Fax: +3531 6771446 Email: needlecraft@iol.ie Mail Order Access/Visa www.ils.ie/needlecraft
Galway - Hickey's Fabrics, Corbettcourt Centre, Williamgate Street Tel: +35391 565 025
Co. Wicklow - The Wool Shop, 71 Main Street, Bray. Tel/Fax: +3531 2760029

FRANCE

DISTRIBUTOR: Elle Tricote, 8 rue du coq, 67000 Strasbourg Tel 03 88 23 03 13 Email elletricote@agat.net www.elletricote.com

ANNECY - ROWAN AT Od'a'laine, 3 rue Joseph Blanc, 74000. Tel 04 50 51 38 46
BESANCON - ROWAN AT La Pastourelle, 4 rue Delavelle, 25000 Tel 03 81 80 96 51
Cadenet - Mylene Creations, 14 rue Victor Hugo, 84160 Tel 04 90 77 16 09
Le Havre - Feelaine, 90 bis rue Victor Hugo, 76600 Tel 02 35 43 19 92
PARIS (3) - ROWAN AT Entree des Fournisseurs, 8 rue de Francs Bourgois Tel 01 48 84 58 98 Fax 01 48 87 77 40. Email: edf@club-internet.fr www.entreedesfournisseurs.com
PARIS (6) - ROWAN AT Entree Des Fournisseurs, 9 rue Madame Tel 01 42 84 13 97. Email: edf@club-internet.fr www.entreedesfournisseurs.com
PARIS (7) - ROWAN AT Le Bon Marche, 115 rue du Bac, 75007 Tel 01 44 39 80 00 Fax 01 44 39 80 50
Paris(18) - Mme Ceresa, 4 rue Saint Isaure, 75018 Tel 01 42 51 62 37
Ramonville - Le Sabot des Laines, 15 avenue d'Occitanie, 31520. Tel 05 61 73 14 38
Rennes - L'écheveau, 11 rue de la Monnaie, 35000. Tel 02 99 79 14 86
Saint Dié - Tricot Conseil, 11 rue d'Amerique, 88100. Tel 03 29 56 76 16
Saint-Pierre Reunion - Fath Creation, 10 rue Marius et Ary Leblond, 97410 Tel 02 62 96 18 78
SARZEAU - ROWAN AT Les Chemins Buissonniers, 1 Place Marie le Franc, 56370 Tel 02 97 48 08 30
STRASBOURG - Rowan AT Elle Tricote, 8 rue du coq, 67000 Tel 03 88 23 03 13 Fax 03 88 23 01 69 Email elletricote@agat.net www.elletricote.com
THONON LES BAINS - ROWAN AT Au Vieux Rouet, 7 rue Ferdinand Dubouloz, 74200 Tel 04 50 71 07 33
Toulon - D'un Fil a L'Autre, 53 rue Jean Jaurès, 83000. Tel 04 94 92 63 76
Vincennes - L'après-midi, 8 rue Lejemptel, 94300 Tel 01 41 93 12 90 Fax 01 43 74 73 12

GERMANY

DISTRIBUTOR: Wolle & Design, Wolfshovener Strasse 76, 52428 Julich-Stetternich Tel 02461/54735

AACHEN - ROWAN AT Martin Gorg Wolle, Annastrasse 16, 52005 Tel 0241/4705913
ADELSDORF/AISCH - ROWAN AT 'LanArt' Susanne Wettendorf, Hohenstrasse 3, 91325 Tel 09195/50515
Ahrweiler - Dat Laedche, Niederhut Str. 17, 53747 Tel 02641/4464
AUGSBURG - ROWAN AT Die Masche - Gertrud Egger, Ludwigstr 4, 86152 Tel 0821/3495607
Backnang - Wollstube Wollin, Hohenheimer Str 29, 71522. Tel 07191/84375.
Bayreuth - Strick-Art, Kirchgasse 16, 95444 Tel 0921/5304870.
BIELEFELD-BABANHAUSEN - ROWAN AT Woll-Deele - Reinhild Uffmann, Babenhauser Str. 70, 33619 Tel 0521 887909
Berlin - Tausend Und Eine Naht - Jutta Neubert, Damaschkestrasse 33, 10711 Berlin - Charlottenburg Tel 030 32701523
Detmold - 'Die Spindel' A Schulze-Wermeling, Unter der Wehme 5, 32756 Tel 05231/33882
Duisburg - Natur-Werkstatt, Lohstr. 16, 47228 Tel 02065/82259
Hamburg - Gaarnhuus - Helena Tiihonen-Gleitsmann, Ottenser Hauptstrasse 26, 22765 Tel 040/394794
Hamburg - Horn-Modedesign, Alardusstr. 12, 20255. Tel 040/40197414.
Hamburg - Pur-Pur-Woll, Hellkamp 9, 20255 Tel 040/4904579
Hamburg - Woll-Eule - Ilse Jalloul, Stormarnplatz 1, 22393 Tel 040/6012920
HANNOVER - ROWAN AT Textilwerkstatt - Minke Heijstra, Friedenstr. 1, 30175 Tel 0511 818001
Itzehoe - Allerhand von Hand - E Seligmann, Oelmuhlengang 2, 25524 Tel 04821/2807
JUELICH - ROWAN AT Wolle & Design - R Kaufmann, Wolfshovener Str. 76, 52428 Tel 02461/54735
Kirchgellersen - Klexx - Ute Rudat, Im Dorfe 7, 21394 Tel 04135/8423
LANGEN - ROWAN AT Wollwerkstatt - Petra Schroeder, Wassergasse 24, 63225 Tel 06103/22772
Leimem - Mausebae, Bahnhofstr. 45, 69181 Tel 06224/50560
Pforzheim Buchenbronn - Wollwerkstatt - M Weinmann, Schonblickstr 8, 75180 Tel 07231/71416
Reutlingen - Wolle & Mer, Metzgerstr.64, 72764 Tel 0721/310488.
SCHALLSTADT - ROWAN AT Senfkorn - A & C Bienger, Erlenweg 16, 79227 Tel 07664/978787
STUTTGART - ROWAN AT Strick Art - Silvia Grosse, Alexanderstr 51, 70182 Tel 0711/245218
VELBERT - ROWAN AT mit Nadel & Faden - Barbel Hoppe-Abe, Bahnhofstr 29, 42551 Tel 02051/50712
Wenden - Handarbeiten - B Klur, Severinusstr. 2, 57482 Tel 02762/1351

HOLLAND

DISTRIBUTOR: de Afstap, Oude Leliestraat 12, 1015 AW Amsterdam Tel 020-6231445

Amersfoort - H W Mur, Langestraat 13, 3811AA Tel 033-4617837
AMSTERDAM - ROWAN AT de Afstap (Lonnie Bussink), Oude Leliestraat 12, 1015 AW Tel 020-6231445
Bergen - Finlandia, Kleine Dorpsstraat 26, 1861 KN Tel 0725 894642
Bussum - Charmant, Huizerweg 26, 1402 AB Tel 035-6919098
Deurne - De Kaarde, (Meur. Fonteyn), Raadhuisstraat 2, 5751 LX Tel 1493 314672
Oldenzaal - Lohuis, Steenstraat 26, 7571 BK Tel 05415-12626
Someren - Het Weverke, Molenstraat 24, 5711EW Tel 0493-492092
Utrecht - Modilaine, Lÿnmarkt 22 Tel 030-2328911
Wormerveer - Priegelmee, Zaanweg 8, 1521DH Tel 075-621626
Zuidlaren - Ryahuis (Lucy van Zanten) Telefoonstraat 26, 9471 EN Tel 050-4092618.

HONG KONG

DISTRIBUTOR: East Unity Company Limited, Room 902, Block A, Kailey Industrial Centre, 12 Fung Yip Street, Chai Wan Tel (852) 2869 7110

ICELAND

DISTRIBUTOR: ROWAN AT Storkurinn, Kjorgardi, Laugavegi 59, ICE -101 Tel 551 8258 Fax 562 8252 Email: stork@mmedia.is

Akureyri - Hnotan, Kaupangi, 600 Akureyri Tel 462 3508
REYKJAVIK - ROWAN AT Storkurinn, Kjorgardi, Laugavegi 59, 101 Reykjavik Tel 551 8258 Fax 562 8252 Email: stork@mmedia.is
Skrinan - Eyrarvegur 27, 800 Selfoss Tel 482 3238

JAPAN

DISTRIBUTOR: Diakeito Co Ltd, 2-3-11 Senba-Higashi, Minoh City, Osaka 562 Tel 0727 27 6604

NEW ZEALAND

Auckland - Alterknitives, PO Box 47 961 Tel : 64 937 60337
Lower Hutt - John Q Goldingham, PO Box 45 - 083, Epuni Railway Tel 64 4 586 4530 Fax 64 4 586 4531.

NORWAY

DISTRIBUTOR: Ruzicka, Hans Aanrudsvei 48, N - 0956 Oslo Tel : 47 22 25 26 92 www.ruzicka.dk

Aasgaardstrand - Eie's Paletten, Grev Wedelsgt 46, 3155 Tel 33 04 88 80
Haugesund - Strikkeglede, Strandgt. 130, 5500 Tel 55 72 49 65
Kristiansand S - Jonnas Garn & Gaver, Skippergt. 18, 4611. Tel 38 07 03 95
Oslo - Husfliden, Mollergt. 4, 0179 Tel 22 42 10 75

Rowan Stockists - Overseas

For more information on Overseas Stockists and Mail Order details please contact the Rowan distributor/agent listed under each country

'ROWAN AT ....' stockists who carry a large range of Rowan Yarns

Oslo - Colours, Observatoriegt 25, 0252 Tel 22 44 42 60
Oslo - Striestuen, Karl Johans Gate 8,
Stavanger - Olga Evensens Eftf, Laugmannsgt 4, 4006 Tel 51 89 42 66

SOUTH AFRICA
Norwood - Creative Kit Company, PO Box 92043, 2117 (Mail Order only) Tel 11 640 6722

SWEDEN
DISTRIBUTOR: Wincent, Norrtulsgaten 65, 11345 Stockholm Tel (08) 33 70 60

Ahus - P-Persson and Co, Gamla Skeppsbron 10, 29631
Tel (08) 240121
Borlänge - Vävboden, Bygatan 1, 784 34 Tel (0243) 229970
Goteborg - Strikk, Vallgatan 19, 411 16 Tel (031) 711 37 99
Goteborg - Garnbutiken Glamour, Avägen 42, 412 51
Tel (031) 40 80 50
Goteborg - Hannas Garn & Design, Axel Dahlströms Torg, 414 80
Tel (031) 41 86 76
Gustavsberg - Garnpaletten, Odelbergs väg 9a, 13440 Tel 570 310 38
Karlskrona - Cikoria, Amiralitestorget 27, 371 30 Tel (0455) 20750
Löttorp - Mjuk & Tuff, Hagaby, 380 74 (Summershop) Tel:(0485)20750
Malmö - Irmas Hus, Kalendegatan 11, 211 35 Tel (040) 611 08 00
STOCKHOLM - ROWAN AT Wincent, Norrtullsgatan 65, 113 45
Tel (08) 33 70 60
Täby - Trassel, Täby Centrum, 183 34 Tel (08) 638 00 59
Uppsala - Yll & Tyll, Bredgrand 7c, 753 20 Tel (018) 105190

SWITZERLAND
Zurich - Vilfil, Klosbachstrasse 10, Beim Kreuzplatz, 8032
Tel 01 383 99 03-

UNITED STATES OF AMERICA
AGENT: ROWAN USA, 5 Northern Boulevard, Amherst, New Hampshire 03031 Tel (603) 886 5041/5043 Email wfibers@aol.com

ALABAMA
Huntsville - Yarn Expressions, 7914 S Memorial Parkway, 35802
Tel (256) 881-0260

ARIZONA
TUCSON - ROWAN AT Purls, 7862 North Oracle Road, 85704
Tel (520) 797-8118

CALIFORNIA
ANAHEIM HILLS - ROWAN AT Velona Needlecraft,
5701 M Santa Ana Canyon Road, 92807 Tel (714) 974-1570
www.velona.com
BERKELEY - ROWAN AT Straw Into Gold,
3006 San Pablo Avenue, 94702 Tel (510) 548-5243 www.straw.com/sig
Danville - Filati Yarns, 125 Railroad Ave, Suite F, 94526
Tel (925) 820-6614
Laguna Beach - Strands & Stitches, 1516 South Coast Highway.
92651 Tel (714) 497-5648
La Jolla - Knitting in La Jolla, 7863 Grand Ave, 92037
Tel (858) 456-4687
Long Beach - Alamitos Bay Yarn Co, 174 Marina Dr, 90803
Tel (562) 799-8484
LOS ALTOS - ROWAN AT Uncommon Threads,
293 State Street, 94022 Tel (650) 941-1815
Oakland - The Knitting Basket, 2054 Mountain Blvd, 94611
Tel (800) 654-4887
REDONDO BEACH - ROWAN AT L'Atelier, 17141/2 Catalina,
90277 Tel (310) 540-4440
SAN FRANCISCO - ROWAN AT Greenwich Yarns,
2073 Greenwich Street, 94123 Tel (415) 567-2535
www.greenwichyarn.citysearch.com
SAN FRANCISCO - ROWAN AT Yarn Garden, 545 Sutter St,
Ste 202, 94102 Tel (415) 956-8830 www.yarngarden.citysearch.com
Santa Barbara - In Stitches, 5 East Figueroa, 93101
Tel (805) 962-9343
SANTA MONICA -ROWAN AT L'Atelier on Montana,
1202 Montana Ave 90403 Tel (310) 394-4665
www.websites.earthlink.net/~latelier

COLORADO
Colorado Springs - Needleworks by Holly Berry,
2409 W Colorado Ave., 80904 Tel (719) 636-1002
Denver - Strawberry Tree, 2200 S. Monaco Pkwy., 80222
Tel (303) 759 4244
Longmont - Over the Moon, 600 S Airport Road, Bldg A, Ste D,
80503 Tel (303) 485-6778 www.over-the-moon.net
Vail - Yarn Studio, 0771 Stone Creek Dr #2, 81658
Tel (970) 949-7089

CONNECTICUT
Southbury - Selma's Yarn & Needleworks, Heritage Inn Arcade, 06488
Tel (203) 264-4838
WESTPORT - ROWAN AT Hook 'N' Needle, 1869 Post Rd East,
06880 Tel (203) 259-5119 www.hook-n-needle.com

GEORGIA
Atlanta - Strings & Strands, 4632 Wieuca Road, 30342,
Tel (404)252-9662

ILLINOIS
Chicago - Weaving Workshop, 2218 N Lincoln Ave, 60614
Tel (773) 929-5776
Clarendon Hills - Flying Colors Inc, 15 Walker Ave, 60514
Tel (630) 325-0888
Evanston - Closeknit Inc, 622 Grove St. 60201 Tel (847) 328 6760

Oak Park - Tangled Web Fibers, 177 S Oak Park Road, 60302
Tel (708) 445-8385
St Charles - The Fine Line Creative Arts Center, 6 N. 158 Crane Rd,
60175 Tel (630) 584-9443

INDIANA
Bloomington - Yarns Unlimited, 129 Fountain Sq Mall, 47404,
Tel (812) 334-2464
Ft. Wayne - Cass Street Depot, 1044 Cass Street, 46802
Tel (219) 420-2277
Indianapolis - Mass. Avenue Knit Shop, 521 East North Street, 46204
Tel (800) 675-8565

KENTUCKY
Louisville - Handknitters Limited, 11705 Main Street, 40243
Tel (502) 254-9276

KANSAS
LAWRENCE - ROWAN AT The Yarn Barn, 930 Mass Ave, 66044
Tel (800) 468-0035

MAINE
Camden - Stitchery Square, 11 Elm St, 04843 Tel (207) 236-9773
www.stitching.com/stitcherysquare
FREEPORT - ROWAN AT Grace Robinson & Co,
475 US Rte 1, Ste 1, 04032 Tel (207) 865-6110

MARYLAND
Annapolis - Yarn Garden, 2303 I Forest Dr, 21401
Tel (410) 224-2033
BALTIMORE - ROWAN AT Woolworks, 6305 Falls Rd, 21209
Tel (410) 337-9030
BETHESDA - ROWAN AT Needlework Attic, 4706 Bethseda Ave,
20814 Tel (800) 654-6654
BETHESDA - ROWAN AT Yarns International,
5110 Ridgefield Road, 20816 Tel (301) 913-2980
Glyndon - Woolstock, 4848 Butler Road, 21071 Tel (410) 517-1020

MASSACHUSETTS
Brookline Village - A Good Yarn, 4 Station St, 02447,
Tel (617) 731-4900
Cambridge - Woolcott & Co., 61 JFK Street, 02138-4931
Tel (617) 547-2837
Duxbury - The Wool Basket, 19 Depot St, 02332 Tel (781) 934-2700
Harvard - The Fiber Loft, 9 Massachusetts Ave. 01451
Tel (800) 874-9276
LEXINGTON - ROWAN AT Wild & Woolly Studio,
7A Meriam St, 02173 Tel (781) 861-7717
LENOX - ROWAN AT Colorful Stitches, 48 Main St. 01240
Tel (800) 413-6111 www.colorful-stitches.com
Milton - Snow goose, 10 Bassett St, Milton Market Pl, 02186,
Tel (617) 698-1190
Northampton - Northampton Wools, 11 Pleasant St, 01060
Tel (413) 586-4331)

MICHIGAN
BIRMINGHAM - ROWAN AT Knitting Room, 251 Merrill,
48009 Tel (248) 540-3623
Grand Haven - For Knitters.com, MAIL ORDER ONLY,
Tel (616) 638-0073
Howell - A Stitch in Time, 722 East Grand River, 48843
Tel (517) 546-0769
Traverse City - Lost Art Yarn Shoppe, 123 East Front St., 49684
Tel (616) 941-1263
Wyoming - Threadbender Yarn Shop - 2767 44th St, SW, 49509
Tel (888) 531-6642

MINNESOTA
MINNEAPOLIS - ROWAN AT Linden Hills Yarn,
2720 W. 43rd St, 55410 Tel (612) 929-1255
Minnetonka - Skeins 11309 Highway 7, 55305 Tel (612) 939-4166
ST PAUL - ROWAN AT The Yarnery KMK Crafts,
840 Grand Ave. 55105 Tel (651) 222 5793
WHITE BEAR LAKE - ROWAN AT A Sheepy Yarn Shoppe,
2185 Third St, 55110 Tel (800) 480-5462

MONTANA
Stevensville - Wild West Wools, 3920 Suite B Highway 93N , 59870
Tel (406) 777-4114

NEBRASKA
OMAHA - ROWAN AT Personal Threads Boutique,
8025 W Dodge Rd, 68114 Tel (402) 391-7733

NEW HAMPSHIRE
Concord - Elegant Ewe, 71 S Main Street, 03301 Tel (603) 226-0066
Exeter - Charlotte's Web, Exeter Village Shops, 137 Epping Rd, Rt. 27,
03833 Tel (888) 244-6460

NEW JERSEY
Chatham - Stitching Bee, 240A Main Street, 07928 Tel (973) 635-6691
www.thestitchingbee.com
Hoboken - Hoboken Handknits, 720 Monroe St, Ste E504, 07030
Tel (201) 653-2545
Princeton - Glenmarle Woolworks, 330 Gold Soil Road, 08540
Tel (609) 921-3022
Sparta - Yarn Loft, 580 Rt 15, 07871 Tel (973) 383-6667

NEW MEXICO
Albuquerque - Village Wools, 3801 San Mateo Ave, N.E., 87110
Tel (505) 883-2919
Santa Fe - Needle's Eye, 927 Paseo de Peralta, 87501
Tel (505) 982 0706

NEW YORK
Bedford Hills - Lee's Yarn Center, 733 N Bedford Rd, 10507
Tel (914) 244-3400
Brooklyn - Heartmade (Mail Order only), 877 East 10th St, 2nd Flr,
11230 Tel (800) 898-4290
Buffalo - Elmwood Yarn Shop, 1639 Hertel Ave, 14216
Tel (716) 834 7580
GARDEN CITY - ROWAN AT Garden City Stitches,
725 Franklin Avenue, 11530 Tel (516) 739-5648
Huntington - Knitting Corner, 718 New York Ave., 11743
Tel (516) 421-2660
Ithaca - The Homespun Boutique, 314 E State Street, 14850
Tel (607) 277-0954
New York City - The Yarn Company, 2274 Broadway, 10024
Tel (212) 787-7878
NEW YORK CITY - ROWAN AT Yarn Connection,
218 Madison Ave, 10016 Tel (212) 684-5099
New York City - Woolgathering, 318 E 84th St, 10028
Tel (212) 734-4747
SKANEATELES - ROWAN AT Elegant Needles, 5 Jordan St.,
13152 Tel (315) 685-9276

OHIO
Aurora - Edie's Knit Shop, 214 Chillicothe Rd, 44202
Tel (330) 562-7226
CINCINNATI - ROWAN AT One More Stitch,
2030 Madison Road, 45208 Tel (513) 533 1170
Cincinnati - Wizard Weavers, 2701 Observatory Rd, 45208
Tel (513) 871-5750
Cleveland - Fine Points, 2026 Murray Hill, 44106 Tel (216) 229-6644

OREGON
Ashland - Web-sters, 11 North Main St, 97520 Tel (800) 482-9801
Coos Bay - My Yarn Shop, 264 B Broadway, 97420
Tel (541) 266-8230
Eugene - Northwest Peddlers, 2101 Bailey Hill Road S., 97402
Tel (541) 465-9003
Lake Oswego - Molehill Farm, 16722 SW Boones Ferry Rd., 97035
Tel (503) 697-9554

PENNSYLVANIA
Bryn Mawr - Ewe & I, 24N Merion Ave, 19010 Tel (610) 520-0440
Kennett Square - Wool Gathering, 131 East State St., 19348
Tel (610) 444-8236
PHILADELPHIA - ROWAN AT Sophie's Yarns,
2017 Locust Street, 19103 Tel (215) 977-9276
Sewickley - Yarns Unlimited, 435 Beaver St, 15143 Tel (412) 741-8894

RHODE ISLAND
PROVIDENCE - ROWAN AT A Stitch Above Ltd, 190 Wayland
Ave, 02906 Tel (800) 949-5648 www.astitchaboveknitting.com
TIVERTON - ROWAN AT Sakonnet Purls, 3988 Main Rd, 02878
Tel (888) 624-9902 www.sakonnetpurls.com

TEXAS
San Antonio - The Yarn Barn of San Antonio, 4300 McCullough,
78212 Tel (210) 826-3679

UTA H
Ogden - The Needlepoint Joint, 241 Historic 25th St, 84401
Tel (801) 394-4355

VERMONT
WOODSTOCK - ROWAN AT The Whippletree, 7 Central St,
05091 Tel (802) 457-1325

VIRGINIA
Charlottesville - It's A Stitch Inc, 188 Zan Road 22901
Tel (804) 973 0331
Falls Church - Aylin's Woolgatherer, 7245 Arlington Blvd. #318,
22042 Tel (703) 573-1900 www.aylins-wool.com
MCLEAN - ROWAN AT Wooly Knits, 6728 Lowell Ave, 22101
Tel (800) 767-4036 www.clark.net/pub/fbarnako/woolyk.htm
Richmond - The Knitting Basket, 5812 Grove Ave, 23226
Tel (804) 282-2909
Richmond - Got Yarn, 8200 Buford Oaks Rd, 23235
Tel (804) 272-1117 Email 2savages@home.com MAIL ORDER &
INTERNET ORDERS ONLY www.gotyarn.com

WASHINGTON
Bainbridge Island - Churchmore Yarns, 118 Madrone Lane, 98110
Tel (206) 780-2686
Bellevue - Skein's!, 10635 NE 8th Street,Ste. 104, 98004
Tel (425) 557 9206.
Olympia - Canvas Works, 317 N Capitol, 98501 Tel (360) 352-4481
Poulsbo - Wild & Wooly, 19020 Front St., 98370 Tel (360) 779-3222
SEATTLE - ROWAN AT The Weaving Works, 4717 Brooklyn Ave,
N.E., 98105 Tel (888) 524-1221 www.weavingworks.com

WISCONSIN
Appleton - Jane's Knitting Hutch, 132 E. Wisconsin Ave., WI 54911
Tel (920) 954 9001 www.angelfire.com/biz2/yarnshop/index.html
Delevan - Studio S Fiber Arts, W8903 County Hwy A, 53115
Tel (608) 883-2123
ELM GROVE - ROWAN AT The Yarn House, 940 Elm Grove Rd,
53122 Tel (414) 786-5660
Madison - The Knitting Tree Inc, 2614 Monroe St, 53711
Tel (608) 238 0121
MILWAUKEE - ROWAN AT Ruhama's, 420 E Silver Spring Dr.,
53217 Tel (414) 332-2660
Wausau - The Black Purl, 300 Third St, 54403 Tel (715) 843-7875

Rowan Stockists – United Kingdom (for Eire see page 120)

Names in bold type are Rowan dedicated shops or departments, many offering professional help and mail order facilities

BATH & NORTH EAST SOMERSET
BATH – ROWAN AT Stitch Shop, 15 The Podium, Northgate.
Tel: 01225 481134 Mail Order Mastercard/Visa/American Express

BRISTOL
BRISTOL – ROWAN AT John Lewis, Cribbs Causeway.
Tel: 0117 959 1100 Mail Order Mastercard/Visa

BEDFORDSHIRE
LEIGHTON BUZZARD – ROWAN AT Needle & Thread,
2/3 Peacock Mews. Tel: 01525 376456 Mail Order
Internet Stockist – ROWAN AT Buy Mail Ltd,
www.buy-mail.co.uk and www.buy-mail.com,
Email: sales@buy-mail.co.uk and sales@buy-mail.com Internet mail
order service, Mastercard/Visa

BERKSHIRE
READING – ROWAN AT Heelas, Broad Street. Tel: 01189 575955
Mail Order Mastercard/Visa
South Ascot - South Ascot Wools, 18 Brockenhurst Road.
Tel: 01344 628327
Windsor - Caleys, 19 High Street. Tel: 01753 863241 Mail Order
Mastercard/Visa

BUCKINGHAMSHIRE
MILTON KEYNES – ROWAN AT John Lewis, Central Milton
Keynes. Tel: 01908 679171 Mail Order Mastercard/Visa

CAMBRIDGESHIRE
CAMBRIDGE – ROWAN AT Robert Sayle, St Andrews Street.
Tel: 01223 361292 Mail Order Mastercard/Visa
Peterborough - John Lewis, Queensgate Centre. Tel: 01733 344644
Mail Order Mastercard/Visa

CHESHIRE
Cheadle - John Lewis, Wilmslow Road. Tel: 0161 491 4914 Mail Order
Mastercard/Visa

CORNWALL
Penzance - Iriss, 66 Chapel Street. Tel: 01736 366568
E-mail: iriss@penzance.ws http://penzance.ws Mail Order Amex/
Mastercard/Visa
St. Ives - Antiques, Buttons & Crafts, 3A Tregenna Hill.
Tel: 01736 793713
WADEBRIDGE – ROWAN AT Artycrafts, 41 Molesworth Street.
Tel: 01208 812274 Email: artycrafts@ukonline.co.uk Mail Order /
Accepts credit cards

CUMBRIA
Cockermouth - Silkstone, 12 Market Place. Tel: 01900 821 052
Fax: 01900 821 051 Mail Order Mastercard/Visa
PENRITH – ROWAN AT Indigo, 7 Devonshire Arcade.
Tel: 01768 899917 Mail Order Mastercard/Visa

DEVON
Bideford - Wool and Needlecraft Shop, 49 Mill Street.
Tel: 01237 473015
PLYMOUTH – ROWAN AT Dingles, 40-46 Royal Parade.
Tel: 01752 266611 Mail Order Mastercard/Visa
Tavistock - Knitting Image, 9 Pepper Street. Tel: 01822 617410
Totnes - Sally Carr Designs, The Yarn Shop, 31 High Street.
Tel: 01803 863060

DORSET
Christchurch - Honora, 69 High Street. Tel: 01202 486000
Dorchester - Goulds Ltd., 22 South Street. Tel: 01305 217816
Sherborne - Hunters of Sherborne, 4 Tilton Court, Digby Road.
Tel: 01935 817722
Sturminster Newton - Hansons Fabrics, Station Road.
Tel: 01258 472698
WIMBORNE – ROWAN AT The Walnut Tree, 1 West Borough.
Tel: 01202 840722

DURHAM
DARLINGTON – ROWAN AT Binns, 7 High Row.
Tel: 01325 462606 Mail Order Mastercard/Visa

ESSEX
Chelmsford - Franklins, 219 Moulsham Street. Tel: 01245 346300
Colchester - Franklins, 13/15 St Botolphs Street. Tel: 01206 563955
Maldon - Peachey Ethknits, 6/7 Edwards Walk. Tel: 01621 857102
Email: peachey-ethknits@ndirect.co.uk
www.peachey-ethknits.ndirect.co.uk Mail Order Mastercard/ Visa
Southend-on-Sea - Gades, 239 Churchill South, Victoria Circus.
Tel: 01702 613789

GLOUCESTERSHIRE
CHELTENHAM – ROWAN AT Cavendish House,
The Promenade. Tel: 01242 521300 Mail Order Mastercard/Visa
Cirencester - Ashley?s Wool Specialist, 62 Dyer Street.
Tel: 01285 653245 Mail Order

GREATER MANCHESTER
MANCHESTER – ROWAN AT Kendals, Deansgate.
Tel: 0161 832 3414 Mail Order Mastercard/Visa
DIDSBURY – ROWAN AT Sew In of Didsbury,
741 Wilmslow Road. Tel: 0161 445 5861
Email: enquiries@knitting-and-needlework.co.uk
www.knitting-and-needlework.co.uk
MARPLE – ROWAN AT Sew In of Marple, 46 Market Street.
Tel: 0161 427 2529 Email: enquiries@knitting-and-needlework.co.uk
www.knitting-and-needlework.co.uk

HAMPSHIRE
Basingstoke - Pack Lane Wool Shop, 171 Pack Lane, Kempshott.
Tel: 01256 323644
Lymington - Leigh's, 56 High Street. Tel: 01590 673254
New Milton - Smith Bradbeer & Co. Ltd., 126-134 Station Road, .
Tel: 01425 613333
Southampton - John Lewis, West Quay Shopping Centre.
Tel: 0238 021 6400 Mail Order Mastercard/Visa
Southsea - Knight & Lee, Palmerston Road. Tel: 023 9282 7511 Mail
Order Mastercard/Visa
Twyford - Riverside Yarns, Cockscombe Farm, Watley Lane.
Tel: 01962 714380
Winchester - C & H Fabrics, 8 High Street. Tel: 01962 843355

HERTFORDSHIRE
Boreham Wood - The Wool Shop, 92 Shenley Road.
Tel: 0181 905 2499 Also Mail Order
Hemel Hempstead - Needlecraft, 142 Cotteralls. Tel 01422 245383
St Albans - Alisons Wool Shop, 63 Hatfield Road. Tel: 01727 833738
WATFORD – ROWAN AT Trewins, The Harlequin, High Street.
Tel: 01923 244266 Mail Order Mastercard/Visa
WELWYN GARDEN CITY – ROWAN AT John Lewis,
Tel: 01707 323456 Mail Order Mastercard/Visa

KENT
Ashford - Katie's Workbox, 15 High Street, Headcorn.
Tel: 01622 891065 Email: katies.headcorn@breathemail.net
Broadstairs - The Wool Box, 66 High Street. Tel: 01843 867673
CANTERBURY – ROWAN AT C & H Fabrics,
2 St. George's Street. Tel: 01227 459760
Greenhithe - John Lewis Bluewater. Tel: 01322 624123 Mail Order
Mastercard/Visa
Maidstone - C & H Fabrics, 68 Week Street. Tel: 01622 762060
ROCHESTER – ROWAN AT Francis Iles, 73 High Street.
Tel: 01634 843082 Mail Order Mastercard/Visa www.artycat.com
Tonbridge - The Curtain Company, Unit 14, The Pavilion.
Tel 01732 352500
TUNBRIDGE WELLS – ROWAN AT C & H Fabrics,
113/115 Mount Pleasant. Tel: 01892 522618

LANCASHIRE
Accrington - Sheila's Wool Shop, 284 Union Road, Oswaldtwistle.
Tel: 01254 875525 Email: sheilaswoolshop@compuserve.com

LEICESTERSHIRE
OAKHAM – ROWAN AT The Wool Centre, 40 Melton Road.
Tel: 01572 757574 Mail Order/Knitting up service available/
Mastercard/Visa

LINCOLNSHIRE
Louth - Tudor Wool Shop, 13 Queen Street. Tel: 01507 604037

LONDON - CENTRAL
ROWAN AT Liberty, Regent Street, W1. Tel: 020 7734 1234 Mail
Order Mastercard/Visa
ROWAN AT John Lewis, Oxford Street, W1. Tel: 020 7629 7711 Mail
Order Mastercard/Visa
ROWAN AT Peter Jones, Sloane Square, SW1. Tel: 020 7730 3434
Mail Order Mastercard/Visa
Chiswick - Creations, 29 Turnham Green Terrace. W4 1RS
Tel: 020 8747 9697 Mail Order
Debbie Bliss, 365 St John Street, EC1V 4LB Tel: 020 7833 8255
Fax: 020 7833 3588 Email: debbie@debbiebliss.freeserve.co.uk
www.debbiebliss.freeserve.co.uk
West Ealing - Bunty's at Daniels, 96/122 Uxbridge Road W13 9RA.
Tel: 020 8567 8729 www.bunty-wool.fsnet.co.uk

LONDON - NORTH
ROWAN AT John Lewis, Brent Cross Shopping Centre, NW4.
Tel: 020 8202 6535 Mail Order Mastercard/Visa

LONDON - SOUTH
Penge - Maple Textiles, 188/190 Maple Road. Tel: 020 8778 8049
E-mail: mapletextiles@hotmail.com
Barnes - Creations, 79 Church Road, SW13. Tel: 020 8563 2970 Mail
Order

MERSEYSIDE
LIVERPOOL – ROWAN AT George Henry Lee, Basnett Street.
Tel: 0151 709 7070 Mail Order Mastercard/Visa
Prescot - Prescot Knitting Co. Ltd., 32 Eccleston Street.
Tel: 0151 426 5264
St. Helens - The Knitting Centre, 9 Westfield Street. Tel: 01744 23993

NORFOLK
HOVETON – ROWAN AT Sew Creative, Wroxham Barns Limited,
Tunstead Road. Tel: 01603 781665 Email:
sewcreative@sylvia79.fsbusiness.co.uk Mail Order Mastercard/Visa
Norwich - Bonds, All Saints Green. Tel: 01603 660021 Mail Order
Mastercard/Visa
Sheringham - Honore Mae's, 47 Station Road. Tel: 01263 823153

NOTTINGHAMSHIRE
NEWARK - Chameleon, 33-35 Cartergate. Tel: 01636 671803
Ansphone
NOTTINGHAM – ROWAN AT Jessops, Victoria Centre.
Tel: 0115 9418282 Mail Order Mastercard/Visa

OXFORDSHIRE
Burford - Burford Needlecraft Shop, 117 High Street.
Tel: 01993 822136 Email: rbx20@dial.pipex.com
www.needlework.co.uk Mail Order Mastercard/Visa
OXFORD – ROWAN AT Rowan - 102 Gloucester Green.
Tel: 01865 793366 Mail Order Mastercard/Visa 24 Hr Ansphone

SOMERSET
Burnham-on-Sea - The Woolsack, 7 College Street. Tel: 01278 784443
Glastonbury - Penny Juniors, 40 High Street. Tel: 01458 831974
Taunton - Hayes Wools, 150 East Reach. Tel: 01823 284768 Mail
Order Mastercard/Visa
Yeovil - Enid's, Wool & Craft Shop, Church Street. Tel: 01935 412421

SUFFOLK
BURY ST EDMUNDS – ROWAN AT Jaycraft, 78 St John's Street.
Tel: 01284 752982 Mail Order/Accepts credit cards
Ipswich - Spare Moments, 13 Northgate Street. Tel: 01473 259876

SURREY
Banstead - Maxime Wool & Craft Shop, 155 High Street.
Tel: 01737 352798
KINGSTON – ROWAN AT John Lewis, Wood Street.
Tel: 0181 547 3000 Mail Order Mastercard/Visa
GUILDFORD – ROWAN AT Army & Navy, High Street.
Tel: 01483 568171 Mail Order Mastercard/Visa

EAST SUSSEX
Battle - Battle Wool Shop, 2 Mount Street. Tel: 01424 775073
Brighton - C & H Fabrics, 179 Western Road. Tel: 01273 321959
Eastbourne - C & H Fabrics, 82/86 Terminus Road.
Tel: 01323 410503

East Hoathley - The Wool Loft, Upstairs at Clara's, 9 High Street.
Tel: 01825 840339 Email: Claras@netway.co.uk Mail Order
www.netway.co.uk./users/claras
Forest Row - Village Crafts, The Square. Tel: 01342 823238
Email: village.crafts@virgin.net
LEWES – ROWAN AT Kangaroo, 70 High Street.
Tel: 01273 478554 Mail Order/Mastercard/Visa Mail Order
www.kangaroo.uk.com

WEST SUSSEX
ARUNDEL – ROWAN AT David's Needle-Art, 37 Tarrant Street.
Tel: 01903 882761 Fax: 01903 885822 Mail Order/Accepts credit cards
Chichester - C & H Fabrics, 33/34 North Street.
Tel: 01243 783300
HORSHAM – ROWAN AT The Fabric Shop, 62 Swan Walk.
Tel: 01403 217945
SHOREHAM BY SEA – ROWAN AT Shoreham Knitting,
19 East Street. Tel: 01273 461029 Fax: 01273 465407
Email: skn@sure-employ.demon.co.uk www.englishyarns.co.uk
Mail Order
WORTHING – ROWAN AT The Fabric Shop, 55 Chapel Road.
Tel: 01903 207389 Mail Order Mastercard/Visa

TEESIDE
HARTLEPOOL – ROWAN AT Bobby Davison, 101 Park Road.
Tel: 01429 861300 Email: sales@woolsworldwide.com
www.woolsworldwide.com

TYNE & WEAR
GATESHEAD – ROWAN AT House of Fraser, Metro Centre.
Tel: 0191 493 2424 Mail Order Mastercard/Visa
NEWCASTLE UPON TYNE – ROWAN AT Bainbridge,
Eldon Square. Tel: 0191 232 5000 Mail Order Mastercard/Visa

WARWICKSHIRE
Warwick - Warwick Wools, 17 Market Place. Tel: 01926 492853

WEST MIDLANDS
BIRMINGHAM – ROWAN AT Rackhams, Corporation Street.
Tel: 0121 236 3333 Mail Order Mastercard/Visa
Solihull - Stitches, 355 Warwick Road, Olton. Tel: 0121 706 1048
WOLVERHAMPTON – ROWAN AT Beatties,
71-78 Victoria Street. Tel: 01902 422311 Mastercard/Visa

WILTSHIRE
Calne - Handi Wools, 3 Oxford Road. Tel: 01249 812081

NORTH YORKSHIRE
WHITBY – ROWAN AT Bobbins, Wesley Hall, Church Street.
Tel/Fax: 01947 600585 Email: bobbins@globalnet.co.uk
www.bobbins.co.uk Mail Order Mastercard/Visa
YORK – ROWAN AT Craft Basics, 9 Gillygate. Tel: 01904 652840
Mail Order/Mastercard/Visa:

SOUTH YORKSHIRE
SHEFFIELD – ROWAN AT Cole Brothers, Barkers Pool.
Tel: 0114 2768511 Mail Order Mastercard/Visa

WEST YORKSHIRE
HEBDEN BRIDGE – ROWAN AT Attica, 2 Commercial Street.
Tel: 01422 844327
Email: info@attica-yarns.co.uk www.attica-yarns.co.uk
Mail Order/accepts credit cards
HOLMFIRTH – ROWAN AT Up Country,
78 Huddersfield Road. Tel & Fax: 01484 687803
Email: gpaul@upco.u-net.com www.upcountry.co.uk
Mail Order/American Express/Mastercard/Visa

WALES
CARDIFF – ROWAN AT David Morgan Ltd., 26 The Hayes.
Tel: 029 2022 1011
Conwy - Ar-y-Gweill, 8 Heol Yr Orsaf, Llanrwst.
Tel: 01492 641149
Fishguard - Jane's of Fishguard, 14 High Street. Tel: 01348 874443
Llandrindod Wells - Bon Marche, Middleton Street. Tel: 01597
822328
Penarth - David Morgan Ltd. 20 Windsor Road, Penarth, Cardiff.
Tel: 029 2070 4193
Swansea - Mrs Mac's, 2 Woodville Road, Mumbles.
Tel: 01792 369820
WHITLAND – ROWAN AT Colourway, Market Street.
Tel: 01994 241333 Email: shop@colourway.co.uk
www.colourway.co.uk/ Mail Order Mastercard/Visa 24 Hr Ansphone

SCOTLAND
Aberdeen - John Lewis, George Street. Tel: 01224 625000 Mail Order
Mastercard/Visa
Beauly - Linda Usher, 50 High Street. Tel: 01463 783017
Crief - Lint Mill Knitwear, 1 Dunira Street, Comrie.
Tel: 01764 670300
EDINBURGH – ROWAN AT John Lewis, St James Centre.
Tel: 0131 556 9121 Mail Order Mastercard/Visa
EDINBURGH – ROWAN AT Jenners, 48 Princes Street.
Tel: 0131 225 2442 Mail Order/Mastercard/Visa
Glasgow - John Lewis, Buchanan Galleries. Tel: 0141 353 6677
Mail Order Mastercard/Visa
HUNTLY – ROWAN AT Not Just Wool, 9 Bogie Street.
Tel: 01466 799045 Mail Order/Credit Cards/Ansphone
Isle of Arran - Traeoch Craft Shop, Balmichael Visitors Centre,
Shiskine. Tel: 01770 860515
Isle of Skye - Di Gilpin, The Old Mission Hall, Struan Workshop,
Struan. Tel: 01470 572 284 Email: di@handknitwear.com
www.handknitwear.com/
Kilmalcolm - Strathclyde, Threads, 3 Drumpellier Place.
Tel: 01505 873841
Lanark - Strands, 8 Bloomgate. Tel: 01555 665757 Mail Order/
Mastercard/Visa
Linlithgow - Nifty Needles, 56 High Street. Tel: 01506 670435
Stirling - McAree Bros Ltd., 55-59 King Street Tel: 01786 465646
Fax: 01786 464759 www.mcadirect.com

SHETLAND ISLANDS
Wimberry, Gardens, Skeld. Tel: 01595 860371 Mail Order

ROWAN YARNS, GREEN LANE MILL, HOLMFIRTH, WEST YORKSHIRE, ENGLAND TEL: +44 (0)1484 681881

122